STALIN, CHURCHILL, AND ROOSEVELT DIVIDE EUROPE

STALIN, CHURCHILL,

AND

ROOSEVELT DIVIDE EUROPE

REMI NADEAU

PRAEGER

New York
Westport, Connecticut
London

Library of Congress Cataloging-in-Publication Data

Nadeau, Remi A.
    Stalin, Churchill, and Roosevelt divide Europe / Remi Nadeau.
        p.   cm.
    Includes index.
    Includes bibliographical references.
    ISBN 0-275-93450-0 (alk. paper)
    1. World War, 1939–1945—Diplomatic history.   2. Stalin, Joseph,
1879–1953.   3. Churchill, Winston, Sir, 1874–1965.   4. Roosevelt,
Franklin D. (Franklin Delano), 1882–1945.   5. Europe—Politics and
government—1918–1945.   I. Title.
    D749.N33   1990
    940.53'2—dc20   90-7413

British Library Cataloguing-in-Publication Data is available.

Library of Congress Catalog Card Number: 90-7413
ISBN: 0-275-93450-0

First published in 1990

Praeger Publishers, One Madison Avenue, New York, NY 10010
An imprint of Greenwood Publishing Group, Inc.

Printed in the United States of America

The paper used in this book complies with the
Permanent Paper Standard issued by the National
Information Standards Organization (Z39.48-1984).

10 9 8 7 6 5 4 3 2 1

To Margaret

Contents

Photographs follow page 107.

Maps

Preface

The tidal wave of independence that has swept through Eastern Europe is a watershed event in our generation. Swirling rapidly across six nations, it has revealed the depth of the popular frustration that had churned beneath the surface. Clearly the floodgates had been opened by one pivotal fact—the withdrawal of Soviet military support from the six puppet regimes.

As we examine this astonishing spectacle, a question naturally arises: How and why was Europe divided between East and West in the first place? The purpose of this book is to answer that question.

The issue involves even more than the oppression of two generations of 100 million East Europeans. Occurring in the course of World War II, the division put Joseph Stalin in a position to threaten Western Europe and thereby upset the global balance of power that emerged from the war. More than any other factor, this spawned the Cold War and the arms race that gripped the world in fear for nearly half a century. Could it have been prevented?

The conventional approach to this question has assumed that Stalin took over Eastern Europe in the postwar years 1945–1948. But this should have been a foregone conclusion once he had gained power there through Red Army occupation, unrestrained by prior Allied agreements with teeth.

How this occurred in the years 1941–1945, how Churchill and Eden hoped to block Stalin with diplomatic bargaining and military preemption, how Roosevelt failed to understand Stalin's intentions and repeatedly failed to support the British with U.S. strength—all this is the tragic story that unfolds in these pages. It is not a story of American wrongdoing but of American innocence. The very idealism that made Roosevelt a surpassing global leader in winning the war also kept him, at least in Europe, from winning the peace.

In their initiatives the British were not always right, but with hindsight it must be said that in their responses the Americans were more often wrong. This is not to say that all of Eastern Europe could have been saved from Stalinism. Yet with U.S. power and will thrown into the political balance, much of it might at least have been kept neutral, and free, in the manner of Finland and Austria. We can never know for certain, because the Americans never tried.

Reduced to the simplest terms, Europe was divided because the United States had enough power but did not know how to use it; Britain knew how to use power but did not have enough; and the Soviet Union had enough power and knew how to use it.

Acknowledgments

For assistance in researching and writing this book I am indebted to many people and institutions. A few are cited here.

My wife, Margaret, generously gave encouragement, support, and inspiration throughout this work.

Invaluable suggestions and insight were provided by Dimitrije Djordjević, professor of history at the University of California at Santa Barbara and an elected member of the Serbian Academy of Sciences and Arts (Belgrade, Yugoslavia).

Also helpful in the same manner for a part of this work was the Honorable Géza Jeszenszky, professor of history at the University of Budapest and Minister of Foreign Affairs, Hungary.

I also wish to thank the following institutions and their librarians: the Federal Records Center, Suitland, Maryland; the library of the University of California at Santa Barbara; the Microfilm Office of the Research Library, University of California at Los Angeles; the British Government Archives, Public Records Office, Kew Gardens, London; the Microtext Office, Cecil H. Green Library, Stanford University; and the Hoover Institution, Stanford University.

For the use of photographs I would like to thank the National Archives and Records Center, Washington, D.C.; the Franklin D. Roosevelt Library, Hyde Park, New York; and the Imperial War Museum, London.

STALIN,
CHURCHILL,
AND
ROOSEVELT
DIVIDE EUROPE

1

Desperate Alliance

At dawn on June 22, 1941, Nazi Germany attacked the Soviet Union on a 1,000-mile front from the Baltic to the Black Sea. Surprised by Hitler's blow, the Soviet navy, army, and tactical air force were sent reeling.

In the Kremlin, Stalin and his generals nervously conferred over maps while Foreign Minister Vyacheslav Molotov announced the attack on Radio Moscow. That night in London, while many of his advisers were giving the Soviet Union only a few weeks, Prime Minister Winston Churchill announced on the BBC: "We shall give whatever help we can to Russia and the Russian people."

When an associate asked how such an old Bolshevik-hater as Churchill could take this position, he thundered, "If Hitler invaded Hell I would make at least a favorable reference to the Devil in the House of Commons."[1]

No such trumpet call came from the United States, which was not then at war. President Franklin D. Roosevelt, terribly aware of Hitler's threat to the world, was using all his powers to aid the British. Through Under Secretary of State Sumner Welles, he publicly seconded Churchill's offer to the Soviets.

Compared with the prime minister's thunderclap, it was a relatively faint echo, but Roosevelt knew how far and how fast he could pull the American public and Congress. Many influential persons in the United States—as well as in Britain—saw little difference between Hitler and Stalin; some said it was an ideal war—the two archvillains at each other's throat.

Nonetheless, before the end of 1941 Japan would attack the United States, throwing Roosevelt into a desperate alliance with both Churchill and Stalin. The "Big Three" would, in the course of the war, become the most powerful men in the world. By cablegram and in a few memorable moments in person, their ongoing conversation would determine the course of the war and, more important, the structure of the peace.

The shotgun alliance was, as both Churchill and Stalin knew, born of raw expediency. Roosevelt would attempt to infuse it with ideology, but this only misled the Americans into imagining that the alliance was based on principles other than survival.

A tragic result of Roosevelt's naive approach to the alliance would be to seal the fate of Eastern Europe during the war itself. Beginning in 1941, the British, recognizing the certain Soviet impact on Europe after Hitler's defeat, would try to bind Stalin while his bargaining position was weak. At each attempt Roosevelt would refuse to throw the weight of U.S. might into the balance.

As the war progressed, Stalin would become stronger and the relative negotiating posture of his allies would weaken. By the war's end, Stalin would simply reap the harvest of Roosevelt's four-year policy. In the immediate postwar period, when Stalin would assert iron control of Eastern Europe, it would be too late for an aroused President Truman to stop it. He would only be able to save the independence of Western Europe.

Thus, though millions of common people would fight and die to win the war, it was the character of three leaders at the top that would fix the peace. Though clearly a superb and aggressive leader in winning the struggle against Germany and Japan, Roosevelt would be essentially passive in the inner struggles among the Allies. A result would be the division of Europe that has only now begun to heal.

One who was thoroughly aggressive, though often subtly, was Joseph Stalin. Born of peasant stock in the Caucasus, he had been hardened by the blows of a drunken father. Hatred of authority had followed him to the seminary, where he outraged the priests by distributing revolutionary literature. The cunning acquired in outwitting his father and his schoolmasters became his weapon in rising through the Bolshevik hierarchy. Though Leon Trotsky's role in the October Revolution was much greater than Stalin's, it was Stalin who emerged as the Soviet leader following the illness and death of Lenin.

As Stalin gained power, he used it to eliminate not only Trotsky but also all other Bolshevik leaders who had risen under Lenin. By the 1930s the bloodbath had claimed tens of thousands. The untrustworthy are the least trusting of all; in Stalin's case both perfidy and the fear of it were pathological.

Yet Stalin's actions in defeating his enemies were seldom overt. From the days of his maneuverings to succeed Lenin, he consistently got others to carry out his schemes. His acts of revenge were carefully planned and usually unrelated to the real or fancied injuries. Much of the outrageous Soviet behavior against Stalin's puzzled allies near the end of the war can be traced to his belief that they were secretly negotiating with Hitler. In his remarkable revision of his book on Stalinism, the Soviet historian Roy Medvedev documents repeated cases of Stalin's subtle vengeance. Even Stalin's daughter mentions in her writings an occasion when she overheard her father directing one of his minions to arrange an "accident" for one of his victims.

Despite this streak of utter hardness, and in some measure because of it, Stalin had a natural if unschooled genius in military strategy and international politics. In his discussions with Churchill and Roosevelt he cared only for facts, and the facts were mostly about power. His famous question regarding the pope—"How many divisions does he have?"—was not really surprising. He often talked about divisions, as when he measured de Gaulle and Tito by the divisions they commanded when considering their qualification for postwar influence.

Averell Harriman, Roosevelt's trusted envoy first to Churchill and then to Stalin, wrote of the latter: "I found him better informed than Roosevelt, more realistic than Churchill, in some ways the most effective of the war leaders."[2]

Britain's chief of the Imperial General Staff, General Sir Alan Brooke, joined in this estimate of Stalin:

He had a military brain of the very highest calibre. . . . In this respect he stood out compared to his two colleagues. Roosevelt never made any great pretence at being a strategist and left either Marshall or Leahy to talk for him. Winston, on the other hand, was more erratic, brilliant at times, but far too impulsive and inclined to favor unsuitable plans without giving them the preliminary deep thought they required.[3]

Stalin's military powers did not come automatically. Serious mistakes were made in 1941 as the Germans rolled toward Moscow. But Stalin learned fast, and was showing strong command by the year's end.

As far as his powers of negotiation were concerned, it was Britain's foreign minister, Anthony Eden, who wrote, "[I]f I had to pick a team for going into a conference room, Stalin would be my first choice."[4] After the Tehran conference, Roosevelt gave the press his impression of Stalin: "I would call him something like me—he is a realist."[5]

Pitted against this streetwise master of geopolitics was Winston Spencer Churchill, noble by blood yet, through the rules of British primogeniture, untitled. As a child he had suffered from the benign parental neglect fashionable among the British aristocracy, having been raised by a nanny and schooled away from home. His desperate efforts to attract the attention of his mother and father stamped his character with self-centered showmanship.

The trait showed itself not only in a flamboyant political style but also, more directly, in repeated demonstrations of courage throughout his life. In his youth he had deliberately exposed himself to enemy fire in colonial campaigns; his daring had in it an element of compulsion—as though he needed to go through an exploit as a symbolic gesture. When Churchill visited the western front in 1944, Eisenhower turned down his request to cross the

Rhine and stand on enemy ground. But when Ike left the scene, Churchill, with Montgomery's help, boated across the river and stood triumphantly on the forbidden turf. Later, on a Rhine bridge at Wesel, when he and his companions came under both shell fire and sniper fire, he was enjoying the moment immensely until a U.S. general ordered him to withdraw.

By thus tempting fate Churchill seemed to be asserting a curious belief that he was somehow "special"—mystically touched for greatness. He once confided to a woman friend, "We are all worms. But I do believe that I am a glow-worm."[6] And when, after serving with mixed effectiveness in British politics for four decades, he became prime minister, he told his doctor: "This cannot be accident, it must be design. I was kept for this job."[7]

Despite such overweening self-importance, Churchill was plagued with fits of depression, which he recognized and called, almost affectionately, his "Black Dog." Yet he could, through his eloquence and pugnacity, inspire whole peoples with the will to bring victory out of defeat.

Churchill was, to be sure, a man of violent contradictions. On the one hand, he had a deep compassion for others; shocked by a photo of German prisoners made to stand with their arms in the air, he promptly gave orders against the practice. He protested vehemently that the Italian partisans, in executing Mussolini, had absolutely no right to do the same to his mistress, Clara Petacci.

On the other hand, he was usually insensitive to the needs of those around him; he kept them up into the early morning hours in interminable conferences marked by his harangues and ending without decision. Clement Attlee, deputy prime minister in the War Cabinet, once had the courage to write to Churchill protesting "the PM's lengthy disquisitions in Cabinet on papers which he has not read. . . ."[8] This, of course, stirred more fulminations at 10 Downing Street. Almost all of Churchill's associates considered resigning at one time or another, and stayed on only out of a sense of wartime duty and loyalty to their tormentor.

A master of both the written and the spoken language, Churchill coined many clever aphorisms that have become part of his legend, but aside from his abhorrence of dictatorship in any form he offered little profound philosophy to the twentieth-century world. He led an empire in winning the war but provided little in the way of a postwar agenda.

As minister of defence as well as prime minister, Churchill could rightfully interfere with his generals—a prerogative he fully exercised, to their chagrin. In military strategy he was capable of imaginative ideas, but these were usually in the nature of isolated strokes unconnected with a grand conception, and often without sufficient reckoning of the logistics required.

"He was never good at looking at all the implications of any course he favoured," General Sir Alan Brooke wrote. "In fact, he frequently refused to look at them."[9]

Bulldog tenacity was, in fact, his dominant characteristic and the key to his successful wartime leadership. Enchanted with his own ideas, he championed them in Allied councils to the very end, even after everyone else knew the game was over. The trait was not particularly attractive, especially when accompanied by his evident love of holding the floor and his lack of interest in the opinions of others. Yet the same dogged obstinacy enabled him to lead Great Britain out of defeat in 1940 to victory in 1945.

In facing Stalin, Churchill brought this same unflinching resolution to bear. Added to this was his abhorrence of Bolshevism; a dedicated monarchist, he had been shocked by the murder of the Russian royal family and had been a leader of British intervention into Soviet territory during the civil war. Further, he embodied centuries of British experience in the bare-knuckle arena of European politics. As a negotiator he was less adroit than his foreign minister, Anthony Eden; he tended to declare Britain's rock-bottom position at the outset, withholding little for bargaining. Such openness was commendable in other contexts, but not against Stalin's Byzantine approach. Yet Churchill nursed a healthy skepticism of Stalin's intentions, and recognized that he could be persuaded only by power.

A still different personality was brought to the Big Three by Franklin Delano Roosevelt. Scion of a prestigious New York family, he had been raised in a patrician tradition of public service. As an only child he had been lavished with attention and approval from his parents, especially his doting mother. Being loved was a way of life, and as he made his way among others in the world it remained a necessity. Going to extraordinary lengths to win people, he developed a charm that would serve him mightily in politics. At the same time, defending himself against his mother's dominance, he had cultivated a devious streak—getting his way by indirection—to the point of saying one thing and thinking another as occasion required. While such a trait is not uncommon in the political mind, it courts disaster when one is promising something that cannot be delivered. Thus, in his overweening drive to make people like him, he was apt to tell them what they wanted to hear, even at the risk of being found out later. In international politics this was especially dangerous.

In 1941, as the first president to have been elected a third time by U.S. voters, Roosevelt was at the height of his powers and enjoying them to the fullest. No president had ever been a greater charmer of people; in domestic politics that gift had brought him to the pinnacle of popularity and influence; he had supreme confidence that, as he now plunged into international politics, it would carry him also to unchallenged global leadership. Before he had ever met Stalin, he assured his friend Francis Cardinal Spellman: "Don't worry. I know how to talk to Stalin. He is just another practical man who wants peace and prosperity."[10]

Not that Roosevelt condoned the Soviet police state. Though he had recognized the Soviet government in one of his first actions in 1933, and at first thought of it as a mighty economic experiment worth watching, he was shocked by Stalin's bloody excesses in the 1930s. When Stalin was consorting with Hitler in 1940, Roosevelt had told an audience of pro-Soviet youths that he "abhorred the indiscriminate killings of thousands of innocent victims" by the Moscow regime. And he deplored the Soviet attack on Finland. "The Soviet Union," he had assured his listeners in spite of their jeers, ". . . is run by a dictatorship as absolute as any other dictatorship in the world."[11]

Yet Roosevelt seems to have looked with little concern on the possibility of Soviet domination of all Europe when Germany's defeat would leave a power vacuum. Cardinal Spellman recorded two conversations in September 1943 in which Roosevelt "assumed that Russia will predominate in Europe." This included not only Eastern Europe but also Austria and Germany.

"The European people," he said, according to Cardinal Spellman, "will simply have to endure the Russian domination, in the hope that in ten or twenty years they will be able to live well with the Russians."[12]

If this seemed like exchanging one tyranny for another, thus nullifying the Allied war aims, Roosevelt's initial answer was that after the scourge of war the Soviet Union would desperately need to cooperate with the United States. More than this, he counted on his own powers of persuasion in the face-to-face meetings he would soon seek with Stalin. William C. Bullitt, Roosevelt's first ambassador to Moscow, warned him of Stalin's postwar ambitions in Europe, and later reported FDR's answer: "I just have a hunch that Stalin is not that kind of man. . . . I think if I give him everything I possibly can and ask nothing from him in return, *noblesse oblige*, he won't try to annex anything."[13]

Such a recital might be dismissed as the tainted memory of a Stalin-hater who had broken with his chief over Soviet policy. But the attitude is substantiated by other evidence. Four days after Hitler attacked the Soviet Union, Roosevelt wrote to Admiral William D. Leahy of his hope that "it will mean the liberation of Europe from Nazi domination—and at the same time I do not think we need worry about any possibility of Russian domination."[14] In 1944 Roosevelt assured Eisenhower, "I can handle Uncle Joe."[15] When Labor Secretary Frances Perkins asked FDR to press Stalin on a particular issue, he demurred, saying, "I like this man and I want to keep on good terms with him." And he told her, after the Tehran conference, "I really think the Russians will go along with me about having no spheres of influence."[16]

Such was the chemistry of the Big Three as they joined to defeat Hitler— each of them a consummate politician in his own arena but each marching to a different drummer. In Moscow, a Machiavellian infighter wielding absolute power; in London, a bulldog realist who understood the uses of power; in Washington, a master of expediency who relied on persuasion more than on power. Together they would block the threat of Hitler while jockeying with one another for postwar position.

All three had been among the earliest to warn against Hitler, but Stalin had been the first to act. To his credit, the Soviet Union, through the mid–1930s, tried to rally the League of Nations to stop the rise of Nazi strength. Maxim Litvinov, then the Soviet foreign minister, led a crusade for collective security. "Peace," he preached at Geneva, "is indivisible."

Yet many leaders in France and Britain distrusted Stalin as much as they did Hitler. The Soviet Union was not invited to the Munich conference in 1938. Stalin had told Czechoslovakia's president, Eduard Beneš, that the Soviet Union would stand by his country if France would do likewise. Lacking this support, Czechoslovakia was dismembered and Hitler moved toward his next prize—Poland.

Through the first months of 1939 the British and French fumbled their way through talks with the Soviets aimed at the collective security for which Litvinov had pleaded. But they were slow; they did not try to get agreement from Poland and Romania to allow passage for Soviet troops in case Hitler attacked; they rejected the claims the Soviet Union made to the Baltic states; and they sent what the Soviets believed were second-string subordinates to parley in Moscow. Stalin suspected they were trying to turn Hitler's aggression away from themselves and toward the Soviet Union.

In a startling about-face, Stalin turned to Hitler, whose aim was to attack Poland without incurring trouble with the Soviet Union. When Litvinov was replaced by Molotov in May, the Germans sensed the change of policy. In the contacts that followed, an understanding was reached while the French and British negotiators were still laboring in Moscow. When Stalin agreed to receive the German foreign minister, Joachim von Ribbentrop, and conclude a nonaggression pact in Moscow, Hitler is said to have pounded on the wall and shouted, "Now I have the world in my pocket!"[17]

As the pact was signed on August 23, Stalin clinked glasses with Ribbentrop. "I know how much the German nation loves its Führer," he said. "I should therefore like to drink to his health."[18]

An integral part of the pact was a secret protocol in which the two nations divided Poland equally and Germany recognized the Soviet Union's interest in Finland, Estonia, Latvia, and the Romanian province of Bessarabia.

Having thus set the table, the two dictators sat down to the feast. Nazi Germany invaded Poland on September 1, 1939—an act that brought it to war with Britain and France. On September 17, with the Polish army reeling and the Polish government collapsing from the German blitzkrieg, Soviet troops invaded Poland from the east. The excuse, as announced on the radio by Molotov the same day, was "to take under their protection the lives and property of the population of western Ukraine and western White Russia," and "to deliver the Polish people from the disastrous war into which they have been plunged by their unwise leaders. . . . "[19] Molotov's wording was remarkable, inasmuch as the German attack had been made possible by a pact with the Soviet Union. The truth was that through their secret protocol the Soviet Union and Germany had joined in a fourth partition of Poland.

Smashing Polish resistance on its front, the Red Army proceeded to occupy eastern Poland up to the agreed Ribbentrop-Molotov Line. After the fighting, with an adjustment of territories that placed Lithuania in the Soviet sphere, Germany and the Soviet Union finished carving their victim. As Molotov told the Supreme Soviet on October 31, "one swift blow to Poland, first by the German Army and then by the Red Army, and nothing was left of this ugly offspring of the Versailles treaty. . . ."[20]

Germany and the Soviet Union had, in fact, divided Poland roughly along the so-called Curzon Line, which had been proposed as Poland's eastern frontier by the victorious Allied powers in Paris after World War I. Without Allied approval, the re-created state of Poland had at that time invaded Russia, then wracked and weakened by the Bolshevik Revolution, and in 1921 had forced a settlement of the eastern frontier along what became known as the Riga Line. Comprising about half of the territory in the new Poland, the area between the Curzon Line and the Riga Line included about 5 million Poles and 11 million Ukrainians and Byelorussians. Within it were two key cities, Vilnius in Lithuania and Lwów in the Ukraine, that were predominantly Polish in population and traditional centers of Polish culture. This is the vast area retaken by Stalin in his deal with Hitler—the Ribbentrop-Molotov Line corresponding to the Curzon Line in the center and extending somewhat farther west at the two ends.

In short order Stalin moved to occupy the other territories he had staked out in the secret protocol with Hitler. After vainly trying to get territorial concessions from Finland, the Soviet Union attacked in November 1939 and, despite stout resistance by the Finns, secured their capitulation in March 1940. Three months later Stalin invaded the Baltic states and, after holding parliamentary elections in which there was only one slate (nearly all Communists) on the ballots, absorbed the three nations into the Soviet Union. Before the end of June he gave Romania a 24-hour ultimatum demanding Bessarabia and, to boot, the province of Northern Bukovina. Romania yielded, and the Red Army occupied the territory.

Stalin had now completed the recovery of lands that, before World War I, had been part of the czarist empire (Northern Bukovina had never belonged to Russia). In so doing he gained more buffer ground and shortened his defensive front in case of a later German attack.

Though Stalin had merely been asserting to the maximum his influence in the spheres allotted to the Soviet Union by the Ribbentrop-Molotov pact, Hitler grew suspicious of his ally's intentions—especially at a time (June 1940) when he wanted a secure rear and an assured supply of Romanian oil while he prepared to invade Britain. By the end of 1940 Hitler decided he did not have the world in his pocket, after all. He resolved to attack the Soviet Union the following spring.

His plans were delayed, however, by complications in the Balkans. Yet by the spring of 1941 intelligence reports on German preparations were

- - - Pre-war Polish frontiers to 1939. The Eastern frontier is the Riga Line, created by Polish-Soviet Treaty, 1921.

······ Ribbentrop-Molotov Line, by agreement between Germany and the USSR after their invasion of Poland, September 1939. It was violated by German attack on USSR in 1941.

——— Curzon Line, as demanded by Stalin during the war. This is approximately the Polish-Soviet frontier since 1945.

Baltic Sea

LITHUANIA

GERMANY

Königsberg

EAST PRUSSIA

Danzig

Vilnius

USSR

Posnan

Warsaw

Pinsk

Lublin

Breslau

Kraków

Lwów

CZECHOSLOVAKIA

0   100
Miles

The Polish-Soviet Frontier Question, 1939–1945

flooding into the Kremlin. No fewer than 84 such warnings came from various intelligence sources, including Soviet, British, and American. Stalin's preparations seem to have been minimal. Dominated by suspicion, he believed the British were trying, by stirring him to mobilize, to provoke Hitler to preempt him, thus taking the pressure off themselves. He knew that it had been the czar's mobilization, not only on the Austro-Hungarian but also on the German frontier, that had impelled the kaiser to attack in 1914 and launch World War I.

Stalin therefore added his name to the roll of appeasers of Hitler. He not only took few defensive countermeasures but also stepped up delivery of raw materials to Germany under the Ribbentrop-Molotov pact. The Soviet Union was faithfully delivering goods to Germany up to the day before the invasion on June 22, 1941. Stalin's shock was so great that he went into seclusion for ten days.

In fact, two weeks passed without Stalin's answering Churchill's first promise of support. On July 7 the prime minister cabled Moscow repeating his offer: "We shall do everything to help you that time, geography and and our growing resources allow." He reported the Royal Air force bombing raids on Hitler's "Fortress Europe," and closed with a Churchillian battle cry: "We have only got to go on fighting to beat the life out of the villains."

On July 18 Stalin finally answered: "[T]he Soviet Union and Great Britain have become fighting allies. . . . " He proceeded to justify his 1940 seizures in Eastern Europe; without them "the German forces would have been far more advantageously placed. . . . " And he called upon Britain for a second front: "[T]he best time to open this front is now. . . . "[21]

It was the opening exchange in an intense Big Three dialogue that continued for the next four years. Roosevelt and Churchill met off Newfoundland and issued the Atlantic Charter in mid-August 1941, and Stalin subscribed to it six weeks later. True, the Charter forswore "territorial changes that do not accord with the freely expressed wishes of the peoples concerned." But this did not bother Stalin, who simply exempted any application to Soviet gains during the pact with Germany—the Baltic states and parts of Poland, Finland, and Romania.

On September 3, declaring the Soviet Union to be in "mortal danger," Stalin demanded "a second front this year somewhere in the Balkans or in France, one that would divert 30–40 German divisions from the Eastern Front. . . . " Without this, plus material aid, "the Soviet Union will either be defeated or . . . will lose for a long time the ability to help its Allies by active operations at the front against Hitlerism."[22]

In delivering this message at 10 Downing Street, the Soviet ambassador to London, Ivan Maisky, added his own urgent appeal to Churchill and Foreign Secretary Anthony Eden: "[I]f Hitler were victorious, what would be the fate of Britain?"

Puffing on his cigar, Churchill listened with sympathy but began to detect what he called "an underlying air of menace." He afterward wrote to Roosevelt, "[W]e could not exclude the impression that they might be thinking of separate terms." With rising anger Churchill told Maisky:

Remember that only four months ago we in this Island did not know whether you were not coming in against us on the German side. Indeed, we thought it quite likely that you would. . . . Whatever happens, and whatever you do, you of all people have no right to make reproaches to us.

"More calm, please, my dear Mr. Churchill," put in Maisky. The prime minister then made it clear that Britain could not launch a successful second front in 1941 but would respond fully to Stalin's other plea for material help.[23]

For the next two months the Stalin-Churchill exchanges continued over Soviet demands for a second front and for a British declaration of war against the satellites that had joined Germany on the eastern front. On November 7 Churchill offered to send a military mission to Moscow; Stalin insisted that unless the mission was prepared to discuss war aims and postwar plans, it would "be very difficult for me to find the time for the conversations."

When Maisky brought this message to Churchill at his office in the House of Commons on November 11, he asked Churchill to "treat this with the greatest possible calm." As the prime minister read the message, his face flushed and his left hand began, Maisky noticed, "agitatedly closing and opening." When he reached the part where Stalin questioned the value of a British military mission, he leaped up and paced excitedly across the room. "I send Stalin my best men," he roared, "and he doesn't want to receive them!" What, he asked, did Stalin want? "Bad relations? A rupture? Whom will that benefit?"[24]

Stalin's agitation was undoubtedly quickened by the German threat to Moscow. At one point the enemy was only 20 miles from the city; in an atmosphere of panic, most of the Soviet agencies and the diplomatic embassies were evacuated to Kuibyshev, 600 miles to the east. Stalin was in no mood to quibble with British punctilio over relations with Finland, Hungary, and Romania, which were fighting the Soviets alongside the Germans.

But even with his back to the wall, Stalin still demanded an agreement on "war aims and on plans for the post-war organization of peace." In his cablegram of November 8, he had called for a "definite understanding" and an "agreement"—without this "there will be difficulty in securing mutual confidence." Churchill came back with a suggestion that Eden go to Moscow to discuss "every question relating to the war," as well as postwar plans for "our mutual safety and rightful interests."[25] Stalin agreed, and Eden began preparing for a major political conference in Moscow. Among other things, he hoped to conclude a military pact assuring that neither Britain nor the Soviet Union would make a separate peace with Hitler.

2

Battle of the Boundaries

Tall, handsome, and affable, Anthony Eden appeared to be more show than substance. "I had hitherto been inclined to think that he was one of fortune's darlings," wrote General Sir Hastings "Pug" Ismay, Churchill's liaison with the Imperial General Staff. But on a trip to Moscow with Eden, Ismay realized he had been wrong. "His hours of work were phenomenal, and he was extremely thorough. . . . He could be tough when necessary, but he could also give way gracefully if the situation demanded it."[1]

This was Eden's second tour as secretary of state for foreign affairs—the first ended early in 1938 when he resigned in protest of Chamberlain's appeasement of Hitler. A veteran traveler in Europe's highest circles, he preferred life in his country home. Although a master of negotiation, he "loathes intrigue and is above it," according to Bruce Lockhart, the wartime head of British propaganda.[2] John Gilbert Winant, then the U.S. ambassador to London, wrote of him, "He had no use for shoddy politics whether at home or abroad." And "He was determined, whatever the cost, not to involve his country in secret treaties. . . . "[3]

Eden resented Churchill's incursions into his foreign policy domain, and could be jealous of other competitors. When Harold Macmillan, Churchill's political liaison with the Allied forces in the Mediterranean, seemed ready to encroach on foreign policy, Eden declared, "We already have two Foreign Secretaries; I am not going to have a third." Yet he would not stoop to hold a grudge; as Lockhart commented, "I know no man in politics who is so free from malice."[4] As for Churchill, he early advised the crown that in case of his death, Eden should succeed him as prime minister. "We thought alike," he later wrote, "even without consultation."[5]

On the eve of his departure for Moscow, Eden called in U.S. Ambassador Winant to brief him on the trip. At Winant's request Eden wrote a memorandum that the ambassador forwarded to Roosevelt and Secretary of State Cordell Hull. In it Eden proposed to "allay the suspicion and resentment" of Stalin toward the Western powers and to reaffirm with him the Atlantic Charter points, especially the "undertaking not to interfere in the internal affairs of other nations. . . ."[6]

Hull responded with alarm. "It was clear to us," he later wrote, "that Eden would be confronted at Moscow with specific territorial demands." In a reply approved by Roosevelt, Hull warned, "It is evident that no commitments as to individual countries should be entered into at this time. It would be unfortunate if we should approach the peace conference thus hampered. Above all there must be no secret accords."

For a nation not at war and not allied with Britain or the Soviet Union, this harsh message seemed presumptuous. But the British were obliged to heed American views; they were not only receiving extensive U.S. lend-lease aid, but were hoping to bring the United States into the war.

At the same time Averell Harriman, then in London as special envoy from the president, disagreed with Washington. This, he believed, was an opportunity to negotiate on the borderlands before the Red Army could occupy them; "it might well be too late then for negotiated settlements." But the United States was at the brink of war with Japan over its territorial demands in Asia, and Hull was in no mood for territorial concessions to the Soviets. He ordered Winant to read his warning message to Eden before he could leave for Moscow.[7]

Thus restrained, the foreign secretary left for Scotland and the rough sea voyage around the North Cape to Murmansk. At Invergordon, Scotland, he got a call from Churchill: The Japanese had attacked Pearl Harbor. Roosevelt had told the prime minister on the phone: "We're in the same boat now." Next day Congress declared war on Japan, and on December 11 Germany declared war on the United States.

Among other things, Washington's hand was strengthened in its policy on territorial claims and in its demands on London. Churchill rushed to Washington to discuss war plans with his new ally; Eden traveled to Moscow to talk of "war aims and postwar plans" with one hand tied by that same ally.

It was to be Eden's second meeting with Stalin—the first one had been in 1935. As a gesture toward winning Soviet confidence, Eden had not brought his own interpreter; the Soviet ambassador to London, Ivan Maisky, had accompanied Eden's party to Moscow, and now served as mutual interpreter.

Eden observed after the first meeting on the evening of December 16, "Stalin is a quiet dictator in his manner. No shouting, no gesticulation, so that it is impossible to guess his meaning, or even the subject of which he is speaking until the translation is given."[8] Others, from Americans such as Harry Hopkins and Charles Bohlen to Europeans such as Sir Alexander

Cadogan and Milovan Djilas, have more than confirmed Stalin's unassuming manner and appearance. In dress, a well-fitting tunic, shiny boots, and at most a single decoration. In appearance, surprisingly short (about five feet, five inches) and heavyset, with large hands and an ungainly walk—"like a small bear." His face—swarthy, eyes yellowish and squinting, teeth uneven and stained, a large mustache and bristly hair. In manner, soft-spoken with little inflection, no wasted words, no emotional outbursts, almost never looking at his listener.

Charles Bohlen's first impression: "[I]f he had dressed in Chinese robes, he would have been a perfect subject for a Chinese ancestor portrait."[9] Correspondent Quentin Reynolds agreed with a description of him as "the kindly Italian gardener you have in twice a week."[10] William C. Bullitt, U.S. ambassador to Moscow in the early 1930s, wrote that "with Stalin I felt I was talking to a wiry Gipsy with roots and emotions beyond my experience."[11] Sir Alexander Cadogan, Eden's under-secretary, was the least complimentary:

There he is—a greater Dictator than any Czar. . . . But if one didn't know that, I don't know that one would pick him out of a crowd. With his little twinkly eyes and his stiff hair brushed back he is rather like a porcupine.[12]

Before the first meeting on December 16, 1941, Eden and his associates— Sir Alexander Cadogan and Sir Stafford Cripps, British ambassador to Moscow—hammered out a proposed draft treaty, working in their quarters at the National Hotel to the sound of gunfire during the German siege of Moscow.

The key article called for "the safeguarding and strengthening of the economic and political independence of all European countries either as unitary or federated states." This not only promised noninterference with other nations but also promoted the principle of confederations. The British hoped such confederations would strengthen Eastern Europe against future aggression from either west or east.

Already the governments-in-exile of Poland and Czechoslovakia, as well as those of Yugoslavia and Greece, were negotiating such confederations. Churchill hoped for a Danubian Federation that would include Hungary, Austria, and part of Germany.

All this must have reminded Stalin of the *cordon sanitaire* that the French had constructed against Bolshevism after World War I. But when he met with Eden on December 16, he told him, "[I]f certain of the countries of Europe wish to federate, then the Soviet Union will have no objection. . . ."[13]

Accompanied by Molotov and Maisky, Stalin offered two short treaties of his own—a military alliance and a postwar political agreement for keeping the peace. To Eden these were unobjectionable. But Stalin then dropped the other shoe: "a secret protocol dealing in some detail with European frontiers." He poured forth a flood of boundary changes. The Soviet Union would have its frontiers, not as they stood at the beginning of the war in 1939 but as they became through Soviet seizure in the two-year period of Nazi-Soviet collaboration up to June 1941. This included a few bites of neighboring Finland; annexation of the three Baltic states—Latvia, Estonia, and Lithuania—that before World War I had been part of czarist Russia for a century; eastern Poland as seized by the Soviet Union after Hitler had attacked from the west; and, from Romania, the provinces of Bessarabia and Northern Bukovina.

Adding to these demands, Stalin continued to remake the map of Europe. To all this Eden begged off: "I cannot sign such a document without consulting my colleagues, and we have not as yet applied our minds to these problems."

"Not even the Soviet frontiers?" put in Maisky.

"I couldn't do this without consulting the Prime Minister and also talking to the Americans."

Eden was, he said, pledged to the United States not to enter into any secret agreement.

"I am quite agreeable to your informing America," returned Stalin, "and I would be very glad if the United States would participate."

"I doubt whether they would do that," hedged Eden.

Stalin then ended this particular conversation: "My desire is to establish that the war aims of our two countries are identical. . . . If our war aims were different, then there would be no alliance."

On the morning of December 17, Cadogan and Maisky worked together on the texts of the two treaties, which appeared satisfactory to both sides. Late that night, accompanied by Cripps and Cadogan, Eden met again with the Russians.[14] Immediately Stalin gave the disagreeable performance that was his standard procedure in second-day sessions. As Eden later wrote, "Stalin began to show his claws." He had reviewed the two treaty drafts, but what really concerned him was "the question of the recognition of the Soviet claim to the 1941 frontiers. . . ." To Eden's previous objection that Britain had told Poland its frontiers would await the peace settlement, Stalin conceded that "the Polish frontier might be left an open question." But he wanted Britain to recognize at once, in a secret protocol, the Soviet Union's other 1941 frontiers.

"I had not come for this," Eden answered. He was in no position to give such a promise. Stalin retorted that he "would rather have no agreement." The issue grew so heated that they never considered the drafts of the treaties. But at length the question of the Atlantic Charter arose.

"I thought," argued Stalin, "that the Atlantic Charter was directed against those people who were trying to establish world dominion. It now looks as if the Charter was directed against the U.S.S.R."

The session broke up at 3 A.M. in a deadlock. The next day Eden again worked with Maisky on proposed drafts, but when the third session began that evening at 7 P.M., neither side could accept the other's version. Stalin proposed a sentence in which the two nations would have full regard to "the desire of the U.S.S.R. in the restoration of its frontiers violated by the Hitlerite aggression."

With this sentence Stalin appeared to be trying to slip in his point despite British resistance. Eden observed that this "either has no definite meaning or else it means that we bind ourselves to agree to your frontiers as they were in 1941, and that is the proposition that we have already discussed at such length."

"All we ask," Stalin explained, "is to restore our country to its former frontiers. We must have these for our security and safety. . . . if you decline to do this, it looks as if you were creating a possibility for a dismemberment of the Soviet Union."

A moment later Molotov added: "We are going to sign a treaty of mutual assistance or alliance and we must know what we are fighting for and where we stand."

"We are fighting to beat Hitler," snapped Eden.

"My formula must stand," insisted Stalin, after further argument.

"I am afraid I cannot possibly accept it."

"That is very regrettable."

The meeting broke up in an atmosphere that Eden called "frigid." As he drove to the National Hotel with his colleagues, Eden pointed out that, since their rooms were probably bugged, they might proceed to give the Soviets an earful. In his sitting room Eden paced back and forth, ranting about Russian behavior while Cripps and Cadogan heartily agreed. They regretted coming to Moscow at all. Eden's sharp conclusion was that, "with the best will in the world, it was impossible to work with these people even as partners against a common foe."

Next day, while Eden toured the war zone in company with Maisky, he added to his performance the night before by lecturing the Soviet ambassador directly. Cripps was doing the same thing with Molotov in Moscow. But while the Russians thawed enough to resume their earlier hospitality, there was only an agreement to disagree. Eden could go back and consult with the Americans. Molotov had told Cripps in his characteristic icy tones, "In the absence of a settlement on the frontier question, no sound basis would be created for relations between Great Britain and the Soviet Union."[15]

After a rousing banquet and entertainment lasting from 10 P.M. to 5 A.M. on the night of December 20–21, Eden and his party left Moscow. Bound by a U.S. admonition against territorial deals, Eden had not softened Soviet suspicions. Stalin, relieved somewhat by Red Army counterattacks that had driven the Germans back 60 miles from Moscow, was still fighting on the political front like a cornered bear. He was more determined than ever to get either a second front or recognition of frontiers or both.

For his part, Eden left Moscow resolved to soften the British and the

Americans. "U.S. policy is exaggeratedly moral," he soon wrote, "at least where non-American interests are concerned."[16] To Churchill, still visiting in Washington, he cabled an urgent message recommending that Stalin's territorial demands be recognized. Churchill's indignant answer: Such questions should await the postwar peace conference. In London the War Cabinet agreed.

But by early February, aided by Ambassador Lord Edward Halifax in Washington, Eden had persuaded Churchill and the War Cabinet that Britain could get a Soviet alliance only if it recognized Stalin's frontiers. The crucial value of such an alliance was unspoken but obvious: Britain hoped to assure that Stalin would not make a separate peace with Hitler.

On February 10 Eden wired Halifax to approach Roosevelt on the issue, priming him with arguments. And he added what became, in retrospect, a key point: "It would not do to make any concessions to Stalin without requiring suitable quid pro quo and by insisting on any concessions made to him being part of bargain. . . ."[17]

These demands, as Eden outlined them, could be: no territorial seizures, as promised in the Atlantic Charter; formal approval of confederations, "especially in Balkans and as regards Poland and Czechoslovakia"; and reconstruction of all European states to strengthen their independence, but with "no aggrandisement and no interference."

This was a tall order. For the Western powers it would mean that, in return for giving up the territories and peoples demanded by Stalin, the rest of Europe could be withheld from his grip. Whether such self-denial by Stalin would later have proven enforceable, once the Red Army had overrun Eastern Europe, is another question. But sealing it into the bargain would have made subsequent violation more difficult.

Actually, Stalin later showed his willingness to honor a bargain by leaving an independent Greece. Certainly in early 1942, with Hitler occupying most of the European portion of the Soviet Union and preparing for a second mass offensive, Stalin's bargaining position would never again be so weak. Since he seemed so intent on getting Britain's approval of his frontiers, this was surely the time to get Eden's quid pro quo.

Moreover, Eden had still another motive in striking a bargain with Stalin. It was possible, he wrote Halifax, that Germany would be defeated mainly by the Soviet Union before the Western Allies could bring their strength to bear.

"In that event," he warned with striking foresight, "Russian prestige would be enormous and the Soviet Government would be tempted to work for the establishment of Communist Governments in the majority of European countries."

If Britain wanted Russian cooperation after the war, he added, it needed to make cooperation advantageous.

"We must therefore recognize that our refusal to satisfy Stalin's demand

. . . might encourage Soviet policy to revert to the pursuit of purely selfish aims with incalculable consequences for post-war period."[18]

But Eden's arguments, though remarkably prescient, were wasted. The initiative in the issue now shifted to Washington and Franklin D. Roosevelt.

On February 17 and 18, Halifax saw first Roosevelt and then Under Secretary of State Sumner Welles, leaving Eden's cables with them. FDR coolly asked Welles to tell Halifax he thought the British arguments for recognizing Stalin's territorial claims were "provincial." He understood Stalin's desire for Russian security, but this should be accomplished by the disarmament and dismemberment of Germany, as promised in the Atlantic Charter, and not by a secret agreement on territorial questions that should await the war's end. Finally, Roosevelt himself would take up the matter with Stalin through the Soviet ambassador in Washington, Maxim Litvinov.

Obviously shaken by this rebuff, Halifax quarreled heatedly with Welles on February 20; "if the President now undertook to discuss this matter directly with Stalin, Mr. Eden would be left in a very embarrassing position."[19]

In both Washington and London, the British thought Roosevelt was butting into a matter between Britain and the Soviet Union. Eden's courtesy in seeking U.S. acquiescence in a Soviet treaty was being abused; Roosevelt was stepping in where he had not been invited. No one had suggested to him that there would be a secret deal, and no one had suggested a treaty involving the United States.

The British now proposed to both Washington and Moscow that it might be best for territorial claims to be discussed by the three governments together. But, as Eden later wrote, Roosevelt thought "he could get better results with Stalin direct than could the three countries negotiating together. This was an illusion."[20]

Meanwhile, Stalin was growing restless at British delay. Ambassador Maisky prodded Eden about it on February 12. Worried about Moscow's reaction, Maisky applied pressure by talking to the press about British foot-dragging. Behind the pressure lurked a possibility that terrified the British— that Stalin, threatened by Hitler and suspicious of the British and Americans, might negotiate a separate peace.

On February 23 Stalin gave his annual "Order of the Day" speech to the Red Army. In it he seemed to indicate a shift of attitude. He made no mention of Soviet allies; in fact, he claimed that while Germany had the "direct support" of Italy, "the Red Army has no such support"—a clear jibe at the lack of a second front. As for the German people, the Soviet Union intended them no harm. The Soviet war aim was to expel the invaders from Russian soil: "It is very likely that the war for liberation of our Soviet land will result in the ousting or destruction of Hitler's clique. We should welcome such an outcome."[21]

If Stalin intended thus to play on British fears of a separate peace, he was successful. British diplomatic channels were aflame with speculation. Did this mild stance on Hitlerism signal an offer of negotiation?

The blow came at a time when Allied war fortunes were at their lowest. The Japanese had taken Singapore and sunk two British battleships. The Americans had lost the Philippines, and the British were losing to Rommel in the African campaign. The German menace on the seas was dramatized by two enemy warships cruising unchallenged through the English Channel. Some of Churchill's supporters feared his government might fall under British indignation. At this moment, on urging from Eden, Churchill stepped into the drama with a cable to Roosevelt on March 7:

The increasing gravity of the war has led me to feel that the principles of the Atlantic Charter ought not be construed so as to deny Russia the frontiers she occupied when Germany attacked her. This was the basis on which Russia acceded to Charter. . . . I hope therefore that you will be able to give us a free hand to sign the treaty which Stalin desires as soon as possible.[22]

To Stalin, the prime minister rushed an encouraging cable: "I have sent a message to President Roosevelt urging him to approve our signing the agreement with you about the frontiers of Russia at the end of the war." He added assurances about keeping war supplies coming as promised, remounting day and night bombing of Germany, and "continuing to study other measures for taking some of the weight off you."[23] The Soviet Union must, Churchill knew, be kept in the war at all costs.

In Washington, Halifax was trying to talk Roosevelt into the proposed treaty, or at least to keep him from tangling the issue by direct contact with Stalin. To the British fears of a separate peace, Roosevelt demurred: "We need not be afraid of Russia quitting the war on this."[24] And he revealed the real source of his own opposition, confirming what the British had assumed: Protests had come from American voters of Baltic descent. The tail of U.S. politics was wagging the dog of global war. To Halifax's report on March 9, Eden fired back an answer calling FDR's position the "height of unwisdom."[25]

Through Welles, Halifax now asked that Eden have a final look at Roosevelt's proposed arguments before he saw Litvinov. But the president refused. Halifax told Welles this decision was "in the highest degree embarrassing," and he was "much disturbed to hear it."[26]

Seeing Litvinov on March 12, Roosevelt told him he was "somewhat put out by the fact that M. Stalin had not approached" him directly on a question of such vital concern. Under no circumstances would he participate in a secret treaty. U.S. public opinion would not stand for recognition of the 1941 Soviet frontiers now. Nor would he "subscribe to any open public treaty with regard to definite frontiers until the war had been won." At that time, any legitimate steps that Soviet Union required for its future security would be approved and supported by the United States Government solely provided that these steps were in reality based on the legitimate needs of the Russian people for their security.

In London the British were aghast at Roosevelt's imperious tone with the only ally fighting Hitler in Europe. One Foreign Office figure observed that Stalin could ask "whether the United States is to be the judge of what the legitimate needs of the Soviet Union are." Eden's verdict: "A dismal tale of clumsy diplomacy. President Roosevelt has shown no consideration for our views, and has increased our difficulties."[27]

But Roosevelt was pleased with his action. He cabled Churchill, "I think I can personally handle Stalin better than either your Foreign Office or my State Department. Stalin hates the guts of all your top people. He thinks he likes me better, and I hope he will continue to do so."[28] Roosevelt was in for a shock. From Moscow, after two weeks of silence, came a one-sentence reply through Litvinov. "[T]he Soviet Government has taken note of the President's views."[29]

The cool response, as Maisky told Eden, was because the Soviets had not approached the United States either for a treaty or for its opinion. Thus brushing aside Roosevelt's intrusion, Stalin was ready to resume negotiations. So, for their part, were the British. They had promised to consult with the Americans, not to obey them. On March 27 Eden told Halifax to notify Roosevelt of the British decision, despite U.S. public opinion:

I should have naturally wished to spare them this embarrassment, but things being as they are I cannot take the risk of keeping Anglo-Soviet relations in a state of suspended animation any longer. The war situation has now become too serious for such dilatory tactics.[30]

Still Roosevelt could not hold off. When Halifax tried to see him, FDR saw "no useful purpose" in such a meeting and had "nothing to add."[31]

On April 10 Eden presented the War Cabinet with a revised draft agreeing to the Soviet frontiers except for the disputed line with Poland. More important, it upgraded the section on confederations, specifying all Eastern and Southeastern European countries and declaring the purpose: "to safeguard and strengthen the political, military and economic security of such States. . . . " Here was the most practical weapon in Eden's quid pro quo.

Three days later Eden presented the draft to Maisky, who forwarded it to Moscow. For the next two weeks the Soviets were silent. During this time Roosevelt was active in urging a tête-à-tête between himself and Stalin— perhaps in the Bering Strait or Alaska. Failing this, he invited Molotov to Washington. His purpose: to discuss the second front, which Harry Hopkins and U.S. Army Chief of Staff George C. Marshall were at that moment planning with the British in London.

The U.S. plan for a landing in France in 1943, and perhaps as early as late 1942, had been approved reluctantly by the British, though Churchill had terrible misgivings about the earlier date. Among other things, Roosevelt intended to use an early second front to satisfy Stalin about his Western allies and forestall his considering a separate peace. Equally important, as Hopkins told Eden in mid-April, the promise of a second front would "take the heat off Russia's diplomatic demands upon England."[32]

For his part, Stalin decided to send Molotov to Washington, but with a stop first in London to finish the treaty with the British. He was doing his best to keep Roosevelt's anti-frontiers policy out of the negotiations.

In London, Maisky reopened the talks on May 1 by presenting Stalin's reply on the treaty draft. It not only reopened the issue of the Polish frontier but also included an entirely new demand—British approval of Soviet mutual assistance pacts with Finland and Romania, which amounted to Soviet dominance of those countries.

At this the British despaired of reaching any agreement. Opposition to territorial recognition was also rumbling in the House of Commons. Undersecretary Cadogan declared that "it would be better not to crawl to the Russians over the dead bodies of *all* our principles."[33] And he proposed to Eden a new approach—a simple mutual guarantee of assistance in case of attack, but no mention of frontiers.

Yet few believed the Russians might settle for this, and Eden faced the possibility of a breakdown. So did Churchill, venting his feelings in a Cabinet meeting. "We must remember that this is a *bad* thing. We oughtn't to do it, and I shan't be sorry if we don't."[34]

To Maisky, Eden came back with a British "no." As long as the promise to Poland was subverted, "we could not sign the treaty." It was, he added, "despairing to try to negotiate with the Soviet Government when they invariably raised their price at every meeting."[35]

The issue remained deadlocked until Molotov's arrival, scheduled for May 20.[36]

Vyacheslav Mikhailovich Molotov, the man whom Stalin entrusted with the British negotiations, was more difficult than his master. For the next decade he would symbolize Soviet intransigence as the wooden-faced "Mr. Nyet." After his first meeting with Molotov in 1941, Harriman had warned Roosevelt that the United States "would have great difficulties with the Soviets as long as Molotov" was a key factor.[37]

Though Molotov could be affable, it seemed to be difficult for him. At banquets his toasts were invariably serious and calculated to make a political point. And his appearance was the opposite of Eden's—even shorter than Stalin, with a flat face and a pasty complexion broken only by a dark mustache and thick pince-nez. Quentin Reynolds wrote, "Molotov always looks as though he is watching someone else sucking a lemon." And "when he smiles, the set crust of his face seems to crack reluctantly, and you feel that it cost him a physical effort."[38]

In part, Molotov's stoicism came from his hard-bitten origins. A nephew of the composer Alexander Scriabin, he had changed his name to Molotov ("Hammer") reportedly to elude arrest for his Bolshevik activities. Nonetheless, he was repeatedly imprisoned and exiled before the October Revolution, during which he became a leader in disposing of the Mensheviks. Lenin is said to have pronounced him "the best filing clerk in Russia," but Stalin saw higher talents in him and it was to Stalin that he attached his loyalty. More than one visitor to the Kremlin noted his obsequious behavior in front of the dictator—if Stalin took out a cigarette, Molotov lit it for him.

But with or without Stalin he was an inflexible bargainer who won the respect, in some cases the admiration, but never the affection, of Western negotiators. Eden called him "a most able but ruthless automaton," but also acknowledged that if Stalin gave the signal, Molotov could be downright helpful, for "he was always a superb workman, as skilful at disentangling as at stalling."[39] Under-secretary Alexander Cadogan was more biting. After one negotiating session he wrote in his diary, "Molotov had all the grace and conciliation of a totem pole."[40] Charles Bohlen, whose State Department career was capped as ambassador to Moscow, wrote: "I never saw him pull off any delicate maneuver; it was his stubbornness that made him effective."[41] Churchill was perhaps the most devastating of all; while showing a flicker of sympathy for Molotov's triumph in surviving the Russian Revolution, Churchill considered him the ideal exponent of cold Soviet policy. "I have never seen a human being," he wrote, "who more perfectly represented the modern conception of a robot."[42]

When Molotov arrived in Britain on May 20, 1942, Maisky boarded his train as it rolled from Scotland to London and briefed him in his compartment. To the ambassador's conviction that the British would not approve the Soviet draft, Molotov gave a stony answer: "We shall see."[43]

Next morning, in what Eden called "an uncompromising mood," the Russians arrived at 10 Downing Street for a meeting with Churchill, Deputy Prime Minister Clement Attlee, Eden, and Cadogan. Again Molotov insisted on the new Soviet demands—otherwise it would be better to postpone the treaty.

More important than the treaty, in Molotov's mind, was the question of the second front. With the failure of the Red Army's Kharkov offensive, the Wehrmacht was now poised for its massive spring campaign. Once again, survival through the relief provided by a second front was the main Soviet concern. Without it, there was always the alternative of a separate peace with Hitler, which would enable him to concentrate again on Britain. This possibility, though unspoken, clearly hung over the discussion.

When Churchill responded that a second front was mainly a technical matter that should be discussed between the generals, Molotov retorted that he wished to discuss it "on the political plane"—a sly hint of a possible separate peace. "Blackmail!" Cadogan noted in his diary.

That afternoon and for the next two days, Molotov continued the battle with Eden and Cadogan. The key problem was, first, that the Soviet Union wanted the general phrase "the restoration of its frontiers violated by the Hitlerite aggression"; the British could not accept this without specifying Poland as an exception. To the Soviets, that would appear to put Britain on the side of the Poles in the issue, and tend to downgrade the Soviet claim against Poland in comparison with the other claims.

Thus the same issue that had blocked agreement during Eden's trip to Moscow was still alive when Molotov visited London. The mere mention of frontiers in the treaty was causing the Soviets a bigger problem than it solved. Nor could the two sides agree on other major issues. Molotov's new draft had omitted reference to confederations. "The Soviet Government," explained Molotov, "had certain information to show that some federations might be directed against the Soviet Union." Behind their charge of a *cordon sanitaire* being created against them, the Soviets were assuring that the weak Eastern European states would remain weak; if there were to be a *cordon sanitaire*, it would be aimed westward, not eastward. Thus the teeth of Eden's quid pro quo would be drawn.

As for the frontiers issue, Churchill summarized the British position in a cable to Stalin on May 23: "We cannot go back on our previous undertakings to Poland and have to take account of our own and American opinion."

On the same afternoon Eden answered Molotov with his alternative—a simple mutual defense treaty with no reference to frontiers. By promising British military alliance in case of a future attack on the Soviet Union, Eden declared it "a bigger offer than His Majesty's Government had ever made in the course of history." But Molotov would not budge from his demand for recognition of frontiers.

Next day Molotov was back with a concession—accepting the British position on Poland. But on Finland and Romania he proposed that if the British would not support Soviet pacts with them, it could recognize that the Soviet Union had "special interests" in them—a phrase reminiscent of Stalin's 1939 pact with Hitler. When Eden balked at these offers, Maisky took him aside. "I cannot understand your attitude," he declared. "We have made many concessions, yet you seem as though you did not want an agreement."

For their part, the British thought the Soviets just as difficult. After the meeting Cadogan wrote in his diary: "They *are* extraordinary people to deal with—they wear their suspicions on their sleeve!"

When the meeting ended, Molotov offered no hope. But, without telling Eden, he cabled Stalin recommending the "no frontiers" draft.

Meanwhile, though the British were playing their hand alone, the Americans had not dealt themselves out. On the evening of May 21 Ambassador Gil Winant had cabled Roosevelt and Hull about the London negotiations: Molotov was still demanding the Baltic states and a part of Finland. When Eden had referred to U.S. public opinion, Molotov had answered that there was "also a public opinion in Russia that had to be considered."

Cordell Hull had been away from Washington on sick leave when Roosevelt had tackled the treaty issue in March and April. But he now returned to the fray with a cable to Winant, approved by the president, threatening that if the "frontiers" treaty were signed, "we might have to issue a separate statement clearly stating that we did not subscribe to its principles and clauses."[44]

In London, Winant had already asked to see Molotov, which he did on the night of May 24 in the Soviet embassy. Molotov again brought up the second front, which Winant simply asked him to defer until he reached Washington. As for the "frontiers" treaty, Winant emphasized that Roosevelt and Hull were "set against introducing frontier problems at this time. . . ."

The Russians listened with what Winant called "great attention." Molotov's answer: "[T]he president's position on this question" deserves "serious consideration." The Russians were, as Winant told Eden, "frightfully nice." When Winant left, Maisky phoned Eden for an appointment next day to discuss the "no frontiers" draft; Molotov thought "something could be done on basis of it."

Despite Stalin's initial rebuff, Roosevelt's argument was getting through to the Soviets even more than to the British. Cadogan wrote that Winant had been twisting Eden's tail and now "twisted *their* tails." Whether the Soviets would have accepted the "no frontiers" treaty without U.S. intervention is a question. Churchill afterward wrote to Roosevelt that Winant's effort was "largely instrumental." And FDR wrote to Winant, "You certainly managed to work out that British-Russian Treaty in thoroughly acceptable form. . . ."[45]

By the time Molotov met with Eden and Churchill at 10 o'clock that night, he had received an answer from Stalin: "authority to sign." That night and next morning the two sides refined the language, and in the afternoon the public signing took place in Eden's study.

Why did the Soviets drop, for the time being, their demand for territorial recognition? The British, in fact, had asked themselves why Stalin had been insisting at all on recognition of territorial claims that he could—and would, if the Allies were victorious—enforce by Red Army occupation. They shuddered at the answer: As in 1939, when their prewar negotiations had foundered partly on the issue of the Baltic states, Stalin was now making territorial recognition the "acid test" of their alliance. As he had turned to Hitler for a bargain in 1939, he might do so again in 1942, especially if he could not be promised a second front.

Now, with Hitler consolidating his grip on the Crimea and preparing for an all-out drive to smash the Soviet Union, survival was again paramount.

A second front in the west to draw German divisions from the Russian front was far more critical than British recognition of frontiers. The Soviets considered their abandonment of territorial recognition to be a concession that strengthened their expectation of a second front. Both Eden and Harriman, who was in London at the time, came to this conclusion.

Harriman pinpointed "the more urgent need of a second front. By their reckoning, a timely concession on the terms of the treaty could avoid a profitless squabble. . . . Conceivably it might hasten the day when the British and Americans would launch their great assault on the continent."[46] Eden agreed:

The chief purpose in the Soviet Government's negotiations was to secure a second front in Europe as soon as possible. At some stage in our talks Molotov probably became convinced he could not get his way over frontiers and decided that more was to be gained in the military field by accepting our new terms, and going to Washington with the Treaty signed, than by failure to agree.[47]

For the Western powers, this Russian strategy carried a crucial meaning. To achieve reasonable relations with the Soviets, and forestall any thought of a separate peace, the promise of an early second front was now imperative.

Thus the "no frontiers" treaty seemed a victory for Roosevelt in his first confrontation with Stalin. Yet this noncontroversial treaty carried an ominous burden. Since it demanded no political concessions from the British, it included no quid pro quo from the Soviets. True, it did retain "the two principles of not seeking territorial aggrandisement for themselves and of non-interference in the internal affairs of other states." But these phrases borrowed from the Atlantic Charter had already been subscribed to by Stalin, involved no new concession by him, and were so general as to be open to peculiar Soviet interpretations. The more specific wording in the earlier British drafts—especially an agreement to encourage confederations in Eastern Europe—would have given some teeth to the British goal of saving that region's independence.

Whether or not the British would ever have won Russian acceptance of this or any part of Eden's quid pro quo is questionable. Yet in 1941 and 1942 Stalin's bargaining power was at a low ebb. Eden wrote:

[I]t seemed inescapable that, if Hitler were overthrown, Russian forces would end the war much deeper into Europe than they began it in 1941. It therefore seemed prudent to tie the Soviet Government to agreements as early as possible.[48]

But the opportunity was missed by Roosevelt's insistence on a "no frontiers" treaty. Refusing to abandon the Baltic peoples was a worthy but unrealistic political gesture, since a Soviet victory would certainly seal their fate. And with no bargain in the treaty, a chance to restrain Stalin in the rest of Eastern Europe was lost.

Why did Roosevelt fail to seize this chance? The outright annexations that Stalin demanded were too flagrant for a U.S. president to accept publicly, especially in view of the power of American ethnic voters. True, the treaty was between the British and the Soviets only, and could have been shunned as a European matter. But this would have made Roosevelt less than the global leader he intended to be. Ironically, within little more than a year FDR would be telling his friend Cardinal Spellman that Stalin would annex Finland, the Baltic states, Bessarabia, and the eastern half of Poland. "There is no point to oppose these desires of Stalin," he added, "because he has the power to get them anyhow."[49]

As for the value of Eden's quid pro quo in saving the rest of Europe, this was a subtlety peculiar to British experience in European politics. The spread of Soviet power across Europe was, to the British, a reality unless blocked; to the Americans, a future possibility and therefore of less immediate importance than Stalin's clear-cut annexations. Though Roosevelt might be able to say he had saved the Baltic states, the first step was taken in losing all of Eastern Europe.

"It would be a measureless disaster," Churchill soon wrote with rising trepidation, "if Russian barbarianism overlaid the culture and independence of the ancient States of Europe."[50]

As for Stalin, his policy was confided to the Yugoslav leader Milovan Djilas: "Everyone imposes his own system as far as his army can reach."[51]

3

"Second Front Now!"

Though the Anglo-Soviet treaty was hailed in London and Moscow, and was a useful psychological basis of wartime alliance, it indirectly sparked a chain reaction of mischief that impacted the future of Europe. First, it represented a political sacrifice by Stalin, who did not get recognition of his 1941 frontiers. This became a bargaining chip in achieving a more critical goal—the promise of a second front in 1942.

In the councils of the Western Allies, Churchill opposed an early second front as courting disaster. As early as his December 1941 visit to Washington, he proposed instead an invasion of French North Africa to secure the Mediterranean and open the "soft underbelly" of Europe to possible attack.

In April 1942 Marshall and Hopkins had won British concurrence in a second front in France to begin April 1, 1943, with a possible smaller version—a diversionary "lodgment"—as early as September 1942, if necessary, to relieve the Russians. Neither the Americans nor the British had proposed the decisive, full-scale second front to start in 1942.

Almost as soon as Marshall and Hopkins had returned to the United States, the British had second thoughts about 1943 as well. When Molotov visited Britain in May 1942 and demanded an early second front, Churchill had been noncommittal, and had referred him to the Americans.

This was the situation when Molotov, dining in the White House on May 29, spent most of the meal propounding the case for a second front in 1942. Next morning, with General Marshall and Admiral Ernest J. King present, Molotov demanded an answer from Roosevelt.[1]

"If you postpone your decision," he warned, "you will have eventually to bear the brunt of the war, and if Hitler becomes the undisputed master of the continent, next year will unquestionably be tougher than this one."

Roosevelt then asked Marshall whether "we could say to Mr. Stalin that we are preparing a second front."

"Yes," was Marshall's clipped answer.

Roosevelt then told Molotov he could say to Stalin, "[W]e expect the formation of a second front this year." This was more than Marshall had acknowledged and more than had been agreed with the British.

In his last meeting with Molotov, Roosevelt seemed to waffle. While the United States expected to open a second front in 1942, it was short of shipping to its forward base in Britain; if the Soviets could get along with fewer shipments of lend-lease goods, this would speed preparations for the second front. He added, "The Soviets could not eat their cake and have it too."

At this, Molotov was visibly angered: "[T]he second front would be stronger if the first front still stood fast. . . . " With obvious sarcasm he asked "what would happen if the Soviets cut down their requirements and then no second front eventuated." With growing indignation he referred to the "no frontiers" treaty he had brought from England, apparently linking it to the second front. "What is the president's answer with respect to the second front?"

Roosevelt, accustomed to having his way, was perhaps taken aback by Molotov's effrontery. But, as Harry Hopkins put it, "Roosevelt was by no means appalled by the new and strange problem in human relations that Molotov presented. It offered a challenge. . . . "

The president answered that the British and Americans were even now consulting about landing craft and provisions: "We expect to establish a second front."

For his part, Molotov was achieving his purpose. Two days later, when Hull showed him a draft of a joint communiqué about his Washington visit, Molotov inserted a key sentence: "In the course of the conversations full understanding was reached with regard to the urgent tasks of creating a second front in Europe in 1942."

When Hopkins told Marshall about this, Marshall answered that it was "too strong" and wanted to delete the year 1942. Roosevelt, however, kept it in the release. And, without facing the advice of his own military or the wishes of his British allies, he cabled Churchill that he was anxious that preparations for the second front "proceed to definite action beginning in 1942."

Why did Roosevelt persist in this dangerous misrepresentation? Partly it was his belief that the Soviets needed such a promise—even a false promise— to stiffen their resistance to Hitler at a bleak moment when they might be tempted to seek a separate peace. And partly it was his peculiar weakness of telling people what they wanted to hear—a compulsion to make others like him at any cost. Certainly in this instance the cost could be disastrous in terms of a bitter and disillusioned ally.

But for the moment the Soviets were delighted to take Roosevelt at his word. FDR wrote that Molotov "actually got chummy toward the end."[2] Armed with the declaration on the second front, Molotov returned to London. There Churchill and Eden were dismayed at the reference to 1942. Eden called it "explosive." Churchill believed it useful in holding German troops in Western Europe, but realized that "in this effort to mislead the enemy we should not mislead our Ally."[3]

In the communiqué on Molotov's London visits and the Anglo-Soviet treaty, the identical "second front" sentence was included. But while it was being drafted in the Cabinet Room on June 10, Churchill handed Molotov a memorandum. "We are making preparations for a landing on the Continent in August or September, 1942," it began. Then it warned of difficulties and of disaster in a premature venture. "We can therefore give no promise in the matter, but provided that it appears sound and sensible we shall not hesitate to put our plans into effect."[4]

Preferring to ignore this caveat, Molotov flew back to Moscow and wired Roosevelt on June 12 expressing "the great satisfaction I feel in having reached a full understanding concerning the urgent tasks connected with the creation of a second front in Europe in 1942. . . . "[5] In Moscow he continued to nail down Roosevelt's promise. In his speech to the Supreme Soviet calling for ratification of the Anglo-Soviet treaty, Molotov repeated the identical words about the second front in 1942. Many of the deputies made the same reference in their speeches. To Admiral William H. Standley, then U.S. ambassador in Moscow, Molotov and other Soviets expressed enthusiasm for the promised second front in 1942. Standley found Molotov "openly jubilant," and Sir Archibald Clark Kerr, the British ambassador, described him as "a new man."

At the same time both *Pravda* and *Izvestia* ran editorials using language identical to that of the Washington and London communiqués. Tass wire service featured the second-front-in-1942 theme in announcing Molotov's talks in London and Washington. And it repeated stories quoting spokesmen for workers in war factories rejoicing at the promised second front in 1942.

The pressure was so great, the treatment of the promise so wholehearted, that Ambassador Standley warned Roosevelt:

[I]f such a front does not materialize quickly and on a large scale, these people will be so deluded in their belief in our sincerity of purpose and will for concerted action that inestimable harm will be done to the cause of the United Nations.[6]

But the British were more concerned than Roosevelt. On July 14, Clark Kerr told Molotov that he exaggerated the promise. Four days later Stalin received a cable from Churchill referring to a "second front in 1943. . . . " At this, Stalin fired back a hot retort: "In view of the situation on the Soviet-German front, I state most emphatically that the Soviet Government cannot tolerate the second front in Europe being postponed till 1943."[7]

Clearly a major Allied crisis was looming. In mid-July a U.S. delegation headed by Marshall flew to London to settle the second front issue. The British now insisted that even a limited landing in France in 1942 would be disastrous. Roosevelt then notified Marshall that he favored Churchill's North African invasion as the most practical way to engage U.S. troops with the enemy in 1942. This brought agreement in London, but against the better judgment of Marshall, who declared for the record that such a commitment of forces would rule out a second front in France even in 1943.

Roosevelt's promise of a second front in 1942 was now in a shambles. Molotov's mission to the West had failed on both counts—no territorial recognition and no second front in 1942. The understandable sense of double cross in Moscow would be devastating—perhaps would even precipitate a separate peace. Stalin would have to be told—in person.

The president's effort to meet Stalin at some halfway point and exercise his eloquence on him had already failed. Churchill, who gloried in difficult tasks, now undertook to beard the lion.

Accompanied by Averell Harriman as Roosevelt's representative, Churchill flew to Moscow via the Mediterranean on a somber mission that could not have been more awkwardly timed. Hitler's legions were again threatening the very life of the Soviet Union with their summer offensive aimed at the Caucasus and Stalingrad.

"I have a somewhat raw job," Churchill cabled Roosevelt from Cairo on August 5. "It was like carrying a large lump of ice to the North Pole," he later wrote.[8]

On the evening of August 12 Churchill entered the Kremlin and for the first time met Stalin.[9] He lost no time in telling him that there would be no second front in 1942; "[I]t would be folly to invite a disaster which would help nobody." But while the Western Allies simply did not have enough landing craft in 1942, they were preparing for a "very great" cross-Channel invasion in 1943. Such a 1943 operation had by no means been agreed upon between the British and Americans, but apparently Churchill believed it would mollify Stalin. It did not.

"You can't win wars if you aren't willing to take risks," he snapped in a tirade that was almost insulting. "You must not be so afraid of the Germans."

The argument that followed ended in what Churchill called "an oppressive silence." Then, unfolding a map of Europe and the Mediterranean, he turned to the air war against Germany, a subject that thawed Stalin considerably. At this point Churchill showed his hole card—the invasion of French North Africa, code-named "Torch." "If we could end the year in possession of North Africa," he declared, "we could threaten the belly of Hitler's Europe." To illustrate the strategy, he drew a picture of a crocodile, saying that in addition to hitting him on the snout, the Allies could now threaten his "soft belly."

His interest fully aroused, Stalin quickly enumerated the advantages of the move and exclaimed, in what seemed an odd expression for a Bolshevik, "May God prosper this undertaking!"

Next day Churchill cabled Roosevelt a report of this first meeting with Stalin: "I shall establish a solid and sincere relationship with this man. . . . " However, aware of the hot-cold treatment that Stalin had given previous Western visitors, Churchill told Molotov, "Stalin will make a great mistake to treat us roughly when we have come so far."

But that night Stalin put on his expected performance. He handed Churchill and Harriman a memorandum reproaching them for breaking the promise of a second front in 1942. The decision, it stated, "inflicts a mortal blow to the whole of Soviet public opinion" and "prejudices the plan of the Soviet Command." Stalin upbraided Churchill with insulting language: "[I]f the British Army had been fighting the Germans as much as the Russian Army it would not be so frightened of them."

At length Churchill interrupted. He hit the table with his fist. Then he roared his answer: "I have come round Europe . . . hoping to meet the hand of comradeship; and I am bitterly disappointed. I have not met that hand."

His impassioned speech came tumbling so fast that his interpreter fell behind and stopped taking notes. The prime minister turned his ire on the unfortunate interpreter. Poking his arm, he asked whether he had translated first one point, then another.

Puffing on his pipe, Stalin stood up, raised his hand and smiled: "I do not understand the words, but by God I like your spirit."

The impasse was broken. If Stalin had been testing Churchill's fortitude, he had received his answer. But the prime minister left late that night resentful and depressed. Accompanying him in the car back to his quarters, Cadogan asked, "Shall I tell Stalin in confidence that you are hesitating whether to accept his invitation to dinner tomorrow after what has happened?"

"No," answered Churchill, "that is going too far, I think."

When the prime minister arrived next night for the usual Kremlin banquet, he was still smarting from the treatment by Stalin, who now—according to the usual script—was affability itself. Even so, the dinner never loosened up in the prescribed manner, probably due to Churchill's restraint. When the prime minister left the party, Stalin, realizing he might have overdone his performance the night before, solicitously saw him down numerous corridors and staircases to the main door of the Kremlin. Molotov later said this was "without any precedent in the history of the Soviet Union."

Churchill had intended to leave Moscow next day, August 15. Back in his quarters he was despondent: "I ought not to have come." But next morning he reflected that Stalin's recriminations were clearly born of the desperation he felt under the German onslaught. If he himself now left Moscow with such a breach between them, the war might be affected. Ambassador Clark Kerr came round and helped persuade Churchill to try once more.

That evening he met Stalin in his Kremlin office, alone except for interpreters. This time it was Churchill's turn to be friendly, though Stalin seemed unresponsive. After more than an hour the prime minister got up to go. He was leaving Moscow, he said, at daybreak. His host's mood suddenly changed. He seemed embarrassed that the comradeship still had not developed.

"Why should we not go to my house," Stalin ventured, "and have some drinks?"

Churchill, hardly a teetotaler, allowed that he was "in principle always in favor of such a policy."

Off they went, Stalin in the lead, through a maze of corridors and rooms to a narrow street within the Kremlin walls; there, after a short walk, they entered Stalin's four-room apartment—austere and unpretentious. Stalin's attractive daughter, Svetlana, came into the dining room and kissed her father, who looked impishly at Churchill as if to say, "You see, even we Bolsheviks have a family life." To his interpreter Churchill whispered, "I think this is going to be an opportunity not to be missed."

While Svetlana began setting the table, Stalin fell to opening bottles of wine. "Why should we not have Molotov?" he suddenly asked. ". . . There is one thing about Molotov—he can drink." And so the three men, with the two interpreters, dined into the early hours, reminiscing, swapping yarns, comparing notes and ideas about the war, and indulging in some friendly leg-pulling. After midnight Cadogan came in with a draft of the communiqué, which they approved with some amendments by Churchill.

When he left at 2:30 in the morning, the prime minister was exhilarated. Probably the first Westerner ever to enter Stalin's home, he had accomplished in this extraordinary session what Eden's diplomacy and Roosevelt's promises could not. "I was taken into the family," he told his doctor next morning. "We ended friends."

Even after Churchill's departure, as they had done before and during his stay, the Soviets played up the second front for home consumption. Churchill's famous V-sign for victory, photographed more than once in Moscow, was interpreted as a sign for the second front. Stalin needed every morale booster he could get, and seems now to have settled for a second-class second front in Africa.

Anxious to exploit his gains, Churchill cabled Roosevelt: "Everything for us now turns on hastening Torch and defeating Rommel." At Churchill's urging, Roosevelt sent Stalin a bolstering message: "We are coming as quickly and as strongly to your assistance as we possibly can. . . ."[10]

On October 23 Lieutenant General Bernard C. Montgomery launched his offensive against Rommel at El Alamein. On November 8 U.S. and British troops under Lt. Gen. Dwight D. Eisenhower landed in French North Africa. On November 19 the Red Army began its counteroffensive at Stalingrad.

Suddenly the tide of war had turned in favor of the Allies. While Stalin declined to join them on grounds he could not be spared from the eastern front, Roosevelt and Churchill held their first meeting on captured territory at Casablanca, French Morocco, on January 14, 1943.

Primarily a strategy meeting, it settled on Sicily as the next target, thus effectively ruling out a second front in France even in 1943. Obviously this would stir renewed cries of "breach of faith" from Stalin, who continued to demand a second front and rightly looked on the Mediterranean as a diversion from a real assault on Germany. Anticipating this, Roosevelt again sought to soften the blow with brave words—words that would reassure Moscow of the resolve and future action of its allies.

On January 7, before he left for Africa, Roosevelt held a meeting at the White House with the Joint Chiefs of Staff. Abruptly he suggested to Marshall that he "should go to Moscow."

"What would I be expected to accomplish there?" asked Marshall, taken by surprise.

The trip would be, explained Roosevelt, "for the purpose of giving impetus to the Russian morale." Stalin had, he said, "a feeling of loneliness." FDR wanted to propose a summit meeting. And he intended to speak to Churchill "about the advisability of informing Mr. Stalin that the United Nations were to continue on until they reach Berlin, and that their only terms would be unconditional surrender." General Marshall could personally take these tidings to Moscow.[11]

The idea of Marshall's mission to Moscow was later dropped due to Soviet opposition. But the "unconditional surrender" concept was now in full flower. According to Elliott Roosevelt, his father broached the idea to Churchill at luncheon in the president's villa at Casablanca, emphasizing that "it's just the thing for the Russians. . . ."[12]

Yet, in a cable to his War Cabinet, Churchill described the proposed unconditional surrender declaration as a concept jointly arrived at, stating that Roosevelt "liked this idea."[13] It was Churchill who proposed at a meeting with the Combined Chiefs of Staff on January 18 that the communiqué following the conference should state, "[T]he United Nations are resolved to pursue the war to the bitter end, neither party relaxing in its efforts until the unconditional surrender of Germany and Japan has been achieved."[14] He followed by asking and getting approval of his War Cabinet by means of cables between Casablanca and London.

The U.S. military chiefs debated among themselves the value of "unconditional surrender." In particular, Generals John R. Deane and Albert C. Wedemeyer opposed it on grounds that it would stiffen German resistance, drag out the war, and enlarge Soviet power in Europe. But nothing more was said of it in the formal meetings until the conference was over and the two leaders met the press at the president's villa. It was not included in the communiqué handed to the journalists, but it was part of a "draft statement" prepared for the press conference, which Churchill reviewed and amended.

While Roosevelt and Churchill sat in chairs, some 50 newsmen sat around them on the lawn behind the villa. Taking the lead, Roosevelt referred to notes that included the following statement:

The President and the Prime Minister . . . are more than ever determined that peace can come to the world only by total elimination of German and Japanese war power. This involves the simple formula of placing the objective of this war in terms of an unconditional surrender by Germany, Italy and Japan.

When this statement was actually voiced by Roosevelt, he interjected a reference to General Ulysses S. "Unconditional Surrender" Grant. He followed this with, "The elimination of German, Japanese and Italian war power means the unconditional surrender by Germany, Italy and Japan." To emphasize the importance of this declaration, he added, "[T]his meeting is called the 'unconditional surrender' meeting."

Roosevelt afterward said that unconditional surrender was an idea that just "popped into my mind" during the press conference. That night, according to Harriman, Churchill was furious that Roosevelt had volunteered the statement without consulting him. He claimed that Roosevelt's announcement was a surprise to him, but that he went along with it for the sake of Allied unity. Both versions were wrong, and Churchill later corrected himself.

The facts are that the doctrine of unconditional surrender was considered by Roosevelt beforehand, discussed with Churchill at Casablanca, and reduced to a formal statement in which both leaders participated.

But while it was not mere whimsy, it clearly was given little attention in the welter of pressing subjects bearing on the leaders at Casablanca. There is no evidence that Roosevelt discussed the question with his advisers, either before or at Casablanca. He simply told them of his decision. Nor does the record show any discussion of the ramifications of unconditional surrender between Roosevelt and Churchill. The only top-level discussion of any importance seems to have been in London, on short notice, by the War Cabinet.

Nonetheless, "unconditional surrender" was the big news of the Casablanca conference. It was immediately, and for years after, debated in the world press and in countless public forums. One purpose, so far as Roosevelt was concerned, was to avoid any repetition of the 1918 armistice, reached before any part of Germany was invaded, thus enabling the Germans to believe, and claim later, that they were not really defeated.

But if this was an important objective of the decision, publicizing it was a mistake. Ruling out any negotiation by any authority in Germany, it encouraged a leader of Hitler's fanaticism to fight to the death, and discouraged a broad German effort to salvage something by replacing him. While many observers, including Churchill, have defended the unconditional surrender decision, the public announcement of it weighted the scales for a longer war.[15] This in turn meant that the Red Army would roll across Europe until it reached and occupied Germany.

However, while Roosevelt's unconditional surrender decision was partly intended to assure that the Germans would taste total defeat, the first objective that he mentioned to his associates was to placate Stalin. Roosevelt still had been unable to talk face-to-face with Stalin about Soviet territorial demands in Eastern Europe—to offer verbal assurance in lieu of written recognition. He still was unable to mount a second front in France, and it soon appeared that none would be mounted there even in 1943.

After four conferences between Roosevelt and Churchill, Stalin was still outside their councils. Stalin's suspicions of the West, stirred by the intervention of Western powers in the Soviet Union after the Revolution, was still burning beneath the surface. He could say, more than ever, that the British and Americans were willing to fight the Germans to the last drop of Russian blood.

In 1939 Stalin had turned from the British and French to make the deal with Hitler that precipitated World War II. He was perfectly capable of doing it again if separate terms seemed to Soviet advantage. Now that the Battle of Stalingrad was ending with a decisive Soviet victory and the capture of an entire German army, perhaps the Nazis would be receptive.

What better way for Roosevelt and Churchill to forestall such a move than by telling the world they would never negotiate? They would fight until the enemy surrendered unconditionally. Stalin, they hoped, would feel obliged to join in the declaration, and would feel ashamed before world opinion to seek separate terms.

Stalin did question the wisdom, as he later told Harriman, of the unconditional surrender announcement. But the Soviet Union adhered to it when Molotov signed the Four-Power Declaration at the Council of Foreign Ministers at Moscow in October. By that time the Red Army was driving back the Wehrmacht all along the eastern front. A separate peace was no longer an issue.

In fact, it is doubtful that Churchill's and Roosevelt's fears of a separate peace were ever justified. In 1943 rumors of German-Soviet peace talks prompted the British Foreign Office to question Molotov, who answered that Moscow had received no feelers from Berlin. Though private go-betweens seem to have busied themselves trying to arrange meetings in Sweden between German and Soviet representatives, there is no evidence that any took place.[16]

Stalin, however, masterfully played on these fears in pressing his allies for advantages, especially for a second front. When told by them in June 1943 that the cross-Channel invasion would not take place until the spring of 1944, his reaction was thunderous. Reminding them of numerous promises that the second front would take place first in 1942, then 1943, he warned that the new decision, taken without Soviet participation, "may gravely affect the subsequent course of the war."[17]

The main result was that Roosevelt and even Churchill were put on the defensive in their dealings with Stalin until the Normandy landings in June 1944. Even then, though Churchill and Eden would press Stalin for commitments in Eastern Europe, they would have to bargain without the weight of U.S. might, since Roosevelt would not support them.

Meanwhile, to Stalin the unconditional surrender declaration was no substitute for a second front. Its principal effect was to assure that the Germans would hold out until the Red Army swept into Germany. The longer the Western Allies delayed their second front in France, the farther the Red Army would go. Since the Germans had no hope of an armistice, even if they removed Hitler, the Red Army might go clear to the North Sea . . . and the Rhine.

4

The Missing 10,000

Less than three weeks after Hitler attacked the Soviet Union, the British were pressing the Poles and Russians to patch up their differences in order to fight the common enemy.

Leading the Polish government-in-exile was General Wladyslaw Sikorski, a long-standing member of the officer class in the tradition of Polish "democratic autocracy." He had fought under Marshal Jozef Pilsudski in World War I and served in his cabinet in the early 1920s. As a result of disagreements with the Polish strongman he was dismissed from the military service in 1928. Sikorski was outside the country when the Germans and Soviets invaded Poland in 1939, and was available to become prime minister of the Polish government-in-exile.

It was a fortunate choice. Though personally vain and insistent on punctilious observance of his position, Sikorski backed up his egotism with superior capabilities. He had all the emotional Polish pride and patriotism, but he coupled this with a logical realism that was uncharacteristic of Polish leaders at that time. Despite Poland's deep grievances against the Russians, he knew that a rapprochement with the Soviet Union was important to the defeat of Hitler. More than any other Polish leader, he was able to control the excessive views of cabinet members such as General Kazimierz Sosnokowski, a product of Pilsudski's regime and a virulent anti-Soviet.

More than the Poles themselves, the British were ready to consider Sikorski a true statesman. Churchill once exclaimed, "I loved that man." And Sir William Strang, a veteran British diplomat, later told the Polish foreign minister: "We in Britain regarded Sikorski as a very great man—in fact, the greatest of all the European statesmen whom the war has driven into exile."[1]

On July 11, 1941, Sikorski and the Soviet ambassador to London, Ivan M. Maisky, met in Sir Alexander Cadogan's room in the British Foreign Office to discuss a draft agreement. In his memoirs Maisky reports that as Sikorski's party arrived in two limousines, Polish officers jumped out and rushed into the Foreign Office, shouting, "The General is coming! The General is coming!" Resplendent in dress uniform replete with medals and decorations, Sikorski strode into Cadogan's office to find Maisky, by contrast, in a simple summer suit.

Maisky began by saying that the Soviet Union favored "the independence of the Polish State within the limits of Polish nationality." This meant the Soviets were insisting on the Curzon Line, not the Riga Line, as the postwar frontier between Poland and the Soviet Union. Sikorski demanded "the return to the legal situation" before the 1939 German-Soviet treaty. Maisky said that he was not insisting that Poland agree, but only stating "the Soviet Government's general point of view." The two nations could "put aside for the present the question of the frontiers of Poland." Sikorski pointed out that in the meantime certain problems could arise: "For example, what would happen if the Polish and Soviet armies marched victoriously into Polish territory? Who would govern this territory, Poles or Russians?"

Maisky answered that "at this moment this question was perhaps a little academic." Sikorski declared he could not even discuss the question. "It was not possible that the Soviet Government should make a unilateral declaration in this matter. Any declaration should be bilateral and agreed to by both parties."[2]

More wrangling ensued over this and other issues. There followed several days of drafting and redrafting by both sides, with the help of the British. On July 30, little more than a month after Hitler had attacked the Soviet Union, the Polish government-in-exile signed an agreement with the Soviet Union that established diplomatic relations between them and annulled the German-Soviet treaty. They also agreed to aid each other in the war against Germany and to form a Polish Army to fight with the Red Army on the eastern front. The Soviets promised to free all Polish citizens held in the Soviet Union.

Regarding the frontier issue, the Soviet Union "recognizes that the Soviet-German treaties of 1939 relative to territorial changes in Poland have lost their validity." But in a secret protocol the two governments agreed: "Various claims both of public and private nature will be dealt with in the course of further negotiations. . . . " For their part, the British—to promote Polish acceptance of the treaty—promised that Poland's frontiers would not be negotiated until the war's end.

From the beginning the Polish-Soviet détente was marked by disagreement and rancor. Three members of Sikorski's cabinet, including Sosnokowski, resigned in protest. Insisting that the disputed territory east of the Ribben-trop-Molotov Line was Soviet, Moscow refused to restore Polish citizenship to those within that region who were of Byelorussian, Ukrainian, or Jewish extraction.

Other Soviet provocations included delays in releasing Poles from prison, as required in the agreement, arbitrary arrests of Polish citizens in the Soviet Union, drafting of Polish citizens into the Red Army, interference with relief work for Poles who were released from internment in Russia, and withholding of adequate food and supplies from the Polish Army in the Soviet Union.

But the most pressing issue was the continued imprisonment of thousands of Poles interned in the Soviet Union between 1939 and 1941. Of more than 1 million imprisoned, about 42,000 remained in prison by October 1941, by Soviet admission. Several thousand civilians and approximately 8,000 officers, about 85 percent of the total officers, could not be identified anywhere.

Numerous inquiries about the missing officers were made by General Wladyslaw Anders, who had been named to head the Polish Army, while he was recruiting officers among former Polish prisoners taken by the Red Army. But he could get no accounting of them from the Soviets. On October 7, 1941, the Polish ambassador to Moscow, Stanislaw Kot, pressed the matter with Andrei Vishinsky, then deputy commissar for foreign affairs: "Altogether 9500 officers were imprisoned in Poland and deported inside the USSR, while there are only 2,000 officers in our army. What happened to 7500 officers?"

Embarrassed, Vishinsky could give no answer.

"I would have understood the missing of some dozens of people," added Kot, "of, let us say, several hundred, but not several thousand."[3]

This was the first of many official inquiries by the Polish government about the missing officers. Later the Soviets answered that they had all been released. On November 14 Ambassador Kot saw Stalin in Molotov's office in the Kremlin. Among other things, he asked about the missing Poles.

Stalin: "Are there still any Poles who have not been released?"

Kot: "Not one officer has returned to us from the camp of Starobielsk which was wound up in the spring of 1940."

In the discussion that followed, Stalin stood up and paced around the desk, smoking a cigarette. Kot continued: "[T]he officers from Starobielsk, Kozielsk and Ostashkov, who were moved in April and May 1940, are missing."

"We have released all the Poles," said Stalin. In a moment he stepped over and picked up the telephone on Molotov's desk.

"Stalin speaking," he snapped. "Have all the Poles been released from prison? . . . The Ambassador of Poland is here and he tells me that not all have been released." He put down the phone, and Kot assumed he had called the head of the NKVD, the Soviet secret police. In a few minutes the phone rang; Stalin listened in silence and hung up. As he rejoined the others, he muttered, almost to himself, "They say they've all been released."

The issue was dropped for the moment but came up again when Sikorski traveled to Moscow in December 1941. On December 3, accompanied by

Kot and Anders, he met Stalin and Molotov in the Kremlin. After a while Sikorski brought up the missing officers.

"These people are here," he said. "Not one of them has returned."

"That is impossible," replied Stalin, "they have escaped."

"Where then could they escape?"

"Well, to Manchuria."[4]

Whether or not Stalin was serious, Sikorski was not amused.

Altogether, the Poles made over 50 inquiries about the missing officers, with no result. The U.S. and British ambassadors in Moscow joined in the quest, only to be told by Vishinsky that the officers had been "released." But none had ever made contact with Polish families or Polish authorities. The issue continued to aggravate Polish-Soviet relations, which were already strained.

On January 11, 1943, Molotov announced that henceforth all those residing in the disputed territory after Soviet occupation (Poles as well as other nationalities) were considered Soviet citizens—a violation of the 1941 Polish-Soviet treaty, which had annulled territorial changes in the German-Soviet treaty.

On the strength of this the Soviets began drafting all remaining Poles in Russia, including those in prison, into the Red Army. It meant an end to the Polish relief program for Poles in Russia. And it meant that the Soviets were acting unilaterally on their claim to the disputed territory, without further negotiation with the Poles.

Immediately Sikorski fired an angry letter to Stalin. Tadeusz Romer, the new Polish ambassador to Moscow, had a stormy session with Molotov. The Polish government declared that its prewar frontier "is in force."

Late on the night of February 26, 1943, Romer met with Stalin and Molotov in the Kremlin. Stalin's position was that if the Supreme Soviet had passed a law, it was immutable. Romer next met separately on March 9 with Molotov, who again declared that Poland must abide by unilateral Soviet laws. Romer charged him with other, more flagrant cases of forcing Soviet citizenship on Poles.

"We have proof that Polish citizens, men and women . . . are detained for examination for days on end, that they are even deprived of food and drink to break their resistance. . . . Those who resist are thrown into prison." And the Polish embassy was being harassed. "Callers leaving the Embassy are forced to show their identity papers and are arrested. Worse, cases are known in which such persons have been beaten up in public."

Molotov's answer was sharp: "Your reproaches on this subject are unfounded and out of place. I shall not reply to them."

The quarrel had now reached the boiling point. "I would like to ask you, Mr. Commissar," demanded Romer, "to give me an assurance that compulsory methods in the matter of citizenship will not be applied."

Molotov: "I regard this demand as unfounded."

Romer: "Then I have no other choice but to appeal to my Government."[5]

The two parted in utter hostility. The recriminations continued through March. The day after the Molotov-Romer explosion, Ivan Maisky visited Anthony Eden, who was preparing for a trip to Washington. The Soviet Union, he said, "was determined to keep the Baltic States after the war and to have bases in Finland and Roumania. The Russo-Polish frontier should be the Curzon line, with minor adjustments."[6]

In Washington, Eden dined with Roosevelt and Hopkins on March 14 and discussed the Polish problem. Roosevelt seemed unworried. If Poland, he observed, "had East Prussia and perhaps some concessions in Silesia, she would gain rather than lose by agreeing to the Curzon Line." He gave Eden the impression that the United States was ready to solve the Polish question along these lines.

"In any event," he concluded, "Britain, the United States and Russia should decide at the appropriate time what was a just solution, and Poland would have to accept."[7]

These remarks in March 1943 seem to have been Roosevelt's first stated opinion on the Curzon Line. But the Poles would not find it out for a year and a half, and it would not be publicly acknowledged until the Yalta conference. However, Moscow learned of it within a few days. When Eden returned to London, Sir Alexander Cadogan reported Roosevelt's remarks to Maisky. The indiscretion was a serious breach and uncharacteristic of the shrewd Cadogan. The Soviets knew now that they could ignore the intransigent Poles.

On the night of April 13 Berlin Radio announced: "It is reported from Smolensk that the local population has indicated to the German authorities a place where the Bolsheviks had perpetrated secretly mass executions and where the GPU [NKVD] had murdered 10,000 Polish officers." Thus was announced the finding of mass graves in the Katyn Forest, some ten miles west of Smolensk, in Soviet Russia. There were not 10,000 bodies, but there were more than 4,200. The 10,000 figure was apparently used because, as the German broadcast said, this "would more or less correspond to the entire number of Polish officers taken as prisoners of war by the Bolsheviks." The victims had been shot in the back of the neck and put into great pits in full uniform, with even their personal papers intact. These showed that they had been brought there from Kozielsk, one of the three prison camps where the missing Polish officers had last been heard from. Papers on the bodies indicated that this had happened in the spring of 1940, more than a year before the Germans had attacked Russia.

For two days Joseph Goebbels's propaganda machine spewed out accounts of the Katyn massacre. On April 15 the Soviet Information Bureau responded with a feverish attack on "this monstrous invention" and blamed the crime on "the German-Fascist hangmen." When the Red Army had withdrawn from the Smolensk area in the summer of 1941, Moscow explained, the

Polish prisoners of war had been left behind, and had been captured and executed by the Germans.

The same day Sikorski and his foreign minister, Count Edward Raczynski, lunched with Churchill and Cadogan at 10 Downing Street. The Poles told the prime minister they had "concrete proof" that the massacre had been perpetrated by the Soviet NKVD—that the German charges confirmed what the Polish intelligence sources had already reported.

"Alas, the German revelations are probably true," Churchill responded sadly. "The Bolsheviks can be very cruel." But he cautioned against premature accusations that would arouse Moscow. "If they are dead nothing you can do will bring them back."[8]

Seizing on the Katyn discovery as a propaganda windfall, the Nazis pressed gleefully onward. Far from believing the Germans, the Polish people at first thought the whole incident was a hoax and that the Nazis had killed the officers.

On April 16 Stanislaw Kot, who by this time was Polish minister of information, drafted a communiqué describing the history of the missing officers and the repeated inquiries made about them. It closed thus:

We have become accustomed to the lies of German propaganda and we understand the purpose behind its latest revelations. In view however of abundant and detailed German information . . . the necessity has arisen that the mass graves discovered should be investigated and the facts alleged verified by a competent international body, such as the International Red Cross. The Polish Government has therefore approached this institution with a view to their sending a delegation to the place where the massacre of Polish prisoners of war is said to have taken place.[9]

Kot went over this draft with Sikorski, who approved it in principle. He later claimed that it had been read over the phone to him at a time when he was sick in bed with a fever. But Raczynski's diary tells of the decisive meeting in Sikorski's office, and Anthony J. D. Biddle, Jr., U.S. ambassador to the London Poles, wrote that Sikorski had ordered the issuance of the Polish statement. In any case, Sikorski claimed he had second thoughts and contacted Kot again; but by that time the announcement had already been given to the press.[10]

The Kremlin was enraged and alarmed by this invitation to the International Red Cross. Nor did a conciliatory statement next day by the Polish government, excoriating the Germans for their record of atrocities, soften the Soviets. The Germans themselves sent a message on April 17 to Geneva (apparently their second request) inviting the International Red Cross to the site. The Polish press in Britain took up the issue and pressed hard on the Soviets. Finally, on April 20 Foreign Minister Raczynski formally demanded an explanation from the Soviet ambassador to the Polish government in London. Recounting the persistent Polish quest for the whereabouts of the missing officers, he noted that in the communiqué of April 15 the Soviet government "would seem to be in possession of more ample information on this matter than was communicated to the representatives of the Polish Government some time ago. . . . " He therefore asked for such information:

Public opinion in Poland and throughout the world has rightly been so deeply shocked that only irrefutable facts can outweigh the numerous and detailed German statements concerning the discovery of the bodies of many thousand Polish officers murdered near Smolensk in the spring of 1940.[11]

Far more accusative than previous Polish messages, Raczynski's note flatly stated that the officers were murdered at a time when the scene of the crime was held by the Soviets. Next day Stalin wired Churchill and Roosevelt his outraged reaction to the Polish position. "Both the Sikorski and Hitler Governments have enlisted for the 'investigation' the aid of the International Red Cross. . . . " Both the Polish and the German press had launched a simultaneous anti-Soviet campaign following "identical lines":

At a time when the people of the Soviet Union are shedding their blood in a grim struggle against Hitler Germany . . . the Sikorski Government is striking a treacherous blow at the Soviet Union to help Hitler tyranny. . . . For these reasons the Soviet Government has decided to interrupt relations with that Government.[12]

Churchill, shifting to a different stance in dealing with Stalin, wired back his support for the Soviets. "Such investigation," he wrote, "would be a fraud, and its conclusions reached by terrorism." He hoped that the interruption in relations did not mean an actual break.

However, at midnight on April 25 Molotov summoned Romer to the Kremlin and read him a note that was similar to Stalin's message but went further. Poland was using the "slanderous Hitlerite fake" to wrest from the Soviet government "territorial concessions at the expense of the interests of the Soviet Ukraine, Soviet Byelorussia and Soviet Lithuania." Therefore, "the Soviet Government has decided to sever relations with the Polish Government."

Next day Molotov talked first with Sir Archibald Clark Kerr, the British ambassador to Moscow, and then to Admiral William H. Standley, the U.S. ambassador. As the American arrived, Clark Kerr was leaving Molotov's office.

"Try to persuade him to postpone the publication of the note," confided Clark Kerr as they passed. "This is madness—I've been trying for the last hour but am afraid I was unsuccessful."[13]

So was the U.S. ambassador. While he and Molotov were talking, the Soviet announcement was being released to the press. Both Churchill and Roosevelt wired Stalin to reconsider, but he persisted. The International

Red Cross did not investigate Katyn, because its policy was to make such interventions only if all parties to the issue requested it. The Soviet Union had not done so.

On April 30 the Polish government withdrew its request. Next day Averell Harriman, then in London, asked Sikorski why the message had been sent to the International Red Cross; "whether the German accusations turned out to be true or false, the Polish statement was bound to have a disastrous effect in Moscow." Sikorski asked Harriman to tell Roosevelt that he "recognized it had been a great mistake. . . . "[14]

Mistake it was, but understandable in light of repeated inquiries about the fate of the officers, and the obvious emotions involved in the deaths of thousands of Poles. Subsequently a German-sponsored investigation by international experts, apparently using professional methods, found the victims had been killed in 1940, when the Soviets held the territory. At the request of the Polish government-in-exile, a Polish Red Cross team visited the site and reached the same conclusion, but, in the hope of improving relations with Stalin, it was kept secret. After the Red Army recaptured the region later in 1943, a Soviet-sponsored investigation reported that the deaths occurred in 1941, during the German occupation. The hearing and the evidence did not convince the U.S. journalists who were present. Other commissions, from the Nuremberg war crime trials to a U.S. congressional committee, sifted the evidence from a distance and generally concluded the crime had been Soviet (the Nuremberg court simply concluded not to charge it against the Germans).

The Poles themselves did not doubt it was a Soviet crime. The site had been used as an NKVD camp since the 1920s. The forensic arts used by experts indicated the bodies had been dead three years, not two. Of the personal papers, such as letters and newspaper clippings, found on the bodies none had a date later than the spring of 1940. The annual growth rings of the trees that had been planted over the graves showed transplantation three years before the discovery. Pistol ammunition found in the graves was of German origin, but research revealed that such guns and ammunition had been marketed before the war in Eastern Europe and in the Soviet Union, as well as in Germany. Puncture wounds other than bullet holes appeared to have been made by the four-sided Red Army bayonet.[15]

Contributing to this evidence was the history of Soviet evasion and denials, in the face of repeated Polish inquiries, before the discovery. If the Polish officers had really been captured by the Germans, why would the Russians not have said so, rather than insisting for two years that they had been set free? Or escaped to Manchuria?

On April 13, 1990—the forty-seventh anniversary of the first Katyn announcement by the Germans—the Soviets confessed the crime. President Mikhail Gorbachev presented to Poland's president Wojciech Jaruzelski cartons of copied documents that, as Gorbachev stated, "indirectly but convincingly testify" that those 4200 or more who died at Katyn were victims of Stalin's secret police. Even more astounding, the Tass news agency, in reporting the event, stated that the total number of Poles who had disappeared after being turned over to the NKVD was not 10,000 but 15,000! No account of the fate of the missing 11,000 was given.[16]

Somewhere in the steppes of Russia they lie undiscovered, but not unmourned. In this officer corps were the educated, the experienced, the professional—the flower of Poland. They were the very ones to whom Poland would look for leadership in reasserting its freedom after the war. And here lies the motive for one of the monstrous acts in a monstrous war.

The final irony came in Stalin's turning the crime to Soviet advantage. For when the anguished Poles appealed to a neutral body to learn the true cause of the atrocity, Stalin called it an insult to the Soviet Union and broke relations. The way was now open, as the Red Army rolled westward, for him to create his own Polish government—one that would not ask questions about Katyn, that would joyfully embrace the Curzon Line, and that would extend Soviet sway far across Central Europe.

Three days after he broke relations with the London Poles, Stalin fired the first shot in the new phase of his Polish strategy. The Union of Polish Patriots, formed in Moscow after the German attack in 1941, was Stalin's political arm for Poland. Heading it was Wanda Wasilewska, who now attacked the Polish London government in a savage article in *Izvestia*, headlined "The Polish Patriots Are Against the Government of General Sikorski."

A dedicated Polish Communist, Wanda Wasilewska had voluntarily become a Soviet citizen and was a member of the Supreme Soviet. When the Germans and Soviets had attacked Poland in 1939, she had written a book lauding the Soviet Union and calling it her "fatherland." Besides chairing the Polish Patriots, which was said to have consisted of not more than 20 Poles in Moscow, she edited a Soviet magazine in the Polish language. Stanislaw Mikolajczyk, later premier of the London Polish government, called her "a stern, horse-faced fanatic." The British ambassador in Moscow was more objective, describing her as "a tall, large-boned woman, who is very 'mannish' in her appearance, has a well-shaped head, is serious of countenance and looks like a strong character."

In reporting the story of Wasilewska's attack on Sikorski, the U.S. ambassador observed that many in Moscow believed the Union of Polish Patriots would be used as a springboard for a puppet government for Poland, similar to the one the Soviets had tried to establish in Finland during the Finnish War in 1939. By August the Union of Polish Patriots had moved further in that direction by sponsoring a Polish division on the eastern front.

Through the spring and summer of 1943 the recriminations flew between the Soviets and the Poles. Soviet attacks were answered in kind by the Polish press in Britain and the United States. The Polish Army that had been recruited from deportees and prisoners in the Soviet Union by General

Wladyslaw Anders had been so ill treated that Anders had asked that it be transferred to Middle East duty. Already hostile to the Soviets, the Polish Army in Iran was outraged by the Katyn disclosures. At a meeting with Churchill in Cairo, Anders shocked him by declaring that there was "no justice or honor in Russia, and not a single man there whose word could be trusted."[17]

Under the guidance of Sikorski, the Polish government-in-exile remained relatively moderate, though many in the cabinet were belligerent. On July 4, 1943, Sikorski was killed in an airplane crash near Gibraltar. He was succeeded by Stanislaw Mikolajczyk, minister of the interior and acting chairman of the Polish Peasant Party, the largest of the Polish political groups.

Peasant to the core, Mikolajczyk had a refined face but a stocky build and large hands, described by one reporter as "like bear's paws." At the age of 18 he had participated in the Polish revolt against the Germans at the end of World War I, and in 1920 was wounded as a private in the Polish Army fighting against the Russians. From the time he founded the Peasant Youth Association at Poznan in the early 1920s, Mikolajczyk rose in political leadership to become premier of the Polish government-in-exile at the age of 42.

Though he lacked Sikorski's stature and experience, Mikolajczyk nevertheless continued his predecessor's moderate policy and grew swiftly in his new job. He was less effective than Sikorski in curbing the violent anti-Soviets in the cabinet. But he proved to be a tireless and stubborn bargainer with the Soviets and the British, resisting pressure from them, as Raczynski put it, "with vigour and resource, and not without dignity."

Through 1943 the British and Americans were trying to bring the Soviet Union and Poland back together. The British believed that Stalin was primarily concerned with territorial claims, as he had been in 1941, and was using Polish recognition as a bargaining lever. Eden wrote:

I have little doubt . . . Soviet Government would be much easier to deal with on Polish and other matters if [His Majesty's Government] and U.S. Government could let them know that we are prepared in practice to contemplate a substantial measure of satisfaction on what we understand Soviet territorial claims to be. . . .

On August 3, Eden asked Ambassador Halifax in Washington to approach Roosevelt on a solution to the Polish dilemma: In return for Soviet recognition of the Polish government-in-exile, Britain and the United States would accept the Curzon Line, Lwów going to Poland, and agree to compensate Poland in the west—Danzig, East Prussia, and Upper Silesia. To sweeten the offer to Stalin, the deal could also include Western acceptance of Soviet sovereignty over the Baltic states and Soviet claims in Finland and Romania.

But such an array of concessions would be only an unofficial promise of the position Britain and the United States intended to take at the postwar peace table. It could not be official, since it would violate the principle of self-determination for which the war was being waged, as well as Britain's promise to Poland.

"You will appreciate," Eden told Halifax in cryptic cable language, "that our proposals imply driving a coach and horses through Atlantic Charter, and that we would like President to join us on the box."[18]

This daring proposal apparently did not reach Roosevelt before the first Quebec conference in mid-August 1943. There Eden handed to Cordell Hull the same proposal he had forwarded to Halifax. To the Poles he proposed a warning that no solution to their Soviet problem could be expected until the frontier question was settled, that it would be "harder to obtain" once the Red Army reached Polish territory, and that Britain and the United States should "help them" by proposing this solution. He would ask the Soviets "to keep it to themselves until such time as it could be presented as part of a general territorial settlement."[19]

Such a Byzantine idea—in effect, a secret deal in violation of the Atlantic Charter and British assurances to the Poles—was uncharacteristic of Eden and hardly palatable to the lofty-principled Cordell Hull. The suggestion fell flat in Washington, which nonetheless had no alternative to propose—a dangerous drift, since Stalin was strengthening his hand every day with the Red Army's advance.

On October 6, while Hull was preparing for the Big Three foreign ministers' conference in Moscow, Ambassador Jan Ciechanowski met with him in Washington and presented Poland's latest proposal. It opposed Soviet occupation of a liberated Poland except with participation of British and U.S. troops; it called for Polish occupation of eastern provinces of Germany; it opposed Soviet occupation of Romania, Hungary, and Slovakia—all of them naive demands in view of the Red Army's relentless offensive westward toward Central Europe.

Nonetheless, Hull listened and discussed the issues sympathetically. As Ciechanowski left, Hull accompanied him to the door of his office. The ambassador later reported Hull's parting words: "[H]e was decided to defend the cause of Poland as he would defend the cause of his own country."[20]

In the Polish government in London, Count Raczynski was not so sure. He expected the Big Three to "come to terms and start pressing us to accept the Curzon Line," as Churchill and Eden had already hinted in conversations. "The storm has not yet broken," he wrote in his diary, "but it is already visible in the sky."[21]

5

Dr. Beneš Faces East

No one was watching the Polish drama more intently than Dr. Eduard Beneš, president of the Czechoslovak government-in-exile. Like Poland, his country was the creation of the Treaty of Versailles after World War I. But unlike Poland, it had been artificially constructed for the first time out of four provinces or duchies of the prewar Austro-Hungarian Empire—Bohemia, Moravia, Slovakia, and Ruthenia. It was, if anything, more strategically located than Poland—a kind of linchpin in the heart of Europe. Bismarck had said, "Whoever is master in Bohemia is master of Europe."

The dismemberment of Czechoslovakia at the 1938 Munich conference, and Hitler's subsequent invasion in March 1939, had been principal steps in precipitating World War II and had confirmed Czechoslovakia's importance far beyond its size.

Munich had taught President Beneš that he could not count on the West for his country's security against future German aggression. His only hope, even if a dubious one, was to look eastward to the Soviet Union. But the experience of Poland was frightening; in resisting Soviet policy its government-in-exile was digging its own grave. Already Stalin was developing a substitute Polish government of his own. Beneš decided he would not let this happen to his country, or to himself.

The task would require masterful diplomacy, Beneš thought, but this was his specialty. As the leading disciple and protégé of Czechoslovakia's founder, Tomás Masaryk, Beneš had served as his country's foreign minister from 1918 to 1935. During this period he held top posts in the League of Nations and, with Litvinov, was a leading apostle of collective security. His diplomatic triumphs were legion. Representing Czechoslovakia at Versailles, he secured from the Allied powers almost all the desired territorial frontiers.

In 1920–1921 it was largely his handiwork that created the Little Entente—an alliance of Czechoslovakia, Romania, and Yugoslavia—which, with French support, resisted the territorial ambitions of neighboring countries during the 1920s and early 1930s.

With Hitler's rise, Beneš's talents were focused on saving Europe's security structure. At a time when both Britain and France seemed more distrustful of the Soviet Union than of Nazi Germany, Beneš worked to bring the Soviet Union into the power scales of Europe. In 1935, with Beneš as a prime mover, both France and Czechoslovakia concluded mutual military aid pacts with the Soviet Union. That same year, with Masaryk's retirement, Beneš became president of the Czechoslovak republic.

It was partly his years in Geneva that had schooled Beneš as a supremely logical, almost mathematical advocate. With his agile mind he habitually enumerated his points—"firstly, secondly, thirdly"—on his fingers, sometimes running out of them in his masterly command of his subject. His persuasion was not through charisma but through painstaking preparation and unassailable argument. He was famous for devising elaborate formulas to solve the most exasperating international problems. For a former sociology professor, he would have made a great lawyer.

Beneš's disciplined professionalism also grew out of his disciplined personality. Stoic and dispassionate, he prided himself on a modulated temperament that survived any surprise or setback. His endurance in negotiation was phenomenal. As his secretary, Edward Taborsky, put it, compromise "became an integral part of his personality. He would negotiate with the patience of an angel, for hours, weeks or months, never tiring in the rich flow of his rhetoric."[1]

In fact, the sound of his own voice and the astuteness of his own observations thoroughly captivated Beneš. His rhetoric often surpassed his discretion. He gossiped to the British about the Russians. He gossiped to the Russians about the British. One British official called him a "chatterbox." And he readily served as emissary or intermediary—between the Poles and the Russians, the Americans and the Russians, the Russians and the British—until some felt he was an international busybody.

Worst of all, his devotion to compromise tended to dim his sense of indignation and outrage. "Beneš himself was a man of impeccable moral purity," wrote Taborsky. "But he was much too forbearing toward evil and wickedness in others." His great mentor, Tomás Masaryk, refused to deal with scoundrels. But, as Beneš explained, "[I]f the scoundrel was politically important, *someone* had to deal with him, and so it was left for me to do it."[2]

Thus his obsession with compromise—even compromise with injustice or oppression in a moment of crisis—punctuated his career from Munich on. Churchill faulted him for not resisting Hitler with arms, in spite of Munich: "Where he failed—and it cost him and his country much—was in not taking violent decisions at the supreme moment."[3]

It is by no means clear that this would have benefited Czechoslovakia in either the short or the long run. But Beneš did not have to put his signature to the Munich surrender, nor to others in the next ten years. He could at least have made a defiant outcry that would have indicted his enemies before the world.

With Munich seared on his mind, Beneš watched the course of the war from his London post with rising apprehension. Most of all, he was aware of the rift between Stalin and the Polish government-in-exile. At loggerheads with Moscow over the Polish-Soviet frontier, and failing to curb repeated anti-Soviet statements, the London Poles continued to antagonize Stalin. As a result he was clearly preparing his own puppet government for Poland. Beneš knew that the best chance of preserving an independent Czechoslovakia after the war was to convince Stalin that it would be a friendly, cooperative neighbor.

As early as January 1942 Beneš, working to develop a collective security system for the postwar years, had concluded with the Polish government-in-exile an agreement for a Polish-Czechoslovak confederation. This was to be the first step in his plan for a tripartite alliance, including the Soviet Union, against any future revival of Germany's *Drang nach Osten*. But in less than two weeks Moscow objected, and Beneš obediently dropped the plan. Moscow's reason was obvious—it distrusted the London Poles and had its own plans for a Polish government.

By 1943 Beneš was making repeated public statements praising the Soviet war effort and highlighting the mutual interests of the Soviet Union and Czechoslovakia. In June he published an article in *Slavyane*, the periodical of the All-Slav Committee in Moscow, insisting that at the time of Munich, "the Soviet Union was the only Power willing to honour her obligation and was prepared to make war and defeat Hitler then without waiting any longer." Then he sounded his keynote: "I trust that close cooperation between Czechoslovakia and Soviet Russia will be an important factor in the Post War world."[4]

If Beneš was playing a dangerous game, he refused to recognize it. To his old friend Bruce Lockhart he declared that the Soviet Union would not launch "an expansionist program in Europe." In fact, he was basing his entire policy on this assumption. The Soviet Union was, he said, "anxious only for a strategic frontier which would bring her security from attack in Europe."[5]

As early as March 1943 Beneš had approached the Soviet ambassador to the London Czechoslovak government, Alexander Y. Bogomolov, about a treaty between their two countries—one that would extend into the postwar period the wartime treaty he had already concluded with Moscow in 1941. The general wording was worked out in the spring of 1943, including a pledge of noninterference in the internal affairs of the other treaty partner.

In May, Beneš visited Washington and met with the top diplomatic and political leaders, including Roosevelt. He told FDR of his intention to conclude a treaty with the Soviet Union: "[W]e could not accept another Munich in future and . . . this already obliged us to consider a treaty with the Soviet Union." He outlined the main points of the proposed treaty, which Roosevelt approved.

At their last meeting on June 7, FDR asked Beneš to serve as a kind of emissary when he met with Stalin. He was to clarify two points with him. On the Baltic states, the United States did not oppose their annexation to the Soviet Union, but it "must be arranged in a manner which would give the least offence to American public opinion." And regarding Poland, Roosevelt favored the Curzon Line but hoped for "concessions which would render this line more palatable to the Poles." Beneš agreed to "undertake these two tasks."[6]

Back in London, Beneš prepared to leave for Moscow. But he quickly encountered a different attitude from the British, with whom he had been less candid than with Roosevelt. At a luncheon meeting in mid-June, Eden asked Beneš whether he intended "to conclude any kind of treaty with the Soviet Government." Suspecting British opposition, Beneš hedged. That would depend, he ventured, on the situation he would find in Moscow. If he found it "possible and desirable to conclude a treaty," he would do so.

Eden then showed his hand. When Molotov had visited London in 1942, they had agreed "to refrain from concluding treaties with smaller States covering the post-war period; in effect a self-denying ordinance." The purpose was to avoid "competition between ourselves and the Russians to conclude such treaties." The Soviets would be breaking this agreement in making a treaty with Czechoslovakia. Besides, such a treaty "would almost certainly be regarded by the Poles as directed against themselves."[7]

Equally distressing to Eden was Roosevelt's use of Beneš as an emissary on the Polish question. Suspecting that Beneš exaggerated this assignment, Eden asked Halifax in Washington to find out what Roosevelt had told him. On July 7, Roosevelt told Halifax that he had merely "discussed with Beneš the possibility of exploring the Russian mind on the subject, but always entirely as from himself and in no way to appear to be acting on behalf of anyone else." This was not the way Beneš had reported the conversation.[8]

In any case, the British opposed his serving in any such role; Eden went further and opposed Beneš's making a treaty with the Soviets until after the war. Beneš claims in his memoirs that Eden approved the treaty but simply opposed its being signed until an armistice. But Eden's opposition to the treaty itself is clear in his correspondence at the time.[9]

Harriman, who talked with Eden and Beneš in London during that period, confirms this. But as for the United States, he supported Roosevelt's attitude by urging Beneš to "try to work out a permanent relationship with the Soviet Union before the Red Army got control of Czechoslovakia."[10]

Beneš insisted on going ahead with his treaty. He submitted his draft to Bogomolov on August 22, and the wording was essentially finalized by October. But in three discussions with Eden through the summer of 1943, Beneš agreed not to visit Moscow until the treaty draft could be aired at the forthcoming Council of Foreign Ministers meeting in late October.

At this first conference of Big Three representatives in Moscow, Molotov introduced the proposed Czechoslovak treaty on October 24. In the discussion, Secretary of State Cordell Hull excused himself as being unfamiliar with the situation. Eden again argued against such treaties in order to "avoid any scramble for special relations with small powers." Since the U.S. delegation was growing restless, Eden passed Hull a note: "I am sorry to take your time, but behind all this is a big issue: two camps in Europe or one."[11]

Clearly Eden was worried about a partition of Europe between East and West; Hull did not seem to grasp this threat and remained indifferent, especially since he had no instructions from Roosevelt on the matter. U.S. secretaries of state had always had less latitude for action than British foreign secretaries, but Hull played this role with more than usual deference.

Thus the Czechoslovak treaty issue became a duel between Eden and Molotov, who argued that neither the Soviets nor the Czechoslovaks "could understand why the British should have any objection to a treaty of this character which was between two countries with a common frontier for their immediate security." The two countries did not, in fact, have a common frontier, although one would be created through the Soviet territorial claims against Poland. This discrepancy was not challenged.

Lacking any support from Hull, Eden at length conceded that, after reading the draft of the treaty for the first time, "it seemed to . . . be a good treaty. . . . no objection." The green light was now given for Beneš's trip to Moscow.

Failing to prevent a Czechoslovak treaty with the Soviet Union was actually the least shortcoming of Britain and the United States in this matter. It evidently never occurred to Churchill or Eden that Britain should have offered Czechoslovakia a treaty of its own— a guarantee of the type Churchill was trying to provide for Poland. As for the United States, Washington was not even aware of the stakes involved, and was basing all postwar policy on a United Nations organization.

In any case, Beneš had seen enough of Western "guarantees" in the Munich debacle. In fact, it was not until 1942, after repeated Czechoslovak urgings, that Britain and the United States renounced the Munich pact and recognized Czechoslovakia's pre-Munich frontiers. Acutely aware of the British and U.S. mentality, Beneš did not even bother to ask the West for a treaty.

Early in December 1943, Beneš left London for Moscow. Entering the Soviet Union by train through the Caucasus, he saw the terrible devastation wrought by the war, as well as some of the industrial progress made by the Soviet Union since his previous visit in 1935. He was impressed by the spirit of the farmers, workers, and soldiers; he was warmly greeted everywhere and lionized by the Soviet leaders in Moscow. To his colleagues in the Czechoslovak government in London he cabled a report that included his favorable reactions: "The growth of a new Soviet Empire, a decentralized one, with a firm place for the other Soviet Nations in the spirit of a new popular democracy, is undeniable and definitely on the march."[12]

Beneš also believed he had Stalin's goodwill because of an incident that had occurred at the end of the unsuccessful German-Czechoslovak diplomatic negotiations in January 1937. The German negotiator had let slip to Beneš that Germany was in secret communication with an anti-Stalin clique in the Red Army. Beneš had notified the Soviet minister in Prague; this may have contributed to the suspicions of Stalin, who extended the massive purges already under way by trying and executing numerous military leaders.

The day after Beneš arrived in Moscow on December 10, he joined his hosts at Molotov's office in the ceremony for the treaty, which was signed by Molotov and Zdenek Fierlinger, the Czechoslovak ambassador to Moscow. That night, as part of the celebration, the visiting Czechoslovaks and their hosts attended Rimsky-Korsakov's *Snow Maiden* ballet at the Bolshoi. Heading the Soviet group were Molotov and Marshal Kliment Voroshilov, an old comrade of Stalin's.

Unexpectedly, Stalin himself appeared in the government box. In the salon behind the box, the group discussed European politics during intermission and long into the night. In particular, the Soviets wanted the opinion of Beneš, one of the world's most experienced diplomats, on other Allied personalities—especially the Poles. At every point, Beneš proved anxious to please his hosts.[13]

Of the London Poles he said: "In some time, a new government will be formed in the territory of Poland which will have nothing to do with the government in London." And he reported that the Polish ambassador to Czechoslovakia had raised fears of Soviet domination and had asked whether Beneš trusted the Soviets; Beneš told his hosts, "I assured him that I trust you, that we want to remain an independent state forever, that we don't at all contemplate to become part of Russia, and that I believe that you don't contemplate that either."

At this, Stalin was pacing back and forth: "Idiots! We have enough of our own troubles, why should we take on the Polish ones in addition?"

Voroshilov dutifully echoed: "And what Polish troubles!"

Two days later Beneš and Molotov renewed the conversation in the foreign minister's office. Superbly prepared, Beneš offered position papers on every key subject; Molotov let him steer the discussion.

On the breakup of Germany after the war: "I agree with you, we shall adapt our policy toward Germany to yours. . . . "

On punishing German war criminals: "[W]e want to adapt our policy to yours. . . . We want to go very far—same as you."

On disarming Germany: "[W]e agree with you. Our delegates at international conferences will always follow you."

On Hungary: "Here, too, I want to adapt our policy to yours. An internal

revolution must take place in Hungary in order to destroy feudalism. . . .
That's why the occupation of Hungary is so important." He thought Hungary should be occupied "primarily by the Soviet Army. . . . "

On transferring German nationals out of Czechoslovakia: "[T]he British requested from me a definite plan. I procrastinated until I would know your position."

On confiscation of German property in Czechoslovakia: "The transfer of the German property will be the beginning of nationalization. I suppose that you will realize now what else the transfer means for us: . . . the beginning of a great social transformation."

"What about the Czech bankers?" asked one of Molotov's aides.

"Naturally there will be a fight, but we shall win."

In a second meeting two days later, Beneš offered a new tray of hors d'oeuvres. He was so anxious to please that he brought up points for agreement on which the Soviets had not yet formed policy. Molotov, astounded but fascinated, let him continue.

On postwar military collaboration: "[W]e must maintain close military collaboration with you. . . . standardize arms and ammunition, cooperate in air defense. . . . "

On economic collaboration: "So far, we have tended 80 percent toward the West—and that will definitely change. I am thinking about 50 percent East and 50 percent West."

On the organization of Central Europe: "[W]e are not going to do anything without an agreement with you."

On the future of France: "As far as I can see, there is no difference of opinion."

Molotov disagreed, apparently to see how far Beneš would go: "No, there is a difference in shade. We are less optimistic than you are; we are more wary than you."

Beneš was quick to adapt: "What matters to me is that we act in concert and that our policy is coordinated with yours. That is very important to us."

Molotov replied: "It is very important to us, too."

Throughout, Beneš laid before Molotov his inner attitudes toward Western leaders, their conversations with him, detailed political conditions in other countries, and his plans for his own country—even how it would be organized politically. To Molotov it must have been like debriefing a secret agent.

The climax came on the evening of December 18 when a Kremlin meeting of Beneš and Fierlinger with Stalin and Molotov.[14] Here Stalin took charge of the discussion in his usual brittle second-act performance. Did Britain and the United States intend "to pursue this war to the end with all its consequences"—including invasion of the European continent? The question was odd, considering that such an invasion had just been promised at the Tehran conference for the following spring. Beneš, of course, added his assurances.

Stalin went on in the same ominous tone: "[T]here are still many conservative people in England who are afraid of the alliance with the USSR; if, however, the English policy followed them, it would be preparing the doom of England."

It was as though Stalin, having absorbed all that Beneš could give him, was now going to use him to deliver some harsh messages in the other direction. And for Czechoslovakia itself Stalin and Molotov seemed to have a particular message: They trusted Beneš himself, but, as their visitor discerned, "[T]hey were and would remain suspicious about us in the future, so that persons whom they do not like might not get power."

But generally during Beneš's 1943 visit to Moscow, Stalin and Molotov did everything possible to allay any concerns he might have about Soviet intentions. They looked favorably on a Soviet treaty with Poland's government-in-exile in London. The Red Army would turn over every part of Czechoslovakia to its civil administration as soon as it was liberated. The Soviet Union had no designs on the province of Ruthenia, which should be returned from Hungary to Czechoslovakia. This was part of a promise that all of the country's pre-Munich frontiers would be restored.

Stalin even offered, with pencil poised to mark a large map in his office, whatever German territory Beneš would like to add to Czechoslovakia. He seemed disappointed when Beneš mentioned only a minor straightening of the frontier. Beneš later told Molotov, "We do not want the Germans in, we want them out."[15]

Most of all, Beneš was assured that the Soviets would in no way interfere in Czechoslovak domestic affairs. In fact, Stalin and Molotov almost refused to listen when Beneš tried to discuss future plans for his country.

"Throughout our discussions there was not a single occasion," Beneš wrote to his London colleagues, "on which our partners did not stress that whatever question might arise they are not concerned with out internal affairs and that they would not interfere in them."[16]

In their new treaty, in fact, the two governments adhered to "the principles of mutual respect of their independence and sovereignty and non-interference in the internal affairs of the other signatory."

Thus Beneš concluded his meetings with the Soviets in a state of exhilaration. Harriman, by this time U.S. ambassador to Moscow, reported Beneš's feelings with such words as "elated" and "thrilled"—certainly unusual for the reserved and even-tempered Beneš. Highly impressed with Soviet sacrifice and heroism in the war, and convinced of a new and more democratic spirit in the Soviet Union, Beneš believed in the sincerity of the Soviet leaders as they granted his every desire.

"We came to a complete agreement about everything!" he told his colleagues in their Moscow quarters after returning from his last meeting with Stalin.[17] To his fellows in the Czechoslovak government he cabled: "There is a complete unity of views. . . . I consider all our negotiations as wholly successful." In the same message he added, "I think it can be regarded as certain that all treaties and agreements not only with us but also with the

British and with America will be kept."[18] At a Moscow press conference he told reporters that his trip was "the crowning step in Czechoslovakia's struggle for independence."[19]

Also during his 1943 Moscow trip, Beneš met with Czechoslovak Communist leaders who had chosen exile in the Soviet Union rather than Britain. Heading them was Klement Gottwald, who had been chairman of the Czechoslovak Communist Party since 1926.

In what was at times a stormy series of meetings, the Communists declared that the Czechs and Slovaks must rise in revolution against the Germans and their collaborators as the war neared its end; demanded a National Front government in postwar Czechoslovakia composed of all parties except those right-wing parties tainted with Nazi collaboration; and insisted that the premier should be from the left, and after elections should be from the party winning the most votes.

To all these concepts Beneš did not object. But to his offer that the Czechoslovak Communist leaders in Moscow and London join the government-in-exile, they refused. They could do so only if that government underwent "total reconstruction." Specifically, they demanded that either the president or the premier, as well as the ministers of Interior and Defense, should be Communists.[20]

To this ominous condition Beneš could not agree. The Moscow Communists thus remained aloof as a separate body under the aegis of the Kremlin.

But otherwise Beneš believed his Moscow trip was a triumph. For his part, Stalin must have been astonished and perhaps even repelled by Beneš's subservience. Other East European leaders were to reproach Beneš for his treaty with the Soviet Union. In Britain, Lord Beaverbrook—with his usual gift for exaggeration—said Beneš "ha[d] become a Russian agent." Some of Beneš's own countrymen called him Stalin's vassal. Even they would have been shocked had they known his behavior in Moscow.

Clearly this veteran diplomat had a strategy—to convince Stalin that the Beneš government would serve his ends without need of a rival puppet state. Yet for all Beneš's trouble, Stalin remained suspicious of Czechoslovakia.

What about the questions Roosevelt had asked Beneš to probe concerning the Baltic states and concessions for Poland? Since these had meanwhile been discussed by the Big Three at Tehran, Beneš's assignment was now academic. At one point, however, Molotov had volunteered to Beneš: "Lvov is out of the question because it is within the Curzon Line; we cannot yield it to the Poles."

"I told the same to Mikolajczyk," answered Beneš, as agreeable as ever, "and keep in mind that the Americans and British already decided that in 1919."[21]

On his way home from Moscow, Beneš began to explain his tilt to the East. First he stopped in Algiers to see General Charles de Gaulle.

"Look at the map . . . ," he argued. "The Russians have reached the Carpathians. But the Western powers are not yet ready to land in France. Hence it is the Red Army that will liberate my country from the Germans. Afterward, in order for me to be able to establish my administration, it is with Stalin that I must come to an agreement. I have just done so. . . . "

When de Gaulle suggested that the Western powers could provide a "counterbalance" to the Soviet Union, Beneš was dubious.

"Roosevelt . . . is anxious to come to an agreement with Stalin and withdraw his troops as soon as he can after victory. Churchill is little concerned with us; for him, the British line of defense is along the Rhine and the Alps."[22]

It was a capsule summary of Czechoslovakia's dilemma and Beneš's solution.

Finally, Beneš stopped at Marrakesh, French Morocco, to visit Churchill, who was convalescing there from an illness brought on by the strain of the Tehran meeting. Churchill clearly relished the talk in the sunny African garden with his friend of a quarter-century. Beneš told him he was "very hopeful about the Russian situation."[23] But he did not tell Churchill how far he had allowed himself and Czechoslovakia to swing into the Soviet orbit. Having done nothing to insure Beneš against another Munich, Churchill and Roosevelt had lost the first nation to Stalin in the partition of Europe.

6

The Eagles Gather

By the fall of 1943 it was imperative that the Big Three powers gather to decide issues of war and peace. Turning the tables on the Wehrmacht, the Red Army had waged a summer offensive of its own—one that was still rolling into autumn. By October the Soviets were ranged along the Dnieper River, some 150 miles from the Romanian frontier; in the north they were 300 miles from the old Polish frontier.

"Once they were into Poland," wrote Anthony Eden, "our negotiating power, slender as it was anyway, would amount to very little."[1]

But there was still time to negotiate a settlement on Eastern Europe before the Soviets gained possession and nine points of the law. The Council of Foreign Ministers meeting in Moscow, October 18 to November 1, and the much shorter Big Three summit at Tehran, November 27 to December 1, 1943, gave the Western Allies this opportunity.

Early in September, before Ivan Maisky had left his ambassador's post in London to become deputy commissar for foreign affairs in Moscow, he had broached the central issue with Eden. After the war, he said, "we could each have a sphere of influence in Europe, the Soviet Union in the east and Britain and America in the west." The Western powers "could exclude the Russians from French affairs and the Mediterranean, while the Soviets "would claim the same freedom in the east."

However, he went on, if "we could all accept that Europe was one, then we must admit each other's rights to an interest in all parts of the Continent." Moscow preferred this latter choice.

Eden agreed, and hoped such an arrangement could be reached at the Moscow conference.[2]

Thus a Russian, undoubtedly speaking for Moscow, had stated the issue squarely. The West could not hope to participate in the fate of Eastern Europe without the Soviet Union participating in the restructuring of Western Europe.

For the West, the suggestion of a Europe open to influence by all three major powers meant letting the Soviet camel under the tent. But the West European tent could still be preserved for democracy if the West showed strength and resolve. The compensating prize would be an independent or at least a neutral Eastern Europe.

Significantly, Maisky had mentioned France but not Germany. In September 1943, with no second front yet and the Red Army still some 300 miles inside the prewar Soviet Union, it was not at all clear whether Germany would be captured from the west or the east or both. Yet Germany was the hinge of Europe. With the Red Army on the Rhine, France would be no safer than in 1940.

Churchill knew this danger, and was beginning to express it more or less freely. In a cabinet meeting to consider instructions for Eden in Moscow, Churchill said, "We mustn't weaken Germany too much—we may need her against Russia."[3]

When he left for Moscow, Eden had Churchill's written views in his pocket. They included full sovereignty for nations overrun by the Nazis; no nation "in a condition of subjugation or restriction"; democratic governments "based on the free expression of the people's will . . . shall be set up"; and a Soviet-Polish agreement that, "while securing a strong and independent Poland, afforded to Russia the security necessary for her western frontier." The latter seemed to contradict another Churchill point: "all questions of final territorial transference must be settled at the peace table. . . ."[4]

But Churchill and Eden were far more concerned with the independence of East European nations than with their frontiers. In the end they would be willing to trade territory for independence.

Representing the United States was Secretary of State Cordell Hull, who came to Moscow as an elder statesman of international stature. A Tennessee judge and lawmaker, he had left the U.S. Senate to become Roosevelt's secretary of state, serving in that post longer than any other. His chief contributions were promoting the New Deal's "good-neighbor" policy and negotiating tariff reductions around the world.

But Hull was relatively unfamiliar with European affairs and had traveled little outside the United States. His flight to Moscow was his first experience in an airplane. While he had a passionate hatred for the fascist tyrants who had plunged the world into war, he viewed Stalin with more tolerant eyes, and lacked the deep-seated skepticism that is a desirable trait in a diplomat. Time and again in the Moscow meetings he shunned discussion of specific political and military matters, preferring always to deal in lofty principles.

As Charles Bohlen observed, Hull "rejected the concept of power in world affairs."[5]

To the British, hardened in European intrigue, Hull was a kind of white-haired sage, a distinguished bald eagle, but ineffectual in the practical politics of Europe. Cadogan, who had observed him at the first Quebec conference, called him a "dreadful old man . . . and rather pigheaded, but quite a nice old thing, I dare say." And again: Hull was "as vindictive as an old woman about whom someone had been spreading scandal."[6] When Pug Ismay saw Hull at Moscow, he called him "old and frail"—imposed upon by the Soviets in insisting that the conference be held in Moscow.[7] Oliver Harvey, one of the British officials present, was more or less complimentary: "Hull takes little part in the discussion, but when he does, he is helpful and even to the point—quite a new Hull."[8]

From the beginning it was clear that so far as Eastern Europe was concerned, Hull was unprepared and, in fact, uninterested. Averell Harriman had accompanied Hull and would stay on as the new U.S. ambassador to Moscow. When he urged the secretary of state to push the Polish question, Hull replied, "I don't want to deal with these piddling little things. We must deal with the main issues."[9] He had come to Moscow to promote a prime Roosevelt objective—a four-power declaration (including China) on war and postwar aims, especially creation of a United Nations peacekeeping organization. The Soviet threat to Eastern Europe that Churchill and Eden feared went over Hull's head.

Meeting in the ornate guest house of the Foreign Ministry on Spiridonovka Street, the diplomats fell to work on October 19. In the conference room they gathered at a large round table having, as its centerpiece, the flags of Britain, the United States, and the Soviet Union.

A hint of the Soviet attitude on Eastern Europe came with the discussion of Hull's four-power declaration on October 21. In the section covering occupation of enemy or liberated territories, Hull's draft called for the powers to "act together in all matters relating to the surrender and disarmament of the enemy, and to any occupation of enemy territory and of territory of other states held by that enemy." At Molotov's objection the phrase covering "occupation" was eliminated. Further, in the U.S. draft the powers would not, after the war, "employ their military forces within the territories of other states except for the purpose envisioned in this declaration and after joint consultation and agreement." At Molotov's request the words "and agreement" were dropped.[10]

Little was made of these changes, either in the meetings or in the public discussions after the conference. Eden defended the original words in the discussion on October 21, but Hull said almost nothing. Yet with these changes Molotov had prevented any Western interference in the Red Army's occupation or use of force in countries it would seize.

Another clue to Soviet strategy came in the discussion of a British proposal favoring confederations of nations in the Danube basin and the rest of the Balkans. According to the British, this could strengthen them economically and politically (against—though this was not mentioned—Soviet designs). Molotov opposed this outright and presented an official Soviet statement on the subject. One of its points: "[S]ome of the plans for federation remind the Soviet people of the policy of the 'cordon sanitaire,' directed, as is known, against the Soviet Union. . . . "[11] If Molotov was striking close to the true strategy of the British, they believed with equal vigor that the Soviet purpose was to keep the East European states from uniting against Russian inroads.

Through these discussions Hull was conspicuous by his silence. Harvey noted that Eden "does practically all. We are carrying the American delegation."[12]

Yet Hull's difficulties were not confined to his reticence. Eden had proposed that the powers would "facilitate the resumption of authority over liberated territory by the Allied Governments concerned." By this he meant the governments-in-exile in London and Cairo, as opposed to the groups of Communist expatriates from various countries biding their time in Moscow. When this issue came up for discussion on October 27, Hull opposed it in one of his few lengthy statements. He had, he asserted, "an aversion to refugee Governments."

After this gratuitous salvo against what the Soviets had been slurring as "émigré" governments, Molotov's work was done for him. The proposal was referred to a commission, where it later died. As a member of the astonished British delegation commented, "Mr. Hull gets out of his depth easily on even important details."[13]

In a still more important effort, Eden proposed the concept first suggested to him by Maisky in London—joint responsibility for Europe rather than "separate areas of responsibility." Hull thereupon opposed separate areas, but in a vaguely worded statement that was incomprehensible to Molotov he failed to support the concept of joint responsibility. The British proposal was lost in the discussion.[14] There was still no policy at all on either separate or joint responsibility, thus leaving a dangerous void.

So far the Polish issue had not surfaced. As early as October 24 Eden had sought out Hull and tried to solicit his support on this question. Hull seemed hesitant without instructions from Roosevelt. He replied that he "considered it more of a British problem. . . . "

Eden was, as usual, the soul of patience. Hull had, he reminded him, already told the Poles that he would support them at the Moscow conference. At length the two agreed that Eden would approach Molotov about healing the rupture with Poland, and Hull would support him in hoping for renewed relations.

Thus, on the afternoon of October 29 Eden confronted Molotov on Polish relations. Britain would, he said, "make any contribution that it could at this conference looking toward a reestablishment of those relations." Then he proposed sending weapons to the Polish underground. "We did not want to decide without consulting our Soviet allies."

Molotov took the second point first: "[A]rms could be given only into safe hands, when they would be of use. But were there any safe hands in Poland?"

As for resuming relations, Molotov dropped his diplomacy and fired a blast. Poland and the Soviet Union were neighbors. "The question concerned the Poles and the Soviets and practically it concerned only those two countries." In short, Britain should mind its own business.

At this inauspicious moment Hull made his only reference to Poland at the conference: "Mr. Molotov had spoken of Poland and the Soviet Union being neighbors. When two neighbors got off speaking terms the other neighbors did not enquire what the trouble was about, but merely hoped that the two neighbors would come back to terms."

With his usual deference to Hull, Molotov agreed with this platitude. With Eden he returned to a sharp exchange, centering on the attitude of General Kazimierz Sosnokowski, who had returned as minister of defense in the London Polish government. Sosnokowski was the most outspoken foe of the Soviets in the Polish cabinet.

"Sosnokowski objected to the re-establishment of relations," grumbled Molotov.

Eden answered that he hoped he "was not going to be asked to defend individual Polish generals."

Molotov countered that he was "speaking of a general who was important not only as regards military matters."

Eden retorted that he had "been told that Sosnokowski did not take political decisions." At this point Eden broke off the discussion; he had "spoken his piece on the subject of Poland."[15]

Hull then changed the subject to his four-power declaration. This was the end of the Polish issue at the conference. From Moscow the British delegation reported to Churchill in London: "We are no wiser as to the Russian attitude on questions concerning Eastern Europe. . . ."

On most other issues of the conference, agreement was reached by November 1. Hull was at his best in getting Soviet approval of China's inclusion in the four-power declaration. The conference was hailed by all three nations as a success, as indeed it was—on all but the really difficult issue of Eastern Europe's future. Molotov had come to the meeting primed for agreement, and Eden had again demonstrated his diplomatic skills.

But as far as Eastern Europe was concerned, few of the British objectives laid down by Churchill had been achieved. So far from assuring the independence of liberated countries, as Harriman reported to Roosevelt, Molotov had "indicated that although they would keep us informed they would take unilateral action in respect to these countries in the establishment of relations satisfactory to themselves."

This ominous warning seems to have been overlooked by the other British and U.S. participants. Yet while barring joint responsibility in their own sphere, the Soviets were happy to pursue it in Western Europe. As Harriman put it: "As to the states west of the areas bordering on the Soviet Union, they appear fully prepared to cooperate with the British and ourselves in working out problems involved, provided they are given full partnership in the decisions."[16]

Concerning the Polish issue itself, Eden thought Hull "unnecessarily reserved." Harriman later said flatly, "Hull failed to support him."[17] The most telling comment came from Ambassador Clark Kerr in his report to London:

The stateliness and fine presence of Mr. Hull, who looked and moved like a magnificent old eagle, made as handsome a contribution as did his rare interventions in debate. We must also commend Molotov for the dexterity with which, having reached agreement with the Secretary of State [Eden], he swept Mr. Hull with all deference into acquiescence in the decisions that had been taken.[18]

Hull's final ineptitude came at his press conference on November 15, after he had returned to Washington. Asked what was meant by "self-determination for liberated countries," Hull replied, "The application of this principle of self-determination would be left to the military people in immediate charge. . . . " And again: "[T]here were 10 Refugee Governments and whether or not they would be restored to their people would be up to their people."[19]

In London the Polish government and press were aghast. This meant, they cried, that the Red Army would control Poland. The British Foreign Office buzzed with such terms as "premature" and "distinctly inept." One British official wrote to his colleagues: "Fortunately, the Polish Govt. seem at last to have sized up Mr. Hull and the U.S. Government and to realize that they will get little but fair words from them. . . . "[20]

But the Poles only pressed their case more furiously. On November 20 the London Polish government delivered a strong warning to Roosevelt and Churchill:

The entry of Soviet troops on Polish territory without previous resumption of Polish-Soviet relations would force the Polish Government to undertake political action against the violation of Polish sovereignty, whilst the Polish local administration and army in Poland would have to continue to work underground. In that case the Polish Government foresee the use of measures of self-defence wherever such measures are rendered indispensable by Soviet methods of terror and extermination of Polish citizens.[21]

This shot was followed by intense Polish agitation as the Big Three Conference at Tehran approached. Mikolajczyk pleaded for a meeting with Roosevelt, who—apparently hoping to avoid a discussion of Polish frontiers—put him off until January. The Polish ambassador to Washington, Jan Ciechanowski, tried in vain to see Hull and was even put off by James C. Dunn, the State Department's adviser on political relations.

Ciechanowski wrote a heated letter to Dunn on November 17. The Poles were alarmed, he declared, that the Council of Foreign Ministers in Moscow had ignored any restoration of civil administration in Poland by its legitimate government. They were further alarmed at Hull's public statement, which "would be equivalent to delivering Poland to the USSR for immediate and complete sovietization."

As for "popular elections" under such conditions, "One cannot hold a plebiscite on a cemetery and, undoubtedly, by that time Poland would have virtually become a cemetery." Apparently Poland and other European countries "are being surrendered to the mercy of the Soviets rather than encouraged to expect the liberation repeatedly promised them in the Atlantic Charter, the Declaration of the United Nations," and many other U.S. and British statements.[22]

On November 19 Hull received an "extremely agitated" Ambassador Ciechanowski. Before his visitor could speak, Hull launched into a lecture. He scolded him for attacks in the Polish press against U.S. policy and the Moscow conference. The United States was, he assured him, trying to get diplomatic relations reestablished between Poland and the Soviet Union. When the meeting ended, wrote Hull, Ciechanowski "at least went away in good humor."[23]

In London the Poles were insisting that they be consulted before decisions affecting Poland were made. "Even a man condemned to death," Mikolajczyk told the U.S. ambassador to his government, "was granted a last word before the court." A representative of the Polish government should "be on hand at the time of these discussions." And in support of the Polish idea that U.S. and British troops should be stationed in Poland, Mikolajczyk said ominously that "as far west as the Russian armies marched, just so far would Russia's western frontier develop."[24]

Despite these Polish pleas, Washington kept silent. Already Hull and Harriman were briefing Roosevelt for the Tehran conference. Hull outlined the Polish fears and his own efforts to calm them. From Moscow, Harriman wrote of the Soviets, "They regard the present Polish Government-in-Exile as hostile, and therefore completely unacceptable to them. . . . They gave us no indication during the Moscow Conference that they were interested in the extension of the Soviet system. I take this with some reservation. . . . "[25] At another opportunity Harriman's warning was more direct: Unless Roosevelt raised the issue at Tehran, Poland would "probably go by default."[26]

As for the British, Anthony Eden proposed to the War Cabinet a policy on Poland to be discussed at Tehran. In return for agreement on the Curzon Line, the Soviets would renew diplomatic relations with the Polish government-in-exile, permit it to return to Poland as soon as possible, and allow free Polish elections for a permanent government.

Such was the situation when the first Big Three summit began in Tehran on November 28, 1943. Roosevelt came to Tehran determined to win Stalin's friendship and confidence. In avoiding any semblance of huddling with Churchill to Stalin's exclusion, Roosevelt cut short the prior British–U.S. meeting in Cairo and filled it with unnecessary sessions with Chiang Kai-shek. Shunning British efforts to develop a common front against Stalin, he rejected separate meetings with Churchill at Tehran while holding three such meetings with Stalin. And while he could not outwardly recognize Stalin's demands against Poland, due to the sensitive Polish vote in the United States, he intended to do so privately.

The Polish issue came up the first night of the conference—at dinner in Roosevelt's quarters in the Soviet embassy. But the president left the table and retired early with a case of indigestion before Churchill broached the subject. At first Stalin was not disposed to discuss the Polish question, as though he considered it a Soviet matter. He "did not feel the need to ask . . . how to act."[27]

But Churchill continued. Stalin had previously commented that he favored moving Poland's western frontier to the Oder River, at the expense of Germany. Those at the table knew this was intended as compensation for Soviet annexation in the east. Churchill proposed that the three heads of state form a policy on Polish frontiers that "we could recommend to the Poles and advise them to accept." Stalin then asked whether the others thought he "was going to swallow Poland up." The Soviets, he said, "did not want anything belonging to other people, although they might have a bite at Germany." (This seems to be the first Soviet reference to designs on part of East Prussia.)

Eden ventured, "What Poland lost in the East she might gain in the West." Stalin replied that "possibly she might. . . . "

Taking out three matches, Churchill set them on the table. They represented Germany, Poland, and the Soviet Union.

"Poland might move westward," he said, "like soldiers taking two steps 'left close.' "

Stalin, obviously pleased and probably surprised at this gratuitous offer by the British, changed his attitude about discussing Poland. It would be a good idea, he acknowledged, "to reach an understanding on this question." At this, the first day's meetings ended.[28]

For two days the Polish issue languished, then exploded into a major topic on December 1, the last day of the conference. After the luncheon session, Roosevelt asked Stalin to visit him in his quarters. Also present were Harriman (Hull not having been invited to Tehran), Molotov, and, as interpreters, Charles E. Bohlen and V. N. Pavlov.

Roosevelt began by telling Stalin he had invited him because he wished to "discuss a matter briefly and frankly." An election was coming up in the United States in 1944; according to Bohlen's notes, "while personally he did not wish to run again, if the war was still in progress, he might have to."

He had to think of the votes of 6 or 7 million Americans of Polish descent. He "would like to see the Eastern border of Poland moved further to the west and the Western border moved even to the River Oder." According to a later recollection by Roosevelt himself, he said flatly, "[I]n general I am in favor of the Curzon Line." He hoped Stalin would understand that "for political reasons" he "could not participate in any decision here in Tehran or even next winter on this subject" and "could not publicly take part in any such arrangement at the present time."

The issue of Lwów, the predominantly Polish city in the disputed area annexed by the Soviet Union in 1939, was not mentioned in the Bohlen minutes. Nearly a year later, when Churchill and Eden were in Moscow, Stalin told them that in the private meeting at Tehran, Roosevelt "had concurred in the policy of the Curzon Line," though he "expressed a hope about Lwów being retained by the Poles." Churchill passed this on to Roosevelt, who confirmed it during a discussion on Polish frontiers at the Yalta conference.[29]

Thus, although Stalin had been reluctant to discuss Poland with his allies, he was receiving carte blanche from them on the annexation of eastern Poland. Eden later criticized Roosevelt's candor in his meeting with Stalin: "This was hardly calculated to restrain the Russians."[30] Yet Churchill himself was not making an issue over the Curzon Line.

In the same tête-à-tête with Stalin, Roosevelt referred to the Baltic states. He mentioned the Americans of Lithuanian, Latvian, and Estonian origin as though they, too, represented a political constraint on the president's public actions. He recognized that the Baltic states had previously belonged to Russia. And with some jocularity he added that "when the Soviet armies reoccupied these areas," he did not "intend to go to war with the Soviet Union on this point."[31]

Thus Roosevelt accomplished what he had been trying to do since February 1942—to assure Stalin verbally that the United States would acquiesce in his territorial demands, even though it could not be put in writing until after the war, or at least after the 1944 elections. The original pressure to do this—the 1941–1942 negotiations over the British-Soviet defense treaty—had long since vanished. So had the fear of a Soviet separate peace and the uncertainty over the second front. To find Roosevelt's motivation in satisfying Stalin's desires, it is difficult to go beyond his desire to make Stalin like him.

The result was that Roosevelt joined Churchill in giving away the territorial bargaining chip without getting anything in return—not even a guarantee and the machinery for Polish independence. Eden's proposed bargain was ignored by his superiors.

This became painfully obvious when the three-power "Political Meeting" opened at 6 P.M. in the conference room of the Soviet embassy. Roosevelt raised the Polish question by hoping that diplomatic relations could be re-established between the Soviet Union and the Polish government. Stalin's response was adamant: "The agents of the Polish Government who are in

Poland are connected with the Germans. They are killing partisans [Communist guerrillas]. You cannot imagine what they are doing there."[32]

After an interjection by Churchill, Stalin continued with his diatribe against the Polish government. "If it sides with the partisans and if we are given a guarantee that its agents will not have ties with the Germans in Poland, we shall be prepared to have talks with it."[33]

Churchill then reverted to the question of frontiers: "If some reasonable formula could be devised," he would present it to the Polish Government as "probably the best they could obtain." If they refused, "Great Britain would be through with them and certainly would not oppose the Soviet Government under any condition at the peace table."

Stalin gave Churchill his answer: "The Soviet Government stands for this border [the 1939 Ribbentrop-Molotov Line, or roughly the Curzon Line] and considers that this is correct."

There followed a general parley over the exact course of the 1939 line, with Molotov insisting that it was the same as the Curzon Line. All three delegations produced maps, about which the conferees crowded. Eden said that "the Curzon Line was intended to pass to the East of Lvov [Lwów]."

Stalin replied that the British map was wrong. "Lvov should be left on the Russian side. . . . "

After more discussion and reference to the maps, Churchill said he was "not prepared to make a great squawk about Lvov."

According to Bohlen's notes, "the Russians admitted that the city of Lwów was predominantly Polish," but it was "in the heart of an overwhelmingly Ukrainian region." For that reason, said Stalin, "it could not be returned to Poland." As Bohlen noted, Stalin took his pencil and "somewhat contemptuously" drew lines on one of the American maps showing the future boundary.

Throughout the discussion on Polish frontiers Roosevelt was silent except to raise the possibility of transfers of population. As Eden put it, "Roosevelt was reserved about Poland to the point of being unhelpful." And as both Eden and Harriman later recorded, they felt at the time that postponing the settlement of the Polish frontiers would only make the issue worse when the Red Army had occupied the country. During a digression concerning Germany, Churchill drafted a "formula" on Polish frontiers.

"I should now like to return to the Polish question, which appears to me to be more urgent because [this according to the Soviet transcript of the meeting] the Poles can make a great deal of noise."

He then read a formula stating that Poland should be located between the Curzon Line and the Oder River, including East Prussia and Upper Silesia. He offered to take this to the Poles in London as the best he could get. Stalin responded by claiming the northern third of East Prussia, including Königsberg. "If the British agree to the transfer of the said territory to us, we shall agree to the formula proposed by Churchill."

The prime minister then asked about Lwów. Stalin answered that he "would accept the Curzon Line." Since the Soviet version of the Curzon Line ran west of Lwów, Stalin was confirming that the Soviet Union would keep that city. (Actually, the Curzon Line of 1919 had not extended as far south as Lwów, which was to have been included in a proposed autonomous state of Eastern Galicia.) Churchill confided to Eden that he would not break his heart "about this cession of parts of Germany to Poland or about Lvov."

So ended the Tehran discussion of Poland. None of the minutes—British, U.S., or Soviet—said there was an agreement. Even the Soviet version quotes Churchill as concluding, "This is a very interesting proposal which I will make a point of studying." According to Bohlen's minutes, "Although nothing definite was stated, it was apparent that the British were going to take this suggestion back to London to the Poles."

Yet at Tehran both Roosevelt and Churchill had signaled to Stalin that they would not oppose his Curzon Line settlement. Stalin considered it an agreement, and later said so to Churchill.

If Churchill had wished to trade Polish territory for Polish independence, he did not press for this at Tehran. His only excuse could be that, without Roosevelt joining him in a tough stance against Stalin, he could not bargain alone.

As for Roosevelt, his high-minded policy of postponing territorial changes to the peace table was now in ruins. No justification remained for having failed to bargain with Stalin when he was weak in 1941 and 1942. Now, without big-power support, the Poles were left to negotiate alone against Stalin for resumption of diplomatic relations.

This, in turn, seemed to hinge on Polish acceptance of the Curzon Line and on changes in the Polish cabinet demanded by Stalin. But with the British and Americans settling for the Curzon Line, the West's only bargaining chip had been squandered. There was little inducement for Stalin to treat with the London Poles, or to agree with the Western powers on mechanisms for an independent Poland.

Thus, for all their public assurances about support for a free Poland, the Americans by their action, or rather inaction, had stripped Polish hopes. Worse still, due to the upcoming U.S. elections, the Poles were not told of the Tehran concessions. They thus went ahead blindly insisting on conditions that had already been given away. Had they known there was no hope of retaining the lands east of the Curzon Line, they might have fallen back on their only remaining resort—changing the Polish cabinet in return for Soviet recognition.

To all these ramifications Roosevelt seemed, if not indifferent, then oblivious. In his "Fireside Chat" on the Cairo and Tehran conferences, he assured Americans, "I got along fine with Marshal Stalin." And to a congressman from a heavily Polish district he wrote, "[T]here were no secret commitments made by me at Teheran. . . ."[34]

The Invasion That Never Was

When Churchill left London for the Casablanca conference in the first days of 1943, he carried with him the proposals of his chiefs of staff for "American-British Strategy in 1943." Global in scope, they included one recommendation that would foment painful confrontation between the British and Americans for the next two years. It came under the heading "Actions in the Balkans after the Collapse of Italy."

Churchill's fascination with the eastern Mediterranean dated at least from World War I. Then, as first lord of the Admiralty, he had championed a campaign against Turkey to breach the Dardanelles and link with Russia through the Black Sea. There followed the disastrous landing at Gallipoli.

The prime minister had undoubtedly harbored notions of Balkan adventures when he first urged the invasion of North Africa on the Americans. Meetings of the British chiefs of staff in the fall of 1942 were peppered with references to possible Balkan action, usually through Turkey. For the next year Churchill's argument centered on pressuring Turkey to enter the war, capturing Rhodes for air cover of the southern Balkans, and mounting commando-type bridgeheads in Yugoslavia to support the partisans. Later, with the Allies moving up the boot of Italy, he pressed for a genuine invasion at the head of the Adriatic Sea and a drive for Budapest and Vienna.

At Casablanca, Churchill's Balkan ideas were confined to pushing Turkey into the war; afterward he met with the Turkish president, Ismet Inönü, and confided visions of a Balkan front linked with the insurgents in Yugoslavia. But the Turks remained officially neutral.

Whetting Churchill's appetite for the Adriatic invasion was the fast-boiling political pot in the Balkans. In the occupied countries—Yugoslavia, Greece, and Albania—strong guerrilla forces were harassing the Germans. Communist-led partisans in Greece had, in coordination with the Allies in 1942, blown up a key bridge, hindering German supply shipments to North Africa. In Yugoslavia, Communist forces under Josip Broz Tito and royalist insurgents under Draža Mihailović had held large mountain areas from German control.

Also, among Hitler's allies the disastrous defeat at Stalingrad aroused thoughts of defection. As the Red Army rolled westward, the Romanians and Hungarians turned to Britain with offers of surrender if this could prevent Soviet occupation. In August 1943 Hungarian representatives in Istanbul met the British minister and proposed to surrender to the Western Allies (not to the Soviet Union) when and if their forces arrived at the Hungarian frontier. And in September the head of the Romanian government told the British, through his embassy in Turkey, that his country would "cooperate with any Anglo-American force entering the Balkans before the Russians. . . . "[1]

Churchill was already doing his best to fulfill this requirement. At the Washington conference in May 1943, when all of North Africa was falling to the Allies, he was still more excited about the Balkans. Armed with another report from his chiefs of staff, he included the Balkans among the rich opportunities in the Mediterranean. He had already talked the Americans into North Africa, then Sicily. On the question of where to go after Sicily, Churchill declared that "Operations in the general area of the Balkans opened up very wide prospects." In the end the Allies agreed on an invasion of Italy if it did not detract from the second front in France, now code-named Overlord.

Since larger strategy in the Mediterranean was still up in the air, Churchill flew from Washington to Eisenhower's headquarters in Algiers on May 29. To bring on an early decision, he took with him General George C. Marshall, the U.S. army chief of staff.

Marshall's key role in strategy was clear to Churchill. Whereas the prime minister was constantly interfering with his generals, Roosevelt had no pretension to military genius; he depended heavily on his generals, especially Marshall, who in the course of the war became "first among equals" in the Joint Chiefs of Staff. Marshall was on his own for weeks at a time without being contacted by Roosevelt; in contrast, General Sir Alan Brooke, chief of the Imperial General Staff, wrote: "I was fortunate if I did not see Winston for six hours."[2]

Marshall's genius, and his greatest contribution to victory, was in administration and logistics. He built, trained, and deployed the most powerful fighting force in U.S. history. He argued, against conflicting estimates from others, that 89 U.S. divisions would be necessary to win the war; by war's end 87 of the 89 divisions had been sent into action.

It is true that most of Marshall's military career had been spent behind a desk. He had not had a field command since he was a junior officer in World War I. Yet his grasp of global strategy grew mightily during World War II; from the U.S. standpoint the war unfolded as Marshall planned it.

Every inch the Virginia gentleman, Marshall was so thoroughly devoid of pretense that others at first tended to underrate him. Brooke called him "a very great gentleman who inspired trust but did not impress me by the ability of his brain."[3]

But Marshall's restraint was a key to his greatness. As a professional soldier in a democracy, he deplored militarism and tried continually to leave political decisions to the politicians. Churchill called him "a statesman with a penetrating and commanding view of the whole scene." Yet Marshall generally focused on military considerations, even at times when no one else was weighing the political ones.

Most of all, Marshall was a tower of integrity. Brooke wrote of him, "I have seldom met a straighter or more reliable man in my life."[4] Even Stalin, never given to compliment Western leaders, once said, "I would trust General Marshall with my life."[5] And Marshall's boss, Secretary of War Henry L. Stimson, told him, "I have seen a great many soldiers in my lifetime and you, sir, are the finest soldier I have ever known."[6]

Capping these traits was Marshall's singleness of purpose, which at times was the main force in holding the Western Allies' war effort on course. He believed firmly in the second front in France as the knockout blow against Germany; once that decision was made by the Allies, he fought against any diversions from it.

Now, at the Algiers meeting with Churchill and Eisenhower, he was skeptical as Churchill looked beyond an Italian campaign to the Balkans—proposing munitions, agents, and "possibly Commando bands" in support of the guerrillas. Sensing the U.S. resistance, Churchill stated that "His Majesty's Government do not contemplate or desire the provision of any organized armed force for the Balkan theatre, either this year or in any period with which we are now concerned."[7]

On May 31, in the middle of the discussion, Eden arrived; without knowing what had been said previously, he observed that the Turks would be more likely to come into the war "when our troops had reached the Balkan area." This revelation of British plans, involving a dilution of the main effort to come in France, was certain to rekindle the fears of Marshall and Eisenhower. Churchill was quick to contradict Eden. He "was not advocating sending an army into the Balkans now or in the near future." Eden dutifully clarified himself as well.[8]

By mid-July, when the Allies were overrunning Sicily, they agreed on Italy as the next target. With that, Churchill's Mediterranean strategy was in full swing. When Secretary of War Stimson visited Britain in July 1943, Churchill deluged him with his Mediterranean plans; and when the prime minister repeatedly warned of the risks in Overlord—"the Channel full of corpses"—Stimson feared he wanted to kill the cross-Channel invasion with a volley of "Mediterranean diversions."[9]

Forewarned, Roosevelt and the Joint Chiefs of Staff insisted on the undiluted Overlord plan during the meetings in Quebec and Washington in the summer of 1943. At a preliminary huddle in the White House on August 10, Roosevelt told his military chiefs, "[T]he British Foreign Office does not want the Balkans to come under the Russian influence. Britain wants to get to the Balkans first."

But Roosevelt could "not believe that Russians would desire to take over the Balkan states." And it was "unwise to plan military strategy based on a gamble as to political results."[10] With this wave of the hand, U.S. leadership turned its back on Southeastern Europe. But during the Quebec conference Churchill's obsession with stopping the Soviet Union suddenly found new words. At dinner, referring to Stalin, he spoke of "bloody consequences in the future."

"Stalin is an unnatural man," he added. "There will be grave troubles."[11]

And while taking a bath—one of his regular locales for a conference—he tole Eden of his fears. Germany and Italy, he warned, "had been the great restraints upon Russia. We were committed to destroy both." Russia, he concluded, "would then be immensely powerful."[12]

During the subsequent conference in Washington, Churchill saw his chance to revive his Mediterranean strategy. On September 9 the conferees learned of the Allied landing at Salerno, Italy, and the surrender of the Italian government. Churchill immediately wrote out and read to Roosevelt and the Combined (British and U.S.) Chiefs of Staff a review of the Mediterranean opportunities now opened. Among them:

When the defensive line across Northern Italy has been completed, it may be possible to spare some of our own forces assigned to the Mediterranean theater to emphasize a movement North and North-Eastward from the Dalmatian ports."[13]

For the first time Churchill openly revealed a plan beyond simply supplying the Balkan guerrillas—an Allied expedition toward the Danube. But Roosevelt, heeding Stimson and Marshall, was adamant. When the conference ended, the British and Americans had renewed their commitment to Overlord.

Still, Churchill would not forget his Mediterranean strategy, with its ultimate goals in Austria and Hungary. Bad news from Italy gave him another reason to renew his argument. The diversion of troops to Britain in preparation for Overlord had slowed the Allied drive up the boot of Italy, prompting a negative report on October 31 from General Sir Harold Alexander, commander of land forces in Italy. Two days later Churchill cabled Roosevelt asking for a review of the plans for 1944.

Not only the Americans, but some of Churchill's own staff, believed he was again trying to postpone or shelve Overlord. Brooke wrote in his diary of Churchill's "wishing to swing the strategy back to the Mediterranean at the expense of the Channel. I am in many ways entirely with him. . . . "[14]

Attending the Council of Foreign Ministers meeting in Moscow, Eden and his staff were dumbfounded. Oliver Harvey wrote in his diary, "[T]he P.M. is set on not carrying out Overlord. He is almost certainly right on military grounds. . . . "[15] Churchill himself never proposed scrubbing Overlord, but he was ready to slip its schedule in order to keep troops and landing craft in the Mediterranean.

At Churchill's insistence Roosevelt was to meet with him in Cairo before going to the Tehran conference with Stalin. With them both chiefs brought their military leaders. Stopping at Malta, Churchill conferred with Alexander and his other top generals. The scene was reminiscent of so many other informal gatherings in his bedroom or bathroom; this time he was in bed, surrounded by uniformed figures crowded into the room. According to Brooke's diary entry of November 18, Churchill was rehearsing what he was inclined to tell the Americans:

"All right, if you won't play with us in the Mediterranean, we won't play with you in the English Channel."

"All right," the Americans might say, "then we shall divert our main effort in the Pacific."

"You are welcome to do so if you wish," Churchill would answer.[16]

For their part, the Americans were sailing to Cairo with their own apprehensions over the Mediterranean. They believed Churchill was promoting a full-dress invasion of the Balkans. On the day after the British met in Malta, Roosevelt was in the Atlantic, approaching Gibraltar on the U.S. battleship *Iowa*. That afternoon he met with the Joint Chiefs of Staff in the admiral's cabin. They were discussing what they would tell the British about the Balkans. Marshall was saying that a Balkan invasion would detract from Overlord and prolong the war.

"The British," he declared, "might like to 'ditch' Overlord at this time in order to undertake operations in a country with practically no communications. If they insist on any such proposal, we could say that if they propose to do that we will pull out and go into the Pacific with all our forces." Roosevelt agreed.[17]

Thus a fateful showdown seemed to be brewing as the Western leaders headed for Cairo. If Churchill was bluffing, he might well have his bluff called. Brooke wrote in his diary, "I do not think such tactics will pay."[18]

At the same time the U.S. attitude was clouded by a naive belief that the Soviets might welcome a Western invasion of the Balkans. On the *Iowa*, Roosevelt observed that the Red Army was approaching Romania. The Soviets, he suggested, might say: "If someone would now come up from the Adriatic to the Danube, we could readily defeat Germany forthwith."[19]

Marshall was quick to oppose such a move, but Roosevelt would not rule it out until he had heard Stalin's view at Tehran. At Cairo, in fact, the Americans tried to avoid discussing European strategy with the British. The visit of Chiang Kai-shek and Madame Chiang, which more sensibly should have come at the second Cairo conference after Tehran, took up most of the available hours. And Churchill, sensing U.S. suspicions, was cautious in promoting his Mediterranean strategy. At Roosevelt's villa on November 24, the prime minister dismissed sending any troops to Yugoslavia except possibly "a few Commandos." He limited further Balkan talk to saying, "Finally, when we had reached our objectives in Italy, the time would come to take the decision whether we should move to the left or to the right."[20]

But if Churchill had sprung a surprise, so did Roosevelt. At the forthcoming Tehran meeting, he said, the Russians "might suggest a junction of our right with their left. We should be ready to answer this question."

The subject was tabled until Tehran. There, on the morning of November 28, Roosevelt met with the Joint Chiefs of Staff in a preliminary caucus at the U.S. legation. In discussing British proposals in the eastern Mediterranean, he suggested "a small force to penetrate northward from Trieste and Fiume."[21]

Both Marshall and Admiral William D. Leahy advised against Adriatic operations. But in the first plenary session, held that afternoon in the conference room of the Soviet embassy, Roosevelt was persistent. Churchill had just advocated help to the Yugoslav partisans, but had given discreet assurance that "there was no plan to send a large army to the Balkans." It was Roosevelt who now suggested "a possible operation at the head of the Adriatic to make a junction with the Partisans under Tito and then to operate northeast into Roumania in conjunction with the Soviet advance."

At this, Harry Hopkins slipped a note to Admiral King, who was sitting next to him: "Who is promoting that Adriatic business that the President continually returns to?"

"As far as I know," replied King, "it is his own idea."[22]

Since some historians have maintained that Roosevelt always opposed a Balkans adventure, this proposal of his has been a mystery. But Roosevelt's previous comments en route to Cairo, at the Cairo meeting itself, and at his preliminary staff meeting in Tehran all show that his idea was seriously weighed, not impromptu. Usually his words were coupled with the thought that the Soviets might welcome it. So when Churchill disavowed any serious invasion of the Balkans, Roosevelt apparently decided he had to bring it up himself in order to test Stalin's reaction.

The first reaction came from Churchill; a consummate opportunist, he embraced Roosevelt's idea and saddled him with it. After Rome was taken, "we will have a choice of moving west, or, as the President says, east in the Mediterranean. . . . " And again, in response to a question from Stalin, "this force could either move west, or as the President suggested, to the eastern part of the Mediterranean."[23] Adroitly, Churchill had made Roosevelt the author of a Balkan invasion plan, thus hoping to spike U.S. or Soviet suspicions of British imperialist strategy in the Mediterranean.

But Stalin's own reaction was pointed. He opposed "dispersing allied forces" to the eastern Mediterranean, southern France, and northern France. He thought "it would be better to take Overlord as the basis for all 1944 operations; that after the capture of Rome the troops thus relieved might be sent to Southern France. . . . "

Seeing Stalin's attitude, Roosevelt swiftly shifted: "[T]here would be 8 or 9 French Divisions . . . available for an operation against southern France."

Stalin soon tightened the screw by asserting that the southern France invasion should precede Overlord by two or three months to divert German troops. Roosevelt added that "nothing should be done to delay the carrying out of Overlord. . . . " Churchill argued against sacrificing all Mediterranean activity "to keep an exact date for Overlord," but his case was now lost.

To the British, Stalin's promotion of southern France was entirely political—to keep the Balkans for the Red Army and Soviet control. Stalin's aims, wrote Brooke, "could now be best met by the greatest squandering of British and American lives in the French theatre."[24] As for Roosevelt, Brooke confided to a colleague, "This Conference is over when it has only just begun. Stalin has got the President in his pocket."[25] Churchill returned to his quarters in a downcast mood. His physician, Charles Wilson, asked whether anything had gone wrong.

"A bloody lot has gone wrong!" Churchill snapped.[26]

For his part, Roosevelt believed it was Churchill whose motives were political. In their guest quarters in the Soviet embassy, Roosevelt is said to have told his son Elliott, who accompanied him to Tehran:

Whenever the P.M. argued for our invasion through the Balkans, it was quite obvious to everyone in the room what he really meant. That he was above all else anxious to knife up into Central Europe, in order to keep the Red Army out of Austria and Rumania, even Hungary, if possible. Stalin knew it, I knew it, everybody knew it.[27]

Next day, true to his pattern at such conferences, Stalin took his turn at being difficult. He started by demanding, "[W]ho will command Overlord?" The Soviets would not take Overlord seriously until a commander was named. He called for a specific, unbreakable date for Overlord. And since Churchill had persisted in talking so much about the eastern Mediterranean, Stalin asked him directly, "[D]o the British really believe in Overlord or are they only saying so to reassure the Russians?"[28]

That night at dinner Stalin continued his attack on Churchill, though in the manner of good-natured teasing. But next day, when the military had reported agreement on the primacy of Overlord without distracting ventures in the eastern Mediterranean, Stalin's mood changed again. For the rest of the conference he was affability itself. As Churchill put it, "He can be quite friendly when he gets what he wants."

Roosevelt, according to Hopkins, was elated over the Tehran conference:"The President knows now that Stalin is 'get-able' and that we are going to get along fine in the future."[29]

Churchill, with a more profound grasp of the issues in Europe, was despondent. In the face of Stalin's emerging ambitions, as Churchill saw them, Roosevelt was offering no resistance, and Britain alone could not block the Soviet Union. In the prime minister's quarters after the second day's meetings, his doctor sensed in him a feeling of "impending catastrophe." Standing dramatically erect, his eyes bulging, Churchill told Dr. Wilson, "I believe man might destroy man and wipe out civilization. Europe would be desolate and I may be held responsible."[30]

Churchill left Tehran in a state of utter exhaustion. In Cairo he met with President Ismet Inönü of Turkey; in vain he pressed again for Turkey's entry into the war—the only condition that could at that time justify Balkan operations. Desperately, he next insisted on flying to see General Alexander, commander of Allied forces in Italy. When his doctor told him it was "madness" to travel in his weak condition, Churchill flew into a rage.

"You don't understand," he shouted. ". . . I am not going to see Alex for fun. He may be our last hope. We've got to do something with these bloody Russians."[31]

But exhaustion was followed by pneumonia. Wilson got Churchill to Eisenhower's villa near Tunis, then to a resting spot in Marrakesh, where he had recovered enough by January 1944 to return to London.

On January 22 the Allies made their second amphibious landing in Italy at Anzio, south of Rome. But the German response was even more effective than at Salerno. Hampering the Allies was the withdrawal of some strength from Italy to Britain, while the Germans had sent in reinforcements. The capture of Rome, which Churchill had planned for January, did not come until June 4, two days before the Normandy landings. Any chance of a prior assault in southern France, as proposed by Stalin, had been frustrated by the slow progress in Italy.

When the true second front in France proved so successful in the summer of 1944, the need for a southern France invasion, code-named Anvil, came again into question. For if Anvil were scrubbed, the same forces could be used for a renewed Italian offensive and an invasion at the head of the Adriatic. The day after the Normandy landings, General Alexander outlined to Brooke his plans for an Italian offensive; once in the Po Valley he could move either west toward France or east through the Ljubljana Gap toward Austria.

"It was a dazzling idea," he later wrote, "this grand project of reaching Vienna before our Russian allies. . . ."[32] Three days later the Combined Chiefs of Staff told General Sir Henry M. "Jumbo" Wilson, commanding

Allied Mediterranean forces, to develop plans for both the Adriatic and southern France alternatives. This he did in a report on June 19.

Immediate response came from Eisenhower, operating now at SHAEF headquarters in Britain. The Combined Chiefs, he cabled Marshall with obvious irritation, "long ago decided to make Western Europe the base from which to conduct decisive operations against Germany." Departing from this was "potentially dangerous." He was contemptuous of "wandering off overland via Trieste to Ljubljana." And he went on:

Both the enemy and ourselves now consider OVERLORD the vital operation. It is imperative that we obtain and maintain superiority over him, and this must be done in France as quickly as we can. We need big ports.[33]

Marshall and the U.S. Joint Chiefs of Staff quickly agreed, but the issue was now in the hands of the politicians. Calling a meeting with the British Chiefs of Staff on the night of June 22, Churchill reopened the issue of Anvil versus what Alexander was now calling "Operation Armpit." According to Brooke, Churchill "was for supporting Alexander's advance on Vienna."

Brooke himself was unconvinced. Alexander's plan called for launching the attack against the Germans in Italy in September; this meant that at best the Allies would not reach the Julian Alps in Slovenia before winter. As Brooke tried to tell Churchill, "if we took the season of the year and the topography of the country in league against us, we should have three enemies instead of one."[34]

Thus the British Chiefs of Staff were not ready to support Alexander and Churchill in a drive toward Vienna, but they did agree that Allied forces in Italy should not be weakened to support Anvil. They were greatly fortified in this view by a German message, intercepted and decoded, showing that Hitler intended to hold in the Apennines at all costs. This meant to them that Italy was a better diversion from the Normandy front than Anvil would be.

Churchill thereupon renewed the Italian issue with Roosevelt in a cable and a formal paper on June 28 and 29; actually, he was still looking beyond Italy to the Adriatic invasion. In the cable he reminded Roosevelt, "Please remember how you spoke to me at Tehran about Istria. . . . " And in the paper he cited the Wilson-Alexander plan for "an attack eastward across the Adriatic," adding Wilson's belief that they could take Trieste by the end of September.

"Let us resolve," he concluded, "not to wreck one great campaign for the sake of winning the other. Both can be won."[35]

With this volley the verbal battle of the Mediterranean reached new fury. Brooke wrote, "[W]e are in for an all-in struggle with our American colleagues. . . . "[36] Cabling Brooke for a decision, Alexander reported the Americans were already taking troops out of the Italian line.

Roosevelt's prompt answer was even stronger than Churchill's message. He thought the war would be delayed by "a campaign to debouch from Ljubljana gap into Slovenia and Hungary." And he emphasized his real fear: "I cannot agree to the employment of United States troops against Istria and into the Balkans. . . . " With the 1944 U.S. elections approaching, "for purely political considerations over here I would never survive even a slight set- back in 'Overlord' if it were known that fairly large forces had been diverted to the Balkans."

As for Anvil, Roosevelt reminded Churchill about their agreement with Stalin. If they could not agree on Anvil by July 1, they "must communicate with Stalin immediately." Since they were now "fully involved in our major blow, history will never forgive us if we lose precious time and lives in indecision and debate. My dear friend, I beg you let us go ahead with our plan."[37]

The core of Roosevelt's message, drafted by Marshall and his staff, chal- lenged the feasibility of the Adriatic invasion. Yet Marshall may have known little about the terrain involved. According to Harold Macmillan, the British political adviser in the Mediterranean, when Marshall had visited Wilson in Italy on June 17–19, he had remarked at dinner, "Say, where is this Lju- bljana? If it's in the Balkans we can't go there." Macmillan had reassured him it was "practically in Austria."[38] And in Britain, Eisenhower spoke disparagingly of "that gap whose name I can't even pronounce."[39]

The truth is that the U.S. military was not interested in any project that might detract from Overlord, and Roosevelt believed the American voters would oppose sending American soldiers into the Balkan backwater, espe- cially when the fields of France offered a straight line to Germany.

Churchill made the point that no one had proposed "moving armies into the Balkans." According to Brooke, it was a moot question whether the targeted area was in the Balkans. Since the Sava River has been commonly considered to mark the boundary of the Balkans in the northwest, Ljubljana and its gap are technically in the Balkans, but the offensive would have been aimed immediately at Hungary and Austria—not Balkan states.

In disclaiming the Balkans the British were splitting hairs unnecessarily; if they had proven conclusively that Ljubljana was not in the Balkans, it would have made no difference. Roosevelt's political objection to the Balkans was certainly overdrawn; after putting U.S. fighting men in North Africa and Italy, the Balkans would have made little stir. The real American fear was in supporting any venture that might drag strength away from the main invasion of France, which had already been postponed an entire year by the demands of the Mediterranean theater.

Until this point the British military had based its Adriatic plan on pure war strategy; Trieste is closer to Germany than Normandy, if one does not consider the mountains. Churchill kept talking about Mediterranean "vic- tories" and "prizes," as though collecting the greatest number of these was the way to win a war.

Churchill's real aim, expressed so far only in the privacy of his office or bedroom, was to preempt the Red Army and save as much of Eastern Europe as possible from the Soviet brand of totalitarianism. He believed Roosevelt's threat to take the issue to Stalin was pure naiveté, since it was obvious to the British that Stalin favored Anvil to keep the Western Allies out of Eastern Europe. For his part, Roosevelt was naive—at least concerning the oppression that would come with the Red Army's heel. But he was shrewd enough to know that Churchill would shrink from bringing Stalin into the decision.

"We are deeply grieved by your telegram," Churchill answered on July 1. It was Roosevelt himself, the prime minister recalled, who had emphasized at Tehran "the possibilities of a move eastward when Italy was conquered and mentioned particularly Istria." As for Stalin, he might welcome Alexander's army in Eastern Europe. Or, alternatively, "On a long-term political view, he might prefer that the British and Americans should do their share in France . . . and that east, middle and southern Europe should fall naturally into his control."

Churchill had now hinted at his real motive. Rather than bring Stalin into the matter, the prime minister was willing to submit, for the first time, to U.S. dominance in the Western alliance: "If you still press upon us . . . to withdraw so many of your forces from the Italian campaign and leave all our hopes there dashed to the ground, His Majesty's Government . . . must enter a solemn protest."[40]

Roosevelt shot back a final answer late the same night. Opposing the dispersal of force to an Istrian venture, he insisted on Anvil in support of the Normandy front and called for the order to be given.

"Will you ask your Chiefs to despatch it to General Wilson at once."[41]

On July 2, 1944, Wilson was ordered to launch Anvil. Churchill acquiesced, though urging his British colleagues to join in making the Americans understand that Britain had been badly handled. To Ismay he wrote on July 6: "[A]n intense impression must be made upon the Americans that we have been ill-treated and are furious."[42] He nursed the determination that at some point the British alone would strike toward the Danube. "I am not going to give way about this for anybody. Alexander is to have his campaign."

Wilson immediately began preparing the southern France invasion from Italian ports, aiming at a landing on August 15 at St. Tropez, at the west end of the French Riviera. U.S. and French troops were taken out of the Italian front.

In the last week of July the situation changed in northern France. General Omar Bradley's forces broke out of Normandy, striking southward and partially cutting off the Brittany Peninsula. With Brest now appearing within Allied grasp, Churchill saw his chance. Surely Marseilles and Anvil were no longer needed.

On the morning of August 4 the prime minister, lying abed and talking to his visiting doctor, berated Anvil as "sheer folly" when the troops could have been used to invade the Balkans. Despite their reduced strength, Allied forces in Italy were advancing and "would soon be in the valley of the Po." With growing excitement he sat up in bed, his words tumbling faster. He "must see Alex without delay." He would go to Italy. "Two heads are better than one at a time like this."[43]

Before Churchill left for Italy, Eisenhower visited him on August 9 at 10 Downing Street. The prime minister took the opportunity to scold him about Anvil and argue instead for Armpit—this only six days before the scheduled landing in southern France. In an exhausting session lasting seven hours, Churchill used every device of persuasion.[44] Eisenhower wrote to Marshall, "I have never seen him so obviously stirred, upset and even despondent." Churchill charged that the United States "is taking the attitude of a big, strong, and dominating partner" in refusing to consider the British viewpoint.

Eisenhower replied that the British view had been followed on other occasions (such as the invasions of North Africa and Italy). The second front needed Marseilles; the artificial harbor on the Normandy coast had been battered by storm; Cherbourg was "unsatisfactory" because of the long, winding, and slow railroad connection. And the Germans were already demolishing Brest (it was not restored by the end of the war).

Churchill argued that his administration's success was in jeopardy if Alexander were not allowed his northward offensive. Eisenhower recognized the importance of political objectives. He suggested that though Churchill had not mentioned it, the prime minister might be promoting Armpit "in order to have a better positioning of the Allied forces at the end of the war." Perhaps he wanted to cancel Anvil to permit this.

"But if you do that," Eisenhower declared, "you must go to the President and get an agreement to change my orders. If he does, I'll go along."

Again, Churchill protested that the second front was a smashing success without Marseilles. He said that they already had the Germans licked.

"Oh, no, we haven't," insisted Eisenhower.

Finally Churchill played his trump. His voice trembling, he declared that if Alexander's offensive were denied, he might have to visit King George and "lay down the mantle of my high office."

But Eisenhower persisted, and left unmoved. Churchill finally surrendered. When Anvil's code name was changed to Dragoon, Churchill said it was appropriate, since he had "been dragooned into it." And in an effort to "do the civil" by the operation, he accompanied the ships and watched the bombardment at St. Tropez on August 15.

The ease of the landing and the Allied advance up the Rhone Valley was used by both sides of the argument to justify their position. While the Americans hailed Dragoon's rapid success, the British said this same success proved it was unnecessary. A month after the landing Churchill was congratulating the U.S. Joint Chiefs of Staff "on the success of Dragoon, which had produced the most gratifying results." But later he was still critical. Acknowledging that the southern landing had delivered another army on

Eisenhower's right flank, he complained that "a heavy price was paid. The army of Italy was deprived of its opportunity to strike a most formidable blow at the Germans, and very possibly to reach Vienna before the Russians, with all that might have followed therefrom."[45]

Still, Churchill had not given up on the thrust through Ljubljana. On August 20 the Red Army launched an offensive deep into Romania. Crossing the Danube, the Soviets were less than 30 miles from Bucharest by August 29. In nine days the Red Army had made an end run around the barrier of the Carpathian Mountains and the whole plain of the lower Danube Valley lay open. Within a few days the Wehrmacht had started evacuating Greece to avoid being cut off. Now was the time to strike at the head of the Adriatic.

Previous plans to invade Yugoslavia may have been premature; an Allied force marching to the Danube would have had to rely solely on Tito's partisans to protect its flanks, and the Germans had repeatedly shown their ability to mount savage counterattacks. But now, threatened by the Red Army in the east, the enemy was pulling northward. An Allied push into the Sava Valley of northern Yugoslavia could create a giant pincers to interdict the retreating Germans and either contain them in the Balkans or badly maul them in their retreat.

Churchill's Armpit operation now took on a true military justification that it had lacked before. But, more important, as the prime minister was soon to reveal fully, this was the last chance to save part of Eastern Europe from complete Soviet occupation.

On August 29, just two weeks before the scheduled opening of the second Quebec conference (code-named Octagon), Churchill cabled Roosevelt: "I have never forgotten your talks to me at Teheran about Istria, and I am sure that the arrival of a powerful army in Trieste and Istria in four or five weeks would have an effect far outside purely military values." He proceeded to mention Hungary as a possibility.

Next day Roosevelt answered: "We can renew our Teheran talk about Trieste and Istria at Octagon." And Churchill, now fully charged, returned a message next day calling for "a movement first to Istria and Trieste and then ultimately upon Vienna." Admiral Leahy drafted still another presidential reply: "As to the exact employment of our forces in Italy in the future. . . . It seems to me that American forces should be used to the westward. . . . " When this draft reached Roosevelt for his approval, he added, "but I am completely open-minded on this. . . . "[46] When Churchill arrived at Quebec on September 11, he could see British armor rolling into Vienna.

By this time Romania had capitulated to the Soviets, who had also declared war on Bulgaria and overrun that country. Sweeping through Transylvania, the Red Army now reached the Hungarian frontier. The Germans were evacuating the Aegean islands and southern Greece. The British in Egypt were preparing a force to land in Greece.

At the first meeting of the Combined Chiefs of Staff in the Hotel Frontenac's main conference room on September 12, it was Brooke who first mentioned openly the anti-Soviet ingredient in the Istrian stew: "It had not only a military value but also political value in view of the Russian advances in the Balkans." Support came from an unexpected quarter; Admiral Ernest J. King, U.S. chief of naval operations, acknowledged he also "had in mind the possibility of amphibious operations in Istria."[47]

Marshall himself did not speak against the plan; unknown to Churchill, the U.S. army chief of staff had received a surprising message from Eisenhower on September 4. Now that the Germans were retreating in France, he wrote, it was important to keep up the pressure on all fronts, including Italy.

A further consideration is that if that front should disintegrate and we could thrust into Austria we might do much to prevent a later assumption of guerrilla warfare by fanatical Nazis. But under no considerations should the force turn south from Trieste into the Balkans. It should strike northeast toward Vienna.[48]

Suddenly the Americans and the British seemed to be agreeing about an Adriatic thrust. The Combined Chiefs of Staff determined to watch events in Italy, take no more troops or landing craft from that theater, and decide on an Istrian landing by October 15.

Churchill now believed his plan might still be realized. At a meeting next day with Roosevelt and the Combined Chiefs of Staff at the Citadel, he gave his first full-dress exposition of his plan and purpose. He had "always been attracted by a right-handed movement, with the purpose of giving Germany a stab in the armpit":

Our objective should be Vienna. . . . An added reason for this right handed movement was the rapid encroachment of the Russians into the Balkans and the consequent dangerous spread of Russian influence in this area.

Churchill preferred, he went on, "to get into Vienna before the Russians did," since he did not know "what Russia's policy would be after she took it."[49]

Roosevelt was noncommittal, but Churchill believed his Istrian thrust had been approved at Quebec, subject to the success of the Italian offensive.

"The idea of our going to Vienna," he cabled to the War Cabinet after the meeting, "if the war lasts long enough and if other people do not get there first, is fully accepted here."[50]

But the key ingredient was a successful offensive in Italy, and this was still lacking due to the weakened Allied strength and the masterful defense of Field Marshal Albert von Kesselring, the German commander in Italy. When Churchill stopped in Italy to visit Wilson and Alexander on October 8, while en route to a Moscow meeting with Stalin, the news was bitter.

Alexander's offensive, begun so well in August, had been slowed first by German reinforcements and next by the weather. Had the Allied force not been depleted in favor of Anvil/Dragoon, the Allied push might have succeeded. But Alexander now confirmed Wilson's earlier fears—a new offensive could not be launched until the spring of 1945.

"Then," growled Churchill, "it will be too late."[51]

At the same time Wilson, in submitting the Italian front report called for at Quebec by October 10, further punctured Churchill's hopes. He could not plan on an attack on Istria until February or March 1945, and to do so he would need reinforcements by December. As for the Italian fighting, "The Russian advance will be a more decisive factor in influencing the withdrawal of Kesselring's army out of Italy than the advance of General Alexander's army. . . . "[52]

When this report reached Washington and London, even the British generals opposed the Adriatic thrust. And Roosevelt referred to Wilson's report in turning down a plea from Churchill for more divisions to Italy; "no divisions," he concluded, "should be diverted from their destination in France."[53]

Still, in Moscow, Churchill found a surprising supporter. At dinner on October 11 he was talking strategy with Stalin, who advocated the encirclement method strategy that the Red Army had used so well. "Fifteen of the 25 Allied divisions in Italy could hold the present line," Stalin suggested, "and 10 might be sent through Austria to outflank the Germans and assist the Red Army's advance through Hungary into Austria."

Suddenly the astounded Churchill had an invitation from the very power he hoped to foil with his Ljubljana thrust. Now thoroughly frustrated, he could not admit that his own commanders had said the move was impossible before February.

Stalin's sincerity in this suggestion has since been questioned, especially as he had opposed an Allied thrust in the Balkans at the Tehran meeting. But now he had little to lose. The Red Army was already across the Tisza River in both Hungary and Yugoslavia; Szeged was taken on the day of the Churchill-Stalin talk, and the Red Army was preparing to capture Belgrade. The Yugoslav capital may be further from Vienna than Trieste, but the Danube Valley is a far easier avenue than the Julian Alps. Stalin, hardly foreseeing the stubborn German resistance at Budapest, was sure he could reach Vienna first.

Yet the pincers movement around the Germans in the Balkans was an obvious idea, as Roosevelt had foreseen. Stalin and his chief of staff, Alexey I. Antonov, renewed the suggestion with Churchill at the formal military conference on October 14. Stalin confided that "the Russians did not propose to advance westward across Yugoslavia." They would, he said, "prefer to join hands with General Wilson's forces in Austria."[54]

The Soviet purpose seems clear enough: a British invasion at the head of the Adriatic would at best draw German troops from the eastern front and at least hasten the enemy's retreat up the Danube Valley.

As it later turned out, the Germans would block the Red Army at Budapest until mid-February. A British invasion of northern Yugoslavia late in 1944 could have relieved this roadblock. It could also have put the British well into Austria and perhaps into western Hungary, and brought on a British-Soviet race for Vienna.

At the last meeting in Moscow on October 17, Churchill told Stalin he hoped "the Ljubljana Gap could be reached as soon as possible. . . . " But in reporting to Roosevelt on the Moscow meeting he said nothing about Armpit. Instead, on the way back he stopped at Naples to confer with Wilson and Alexander. By this time Wilson, still stalled in Italy by the Germans, knew he could not spare enough troops for the Ljubljana assault. He would not be able to move on Trieste until February. Churchill returned to London with his hopes crashing. On October 30 he wrote to the Chiefs of Staff:

One of the absurd things in all the plans which are submitted . . . is the idea that if they move in February they will be in time to effect anything. In the three months which they say must elapse before they are capable of movement the whole of Yugoslavia will be cleared of Germans, who will either have been overwhelmed or made their escape to the north.[55]

Still worse, even Wilson's February plan was eroded by German resistance in Italy and new political difficulties with Tito. When Wilson sent a liaison officer to Moscow, he learned that while the British would be depending on Tito's partisans to protect their right flank, the Soviets would be depending on them to support their left flank as they advanced on Budapest. Spanning this 150 miles was, in Wilson's view, too far to stretch the Yugoslav guerrillas.

How far they would cooperate with the British was still another question. In August, Churchill had assured Roosevelt, "Tito's people will be awaiting us in Istria." But just how they would be waiting may be indicated by Tito's response in Moscow at this same time when Stalin asked him what his forces would do if the British landed in Yugoslavia: "We should offer determined resistance."[56]

Wilson, in fact, was soon having difficulty getting Tito's cooperation even in the limited objective of supplying the guerrilla forces. When Wilson offered British troops to help take and hold supply ports in Dalmatia, Tito refused and told Wilson that "the Yugoslavs were disturbed at having British troops in their country and were suspicious of [British] intentions."[57]

By early December the Western Allies had agreed to scrub Operation Armpit and any variation thereof. Alexander was to concentrate on beating Kesselring in Italy. At the end of January even Churchill agreed with his military chiefs to send more divisions from Italy to reinforce Eisenhower.

Still, the prime minister nursed his march to Austria when the Western

Allies met at Malta on their way to the Yalta conference at the beginning of February 1945. Most of Budapest, though surrounded by the Red Army, was still defended by the Germans, delaying the Soviet advance up the Danube. Months before, Churchill had given Alexander standing orders that if the war suddenly came to an end, "be ready for a dash with armoured cars" to Vienna.[58] Now, though the Italian front was to be further weakened in favor of the western front, Churchill still harbored his dash for Vienna. In case the German forces in Italy withdrew or surrendered, the prime minister called for "a rapid follow-up." It was, he insisted, "essential that we should occupy as much of Austria as possible as it was undesirable that more of Western Europe than necessary should be occupied by the Russians."[59]

Thus the old lion, frustrated and nearly exhausted as the war neared its end, had written off Eastern Europe and was striving now to save the West. Ten days earlier, when going to bed at 10 Downing Street, he had revealed his grief to his secretary, Jock Colville. "Make no mistake," he rumbled, "all the Balkans, except Greece, are going to be Bolshevised; and there is nothing I can do to prevent it." Then, as a final pronouncement, he added, "There is nothing I can do for poor Poland either."[60]

On the opening day of the Yalta conference, Stalin called on Churchill at the British embassy and suggested again that the British "should send a force from Italy through northern Yugoslavia" to join with the Soviet left flank.[61] Once again the frustrated Churchill could not respond. Nine days later Budapest fell and the Red Army pressed up the Danube toward Vienna. Churchill's invasion to salvage part of Eastern Europe now belonged to history's events that never happened.

In the larger sense it never happened because it was caught in the running feud from 1942 to 1944 between the British and the Americans over a Mediterranean versus a cross-Channel strategy. At first the British had prevailed—hence the invasion of North Africa in 1942 at the expense of a landing in France in 1943, followed by the invasion of Sicily and Italy.

By 1944 the Americans had gained ascendancy first in the supply of matériel for the war effort, and then in the number of troops engaged, so that their counsels bore the greater weight in war strategy. Marshall and Eisenhower used this ascendancy to insist on the U.S. concept—all-out support for the main front in France, including the supporting invasion of southern France, even if this meant a stalemate in Italy.

As for the proposed thrust from the Adriatic to the Danube, the Americans dismissed it out of hand until the Overlord assault was secure and the southern France invasion was completed. When they did join in supporting the Adriatic thrust in September 1944, it was not practical because the Germans still held the upper Italian peninsula, a situation due to Alexander's forces having been weakened for the southern France invasion.

There was something gratuitous about Eisenhower's belated support for the Adriatic thrust, when he himself had made it infeasible. By the time Alexander could get within striking distance of Istria and prepare through the winter of 1944–1945 for a campaign through the Ljubljana Gap, it would be February at the earliest. This, as Churchill knew, was too late.

Thus Kesselring, following Hitler's orders to fight for every inch of Italy, could take credit for preventing the Adriatic invasion. Whether Alexander could have broken German defenses if his forces had not been drained for the southern France invasion is another question. The British, from Churchill to Brooke to Wilson to Alexander himself, believed he could have done it. So did the top U.S. ground commander in Italy, General Mark Clark.

"After the fall of Rome," Clark later wrote, "Kesselring's army could have been destroyed—if we had been able to shoot the works in a final offensive."[62]

All of the British generals deplored the weakening of Alexander's army in Italy (Brooke was especially critical of the Americans for a shortsighted strategy). "We should have had the whole Balkans ablaze by now," Brooke wrote in November 1943, "and the war might have been finished in 1943."[63]

This, considering the problems of terrain and logistics posed by the Balkans, was unrealistic. The truth was that, with particular regard to the Adriatic operation, Brooke was always lukewarm; years after the war he said, "I never supported Winston or Alex in that maneuver, because it didn't seem feasible. . . ."[64]

Wilson was of two minds of the subject at the time, and was never so strong an advocate of the Adriatic-to-Vienna drive as Alexander. Some years later he put his finger on the key problem—logistics: "[I]f we got stuck in heavy battle, the question of the supply and maintenance would have become very difficult then, and perhaps the farther we got the more difficult it would have become."[65]

Still another hazard was that a long drive through enemy territory is vulnerable to counterstrikes on the flanks or the rear—the longer the march, the more danger of encirclement. Such a thrust was on weak military ground if conducted on its own—in effect, climbing out on a limb to be sawed off. Thus, up to August 1944 the military justification for the venture was thin.

With the Red Army moving northwest from Romania, however, the Ljubljana Gap drive suddenly took on military logic as one arm of a pincers against the Germans in the Balkans. It was at this point that not only Eisenhower, but also Stalin himself, suddenly supported it. But it was also at this point that the Western Allies were unable to act.

So the issue boils down to the question: Was the capture of Marseilles as a port to supply the Allies in France worth so much that the West could turn a blind eye to the fate of perhaps two countries in Eastern Europe?

For the East Europeans the issue was clear: It did little good to defeat one oppressor and welcome another. For the British, led by Churchill, the war had reached a classic stage where allies with different objectives had to think not only of beating the enemy but also of winning the peace.

For most U.S. leaders the issue did not really exist, since the impending Soviet impact on occupied countries was not understood. Roosevelt did not believe Stalin wanted to take over the Balkans. To the Americans the decision was strictly military—between two routes to Germany. In such case the choice was clear. Marshall later expressed the U.S. view and the reason why Churchill's invasion never was:

The "soft underbelly" had chrome-steel sideboards. That was mountainous country. There was no question in my mind that the West was the place to hit. . . . Half of Patton's army was supplied from Marseille. . . . It helped to complete the Eisenhower operation in Normandy. . . . The southern France operation was one of the most successful things we did. . . . The differences were so great that it was almost facetious.[66]

So spoke the American military mind. And from a strictly military standpoint, it was right.

As for the American political mind, embodied by Roosevelt, it had never answered the main question raised by Churchill—the political fate of Danubian Europe.

Just as in the previous encounters with Stalin on postwar Europe—the British-Soviet treaty and the continuing Polish question—Roosevelt misread Stalin's intentions. Winning the war was the immediate imperative; they would take up the peace afterward. This order of priorities meant that Stalin, after occupying all of Eastern and Central Europe, would be vastly strengthened at the peace table. Such an outcome was clear to Churchill, if not to Roosevelt.

8

Save Us from Our Allies

In May 1943 the Communist International, headquartered in Moscow, announced its dissolution. Spearhead of the worldwide Communist movement since 1919, the Comintern had become a liability in Stalin's eyes. In a press interview he explained that this step would dispel the notion that various national Communist parties were controlled by Moscow. Nothing, he said, should stand in the way of their working closely with other national groups in fighting Hitler. Actually, the Soviets were opposing any resistance forces except those led by Communists, clearly with a view to influencing the political outcome after the war.

In Yugoslavia, the royalist guerrilla forces headed by General Draža Mihailović were at first supported by London and approved by Moscow. But in the summer of 1942 the Soviets switched support to the partisan forces under Josip Broz Tito, a long-time Communist and Comintern agent. As the partisans emerged as the most active fighters against the Germans, Churchill also shifted his assistance to Tito.

Since it was not yet clear in most of 1943 that the partisans were Soviet-controlled (though they were believed to be leftist), Churchill may have hoped to gain their adherence before the Soviets did so. And as Churchill formed his plan to invade northern Yugoslavia and drive for Vienna, he may have reasoned that Stalin would be less suspicious of that undertaking as a British imperialist plot if it were divorced entirely from General Mihailović, who represented the old regime.

As for Stalin, he cautioned partisan leaders against actions that might alert Western powers to Soviet aims—even opposing the red stars on their uniforms.

In Greece the resistance was also divided, and the British supported the Communists for a time in 1943. Soviet contact with the Greek Communists was tenuous until the Red Army invaded Romania in August 1944, when Soviet agents were secretly landed at an airfield in northern Greece.

In Czechoslovakia and Poland the Communist forces were supported by Moscow from the beginning, but were not the principal fighters against Hitler. During the Ribbentrop-Molotov pact from August 1939 to June 1941, they had earned the disgust of their countrymen by following Moscow in supporting the Germans. Discredited at home, the Communist leaders of Poland and Czechoslovakia exiled themselves for the duration—mostly to Moscow.

Especially in Poland, where the Red Army had joined the Wehrmacht in the 1939 attack, overt Communist activity was believed to be an instrument of the Soviet Union and therefore unpatriotic. To disguise itself, the political party took the name Polish Workers Party (PWP) and avoided Communist objectives in its propaganda. The anti-German efforts of the PWP's military arm, the People's Guards, were insignificant compared with those of the real Polish underground, or Home Army, which was linked with the government-in-exile.

In Czechoslovakia, a strong guerrilla force had developed by the middle of 1944 in the mountains of Slovakia, which had been established as a German puppet state under a quisling president, Monsignor Jozef Tiso. The underground was primarily democratic in leadership and linked with the London government-in-exile. A smaller Communist partisan group was also in operation. But as in Poland, Greece, and Yugoslavia, it was not working with other resistance groups—contrary to an announced purpose in disbanding the Comintern.

As the Red Army approached the Eastern European states in 1944, bands of Communist agents were infiltrated behind German lines, sometimes by parachute, to disrupt enemy logistics and promote political support. This was the situation when the Red Army approached the eastern end of the puppet Slovak republic in the summer of 1944.

As the Slovak underground moved to launch its long-planned uprising, it flew two emissaries behind the lines to coordinate with the Red Army; the Soviet response was to send them to Moscow, where they were held incommunicado.

Meanwhile, on July 24 the Soviets had parachuted a Ukrainian detachment into Slovakia to lead Communist partisans. Around August 20 they launched an active sabotage campaign that precipitated a premature uprising by many Slovaks.

On August 27 the Soviet-led Communist partisans stopped a train carrying 28 German officers and enlisted men, and next day shot them all. This accelerated what was already under way—the invasion of Slovakia by German armed forces, most of them crack SS divisions, on August 29. And that immediately triggered an official uprising of some 50,000 Slovak insurgents under the auspices of the Czechoslovak government-in-exile, announced over captured radio on the same day.

Two days later the U.S. chargé d'affaires to the Czechoslovak government in London was visited by Jan Masaryk, deputy prime minister and foreign minister of the Czechoslovak government. Son of Tomás G. Masaryk, founder-president of Czechoslovakia, Jan Masaryk was one of Europe's most popular and persuasive diplomats. He appealed to the United States for aid to the insurgents, first in the form of bombing raids against German targets.

The request was referred to the U.S. Military Command, which flew a mission consisting of one officer and five enlisted men into Slovakia. The three aircraft arriving with the mission on September 17 brought weapons, ammunition, medicine, and other supplies. A second flight of six large U.S. aircraft, together with a British contingent, landed on October 6 with more weapons, including antitank guns, and medicine. Other British support arrived from weapons stores in Italy.

However, the British officer in charge told the insurgent commanders that the Western Allies could not give military assistance to them because Slovakia was in the Soviet sphere of operations. The aid was to be considered as a "gift," not military assistance. Equipment for 10,000 men had been assembled in Italy for this purpose, but the Soviets had refused permission to deliver it.[1]

Whether or not the British officer was correct, the fact is that as early as September 22 the U.S. Joint Chiefs of Staff had decided that help to the Slovak insurgents "would not be a reasonably feasible operation for American or British aircraft."

"It was considered," wrote Edward Stettinius, the acting secretary of state, "that geography left only the Soviet forces in position to do it."[2]

Meanwhile the British SOE, the organization aiding insurgents in Eastern Europe, had already proposed plans for helping the Slovaks. The Foreign Office had asked the Soviets about such aid, but, having received no answer, opposed any but minimal action.

The Soviets were busy supplying the Soviet-led Communist partisans with weapons, land mines, and several aircraft. The main insurgent army asked the Soviets to fly in the Czechoslovak Brigade that had been assembled behind the eastern front. But the first priority of the Soviets was to fly in, as one of the Slovak insurgent leaders put it, "Soviet partisan officers and political commissars, as well as Czech and Slovak Communist agitators and politicians who had been spending the war in exile in Moscow."[3] Six weeks after the Slovak plea, the Soviets finished airlifting in the Czechoslovak Brigade of 2,800 men.

Meanwhile, the Red Army was about 100 miles away, trying to break through the Carpathian Mountains. Stiff German resistance at Dukla Pass stalled the Soviet drive in that sector. Later the Slovaks charged that the

Soviets wanted the uprising to fail, so that the Red Army and the Communist partisans could be the instrument of liberation. The Soviets denied this and pointed to their heavy casualties at Dukla Pass. What is clear is that the Soviet aid was too little and too late, though probably greater than that of the Western Allies. After an initial modest assistance, the Americans and British left it to the Soviets.

The Czechoslovaks also believed that the British and Americans had made an agreement with the Soviets, possibly at the Tehran conference, that Czechoslovakia was to be in the Soviet zone of influence. This belief was due, first, to the U.S. and British refusal to sign an agreement with Czechoslovakia as to civil administration in liberated areas, as the Soviet Union did in May 1944. Both the U.S. State Department and the British Foreign Office had rejected the need for such an agreement "in the light of the practical considerations involved, including geographic factors. . . . "[4]

This impression that Czechoslovakia had been relegated to the Soviets was fortified when the Americans and British stopped sending aid to the Slovak uprising. It was further reinforced when the arriving British officer had told the insurgents that "Slovakia was in the sphere of Soviet military operations, and there could be no Western interference in this sphere without Soviet permission."

There is no evidence in the record to support any such agreement between the Western Allies and the Soviets. In fact, a message of April 15, 1944, to the U.S. Department of State from the British embassy states that "Czechoslovakia is not within any combined Command. . . . "[5]

By late October the insurgents, short of arms and ammunition but not of valor, were being routed by the Germans. On October 24 Jan Masaryk told the U.S. chargé to his government in London that the uprising was going badly and may be "liquidated." He appealed to the Americans to fill a specified list of machine guns, mortars, bazookas, flamethrowers, and other items. Four days later the Czechoslovak government in London received its next word from the United States: "We Americans salute our Czechoslovak comrades-in-arms who are today so bravely contributing to the liberation of their homeland and the rest of Europe."[6] The message was from President Roosevelt to President Beneš on the anniversary of Czechoslovak independence.

The same day the head of the Slovak insurgents announced on the radio, "[A]n organized resistance of the army as a whole is no longer possible." The Slovak troops were ordered to carry on guerrilla warfare against the Germans, who in turn terrorized Slovakia with reprisals. Whole communities were put to the torch and destroyed. Thousands of soldiers and civilians were killed and buried in mass graves. Tens of thousands were sent to concentration camps in Germany; most of them were executed, including two Americans war correspondents and all the members of the U.S. military mission to Slovakia.[7]

Three weeks after the uprising collapsed, Stettinius replied to Masaryk's last appeal: "Pending Soviet reply United States Chiefs of Staff . . . recommended withholding action."[8]

In London the Czechoslovak government leaders recalled how, at the Moscow meetings in December 1943, Stalin had urged Czechoslovak resistance and had promised to help. But as the Czechoslovaks strove to regain independence, it became only too clear what kind of "help" they could expect from the Americans, the British, and the Russians.

The truth was that the Soviets were opposed to any insurgency that they did not control, the British were paralyzed by the silence from Moscow, and the Americans were guided by military considerations. The responsibility had been shifted to the military by a U.S. State Department headed by Hull and Stettinius—men who were unfamiliar with Central European political currents and who would not make the decision on political grounds.

The results of divided resistance were still more grievous in Poland, where the Soviet strategy had been unfolding since Stalin had broken relations with the government-in-exile in April 1943. Crossing into the disputed territory of prewar Poland in January, the Red Army was pushing the Wehrmacht back toward the Curzon Line through the spring of 1944. By July the Soviets were across that line and pressing toward Lublin, an important Polish city 100 miles southeast of Warsaw.

The Polish government-in-exile had already ordered its underground Home Army to cooperate with the Red Army—even without the Soviet Union's resuming diplomatic relations—by sabotaging German communications behind the lines. Beginning in the disputed area east of the Curzon Line, the Home Army rose openly in support of the advancing Soviet troops. A key objective was to strengthen the legitimacy of the democratic underground and the London government-in-exile by capturing Polish towns and presenting the arriving Red Army with a fait accompli.

But this posed a danger not only from German retaliation but from the Soviets as well. In Wolyn Province of the northwestern Ukraine, a Polish underground division had fought alongside the Red Army. During June 1944 part of the division was pressed into the Polish forces under General Zygmunt Berling that had been sponsored by Moscow's Union of Polish Patriots and the Polish National Council. Its officers were arrested and deported. In July several battalions of the Home Army helped the Soviets take Vilnius, only to have their officers arrested. Again in July, 3,000 Poles helped the Red Army take Lwów; their officers were arrested.

The pattern was clear: Red Army field commanders gladly accepted Polish help. When they moved on, NKVD units moved in and ordered the guerrillas to join the Polish forces that had been trained in the Soviet Union under General Berling. Those who refused (most of them) were interned and sent to the Soviet Union. In either case the officers were arrested and deported, and in some cases shot.[9]

These developments, drawn from Polish sources, are not mentioned in the memoirs of Marshal Konstantine Rokossovsky, the Red Army commander on this front. He states simply that the Polish Home Army acted independently of the Red Army. At a meeting in the forest north of Lublin, representatives of the Polish underground army had told Russian officers: "We shall not use arms against the Red Army, but we do not wish to have any contacts."[10]

By July 22, with the Soviets approaching Lublin, the Moscow-controlled Polish National Council announced formation of the Polish Committee of National Liberation. Calling itself the "de facto authority in Poland," it denounced the Polish government in London as "illegal" and branded the Home Army an outlaw organization. When Lublin fell on July 24, the Committee declared it the capital of Poland; then Moscow signed an agreement with the Committee "on relations between the Soviet Command and the Polish Administration."

This looked to Churchill like recognition of a new government. Stalin explained it to him thus:

The Polish Committee of National Liberation intends to set up an administration on Polish territory, and I hope this will be done. . . . I cannot consider it a Polish Government, but it may be that later on it will constitute the core of a Provisional Polish Government made up of democratic forces.[11]

This ominous declaration, revealing the next step in Stalin's plan for Poland as the Red Army advanced, confirmed Churchill's fears. But the London Poles believed they had one or two more cards to play. On July 25, as the Red Army neared Warsaw, the government-in-exile authorized the Polish underground to rise openly and seize the Polish capital. And Mikolajczyk had succeeded in getting Churchill to make another plea to Stalin for the Polish premier's visit to Moscow. On July 23 Stalin had answered, "I shall certainly not refuse to see him."[12] Interpreting this as an invitation, Mikolajczyk left on July 26. His purpose: to reopen diplomatic relations and to negotiate with Stalin on frontiers. And his credentials would be enhanced if the Polish Home Army could liberate Warsaw.

The stage was now set for Poland's climactic effort to assert its independence. Some 40,000 Polish underground fighters, armed with weapons and explosives smuggled in for months from Britain, made ready to capture Warsaw. To the world and to the Soviets, they would prove they were a military force that could decisively influence the war. And at this critical moment Mikolajczyk would be in Moscow to press their case with Stalin.

The strategy was dangerous. In the disputed territory east of the Curzon Line, the Soviets had accepted help from the Poles, only to disarm, arrest, or shoot them. Even west of the Curzon Line, the three Polish divisions that helped the Red Army take Lublin were one by one surrounded and disarmed as they tried to accompany the Soviets in their drive toward Warsaw. More than 2,500 were sent to concentration camps and later shipped to the Soviet Union.

While news of this treatment raced through Poland and caused some underground units to sit on their arms, it impelled the Polish underground leadership to mount one last blow at the Germans in Warsaw—an effort that must certainly capture the world's attention.

Near the end of July, Soviet forces reached the Vistula River near Warsaw and began converging on the capital. On July 29 their artillery was pounding Praga, an industrial suburb on the east side of the Vistula. That evening the Polish-language radio station in Moscow broadcast a call to "direct active struggle in the streets of Warsaw."

"Poles, the time of liberation is at hand! Poles, to arms! . . . There is not a moment to lose!"[13]

Leading the Polish underground was Lieutenant General Tadeusz Bór-Komorowski, a hard-bitten army commander who had been given discretion by London in timing the uprising. Late on the afternoon of July 31, word came to Bór-Komorowski that Soviet tanks were entering Praga. Unknown to him, a strong German tank force counterattacked the Red Army northeast of Warsaw and interrupted its drive for Praga. But the sound of Soviet artillery was heard in Warsaw. Overhead, Red Air Force planes were fighting the Luftwaffe. The Germans were evacuating their civilians and conscripting Poles to build defenses.

Bór-Komorowski concluded that the Red Army would soon be in Warsaw. If his Home Army were to seize the glory for liberating the capital, it would have to strike now.

Next afternoon, August 1, windows were suddenly flung open all over Warsaw and the streets crackled with machine-gun and rifle fire. The Poles captured whole buildings, then whole blocks. By August 5 the Home Army held most of Warsaw. The Germans counterattacked with tanks, bombs, and artillery. From an observation post on top of a factory chimney near Praga, Rokossovsky could see Warsaw burning. "A pall of smoke hung over the city," he noted, "houses were burning amid the flashes of bombs and shells."[14]

Bór-Komorowski called on the radio for more weapons and supplies from London. It was hoped and believed that the Red Army would cross the river at any moment. When Mikolajczyk saw Stalin in Moscow, he was told: "We hoped to take Warsaw on August 5 or 6, but the Germans were defending it more savagely than we had expected. There would be a small delay in capturing the city."[15]

The German defense, in fact, consisted of five divisions, mostly panzers, that had been thrown against the Soviets. Interviewed at the time in Lublin,

Rokossovsky stated that the Germans had flung the Red Army back nearly 100 kilometers.[16] Even so, Rokossovsky had told Stalin he could start the campaign to take Warsaw by August 25. That date passed without activity.

Meanwhile, the German counterattack against the Polish insurgents was proceeding relentlessly, highlighted by atrocities against noncombatants. Bór-Komorowski contacted Rokossovsky and pleaded with him "to send us assistance and to coordinate our efforts." Rokossovsky denies receiving any such message and faults the Poles for not contacting him beforehand to coordinate their actions.

By this time the Polish fighters were desperate—and outraged. One of their leaders radioed London: "This incomprehensible, passive and ostentatious behavior of the Soviet troops at a distance of a dozen kilometres from Warsaw has its political significance. . . . "[17]

At first the British tried to rush in help. Bombers were dispatched from Italy to drop some 60 tons of equipment and ammunition but suffered heavy losses from German fighters. From one group of seven aircraft, only one returned. The British temporarily halted the effort.

At the same time the Western Allies were pressing Stalin. On August 4 Churchill wired him about the Polish revolt: "[T]hey appeal for Russian aid which seems very near." Stalin answered by belittling the Polish effort.[18] In Moscow, Mikolajczyk also asked Stalin "to order help to be given to our units fighting in Warsaw." The two talked for several minutes about the Warsaw Rising—Stalin explaining why his troops were delayed in assaulting the city and the two of them determining how to air-drop supplies and establish liaison with the insurgents.

"I shall give the necessary order," concluded Stalin.[19]

Yet nothing was done. Two days later Churchill was in Italy; from there, British bombers were flying supplies to Warsaw. Wiring Eden, he asked him to telegraph Molotov about the adverse political reactions to Soviet indifference:

It certainly is very curious that at the moment when the Underground Army has revolted the Russian armies should have halted their offensive against Warsaw and withdrawn some distance. For them to send in all the quantities of machine guns and ammunition required by the Poles for their heroic fight would involve only a flight of 100 miles.[20]

Churchill next received a desperate plea from Jan S. Jankowski, Poland's secret deputy prime minister, who was with the insurgents in Warsaw. The Germans were bombarding the city continuously, he said:

The soldiers and the population of the capital look hopelessly at the skies, expecting help from the Allies. On the background of smoke they see only German aircraft. . . . I repeat emphatically that without immediate support, consisting of drops of arms and ammunition, bombing of objectives held by the enemy, and air landing, our fight will collapse in a few days.

Forwarding this to Stalin on August 12, Churchill added, "[C]an you not give them some further help, as the distance from Italy is so very great?"[21]

In Washington, the Polish ambassador pleaded with the State Department to intervene with Stalin and ask for help. On August 14 Harriman in Moscow urged Molotov to allow the U.S. Air Force to use Soviet air bases in the Ukraine for shuttle missions to drop supplies to the Polish insurgents. The feasibility of this had already been demonstrated in a series of U.S. shuttle bombing raids against German targets.

Next day Deputy Foreign Minister Andrei Vishinsky sent Harriman a note saying that the "action in Warsaw . . . was a purely adventuristic affair and the Soviet Government could not lend its hand to it." With Clark Kerr, Harriman visited Vishinsky that afternoon and pursued the argument.[22] What about Stalin's promise of help to Mikolajczyk? To prevent the U.S. Air Force from assisting the Poles "would have serious repercussions in Washington and London."

Vishinsky: "[T]he outbreak in Warsaw was ill-advised, not a serious matter, not worthy of assistance, and . . . would have no influence on the future course of the war."

Harriman: "[W]e were not requesting Soviet participation . . . I could not understand why the Soviet Government should object to our endeavor to assist the Poles. . . . "

Vishinsky: "[T]he landing of the American planes at the Soviet bases constituted participation and . . . the Soviet Government did not wish to encourage 'adventuristic actions' which might later be turned against the Soviet Union."

This was, of course, the real reason for Soviet intransigence. Harriman reported to Washington:

If Vishinsky correctly reflects the position of the Soviet Government its refusal is based not on operational difficulties or denial that the resistance exists but on ruthless political considerations.

It was, Harriman later declared, "the toughest talk I ever had with a Soviet official."[23]

Meanwhile, Warsaw was in flames. The German counterattack was destroying the city, block by block. A Soviet officer found his way into Warsaw as a kind of liaison; he sent out messages calling for help from the Red Army, but there was no reply. On the night of August 18 Red Air Force planes droned over Warsaw; the Poles hoped for a drop of supplies but instead were deluged with leaflets calling upon them to "cease resistance, as the rising is the irresponsible act of a reactionary clique in London."

Frantically the Poles radioed London for help. Ambassador Ciechanowski in Washington and Premier Mikolajczyk, back in London, begged for assistance. They asked that the Polish paratroop brigade be dropped on Warsaw with supplies; this was refused. They asked the Allies to declare the Polish Home Army a co-belligerent so that prisoners would be protected by the Geneva Convention, instead of being summarily shot by the Germans; after some delay, this was done on August 29. They asked the United States for military supplies to be air-dropped on Warsaw; the Joint Chiefs of Staff told them to go to the British for help. The British decided to resume airdrops. When one damaged British plane made a crash landing at an abandoned Soviet airstrip, its crew was arrested and shipped to Moscow.

On the night of August 17, Harriman and Clark Kerr held a stormy meeting with Molotov in the Kremlin.[24] Clark Kerr objected to a letter from Molotov denying the use of Soviet airfields even for crippled British aircraft. After a long argument on this point, Molotov conceded that "British crews could parachute out on Soviet territory. . . . " After this generous offer, Molotov reiterated the Soviet refusal to have any hand in the Warsaw rising: "It had been started by a band of adventurers and certain elements of the Polish Government in London."

With rising outrage, Clark Kerr reminded Molotov that "the Poles and Poland had been exhorted by the Soviet press and wireless to rise up. . . . This imposed upon the three Governments a strong moral obligation to render assistance." Soviet refusal could affect relations not only "between Poland and the Soviet Union but those between the Soviet Union and Great Britain and the United States."

Harriman joined in the argument. U.S. bombers could fly to Warsaw, but the range was too far for fighter escort. Fighters could, however, accompany the bombers if they could land at Soviet bases. If the bombers had to fly the round trip from Italy or Britain without fighter protection, "our losses would undoubtedly be very heavy—uselessly and without any good reason."

Americans, he went on, were watching the Polish problem with keen interest "as the first case of Allied collaboration in dealing with mutual problems." If aid were denied to Warsaw, collaboration would be seriously questioned. His argument was only a little less pointed than Clark Kerr's.

But when Harriman asked why the Soviets had changed their minds about aiding Warsaw, Molotov spoke of the "adventuristic character of the uprising and . . . the attempts which had been made to take advantage of it for purposes hostile to the Soviet Union." In particular, he was referring to criticism of Soviet inaction in the Western Polish press, which he blamed on the London Poles.

Clearly the Soviets were retaliating with another turn of the screw. And to turn it still tighter, Molotov said in the same conversation that the Ukrainian shuttle bases used for bombing German targets had been available for the summer only and would be closed for winter. In reporting the meeting to Hull, Harriman was despairing:

My recent conversation with Vishinsky and particularly with Molotov tonight lead me to the opinion that these men are bloated with power and expect that they can force their will on us and all countries to accept their decisions without question.

At this point Harriman proposed that Roosevelt send a personal plea to Stalin for help to Warsaw. "Stalin should be made to understand that American public belief in the chance of success of world security organization and postwar cooperation would be deeply shaken if the Soviet Government continues such a policy. . . . " Hull answered that Roosevelt still wanted Harriman to do the talking.[25]

Two days later Hull, bowing to the Soviet threat, told Harriman not to allow the issue to "imperil the continuous and smooth function of the shuttle bombing arrangements. This is a consideration of primary importance to our military authorities. . . . " The British, he wrote, had

a tendency to go considerably farther than the President is prepared to go in attempting to force Soviet cooperation. . . . [W]e feel that since the Soviets are not attempting to prevent our independent actions in this matter our chief purpose has already been achieved. . . .

Harriman could see the fine hands, again, of Marshall and Eisenhower—winning the war came ahead of winning the peace. Still arguing, he wired back:

I do not see how it can be considered that "our chief purpose has already been achieved" and I feel strongly that we should make the Soviets realize our dissatisfaction with their behavior. . . . [26]

While the diplomats parleyed and U.S. crews readied themselves in Italy, Mikolajczyk made another plea to each of the Big Three. To Stalin he pointed out that for 18 days Warsaw had fought "a lonely and bloody battle against the whole strength of the German invader." He called for "arms dropping, strafing of German centres and retaliating to the raids of the German Air Force." To Roosevelt he pleaded for U.S. help as "the last hope for the insurgents after the losses incurred by the British and Polish Air Forces during the night operations undertaken without fighter protection."[27]

Apparently prodded by the plea they received, Eden urged Churchill to wire Stalin again. Roosevelt agreed to join in a message to Stalin on August 20:

We are thinking of world opinion if anti-Nazis in Warsaw are in effect abandoned. We believe that all three of us should do the utmost to save as many of the patriots there as possible. We hope that you will drop immediate supplies and munitions to the patriot Poles of Warsaw, or will you agree to help our planes in doing it very quickly? We hope you will approve. The time element is of extreme importance.[28]

The tone of the plea was obsequious. Stalin's harsh answer came two days later: "Sooner or later the truth about the handful of power-seeking criminals who launched the Warsaw adventure will out." They were only exposing the people of Warsaw to German extermination. Nonetheless, "I can assure you that the Red Army will stint no effort to crush the Germans at Warsaw and liberate it for the Poles."[29]

Stalin did not say when this would happen. And he gave no answer to the immediate plea of Roosevelt and Churchill. FDR reacted in a cable to the prime minister: "I do not see what further steps we can take at the present time that promise results."[30]

For his part, Churchill was astonished at Stalin's grim answer: "I could not believe it."[31] Characteristically, he was not ready to give up. To Roosevelt he had already suggested that U.S. bombers make a daylight drop on Warsaw and then land on Red Air Force fields, thus confronting the Soviets "with an accomplished fact." Mikolajczyk suggested to Eden that "the American Air Force should make a massive air-raid over Warsaw with arms-dropping and after it land on Soviet air-fields."[32] Eden later proposed this to John G. Winant, the U.S. ambassador in London, who passed it to Washington. Churchill sent another message to Roosevelt on August 25: If Stalin refused to allow help, "I feel we ought to go and see what happens."[33] Roosevelt's answer: "I do not consider it would prove advantageous. . . . "[34]

By August 21 the British had sent 134 sorties to Warsaw. Of these, 23 had been lost and only 34 had actually reached Warsaw. Of the supplies dropped, the Polish fighters estimated they had received 77 percent. When losses were evaluated on August 16, the British flights were stopped. Polish air crews were, however, permitted to continue after August 20, sending four planes per night.

On September 4 Churchill sent still another message to Stalin urging help to Warsaw, and another to Roosevelt advocating a U.S. airdrop with landings on Soviet airfields without permission. At first his draft to Roosevelt had included the idea that "we might inform Stalin that in default of assistance to Warsaw we should take certain drastic action in respect of our own supplies to Russia."[35] His proposed joint message would include the words "owing to your refusal to receive American or British planes carrying aid to Warsaw the September convoy will not sail." But Eden had objected, and the message was tempered when it left London. Roosevelt's answer was that it was too late, that there was "nothing we can do to assist them."[36]

"I had hoped," Churchill later wrote, sadly, "that the Americans would support us in drastic action."[37]

But suddenly, on September 9, Stalin reversed himself. In a curious and bitter message to the British, the Soviet government blamed them for the failure of the Warsaw rising and even for the Polish response to news of the Katyn massacre in 1943. Regarding Warsaw, the Soviets had dropped supplies, but they had fallen into German hands.

If you are so firmly convinced, however, of the efficacy of this form of assistance and if you insist that the Soviet Command organize jointly with the Americans and British such aid, the Soviet Government is prepared to agree to it.[38]

Talking with Rokossovsky on the telephone, Stalin asked whether Warsaw could be taken immediately. Rokossovsky said it could not. According to the marshal, Stalin then told him to "give all possible help to the insurgents so as to ease their plight."[39]

Starting on the night of September 13, Soviet planes began dropping supplies on Warsaw. According to the official Soviet history of the war, Red Air Force planes flew more than 2,000 sorties over Warsaw; Rokossovsky claims 4,800. But, according to the Poles, the ammunition that was dropped did not fit the guns dropped, nor did it fit any of the weapons used by the Polish fighters. The food was dropped without parachutes, according to Stefan Korbonski, a leader in the Warsaw rising, "as if they wanted to mock us."

Everything they dropped was smashed to smithereens. It was obvious that these were purely propaganda drops, which would enable the Soviets to tell the West that they were helping the Rising, while in fact they were not.[40]

The starving Poles, who had been reduced to eating horses, pounced on the food and swept it up from the street, dust and all.

On September 11 the Red Army renewed its assault on Praga and captured it three days later. On September 16 four battalions of the Polish forces with the Red Army crossed the Vistula and won a bridgehead on the west bank. But a German attack virtually destroyed them. After ten days, unsupported by the Soviets, the bridgehead was abandoned. For the rest of September the Red Army sat on its arms on the east bank of the Vistula. However, according to Rokossovsky, his aircraft bombed and strafed German forces, his antiaircraft shot at German planes, and his ground artillery "suppressed enemy artillery and mortar batteries."[41]

On September 18, after delays caused by weather, a formation of 104 U.S. bombers, escorted by 200 fighters, dropped supplies over Warsaw and landed in the Ukraine. At the same time Soviet planes cooperated by bombing nearby German airfields. Most of the U.S. supplies, dropped from high altitude, landed outside the area held by the insurgents.

By September 22 Warsaw was a shambles and its defenders exhausted and starving. Korbonski reported to London four days later: "There are no reserves left. The population is already killing dogs for food. We are again faced with the spectre of capitulation. . . . "[42]

On October 2, after 63 days of hopeless resistance, the Warsaw fighters signed a surrender agreement with the Germans. On October 5 the bedraggled Home Army soldiers, nursing their wounds, lined up for their march out as prisoners, under German guns. Led by Bór-Komorowski himself, the ragtail soldiers bared their heads. From the smoking ruins there soared the words of the national anthem, "Poland Shall Never Perish."

Of Warsaw's 1 million population, one quarter had been killed or injured. More than one third of the 40,000-man Home Army were casualties. Of those marched out of Warsaw as prisoners, thousands were sent to the death camp at Auschwitz, where they were packed into mobile gas chambers. On the day after the surrender the leaders of the Warsaw fighters sounded their manifesto "to the Polish nation":

On August 1, 1944, we began an open struggle against the Germans in Warsaw. We chose this moment because Russian troops were on the outskirts of Warsaw. . . . We counted on the aid of Russia and our Western Allies . . . we were deceived. . . . We have been treated worse than Hitler's allies. . . . [43]

Through the smoke of burning Warsaw, and the barrage of recriminations hurled between Poles and Russians since 1944, is it possible to discern some truths?

The Red Army was, in fact, stopped from taking Warsaw early in August by a strong German counterattack. General Heinz Guderian, who then commanded German forces on that front, wrote later, "We Germans had the impression that it was our defence which halted the enemy rather than a Russian desire to sabotage the Warsaw uprising."[44] Moreover, when the Red Army reached the Vistula, it had been on a swift offensive for 40 days; its normal practice was, on reaching a barrier such as the Vistula, to consolidate supply lines and bring up artillery for the next advance.

But this does not explain why the Red Army, after renewing its attack and capturing Praga in mid-September, did not exploit the bridgehead held by the four Polish battalions across the Vistula in Warsaw for ten days.

At the same time it seems clear that the Warsaw Poles, in their eagerness to liberate the Polish capital themselves before the Red Army could, jumped the gun. Forgoing any prior contact with Rokossovsky, undoubtedly because of their distrust of the Soviets, they relied on very limited intelligence efforts to give them the gauge of battle across the Vistula. They were also influenced by German efforts to evacuate Warsaw and to conscript Poles to build defense works. This in itself could have destroyed their plans for revolt and added to their "now or never" decision.

The really crucial issue is the Soviet refusal, for the first six weeks of the nine-week ordeal, to permit the Western Allies to help Warsaw. Here the

Soviet behavior was inexcusable and shocking. The Soviet leaders themselves acknowledged that, as they believed the rising was politically motivated, so was their decision in abandoning the Poles to their fate. This admission not only explained their denial of Allied help from the air but also proved that even if they had been able, they would not have given help on the ground.

Here at Warsaw was, surely, the most critical moment of Allied relations during the war. On September 1, at the height of the Warsaw Rising, Churchill talked seriously of a massive British night drop of supplies, and if the Soviets tried to hold any British planes that were forced to land in the Soviet Union, he would "retort by stopping the supplies to Russia via the Arctic route."[45] George F. Kennan, then the U.S. chargé in Moscow, later wrote:

[T]his was the moment when, if ever, there should have been a full-fledged and realistic political showdown with the Soviet leaders, when they should have been confronted with the choice between changing their policy completely . . . or forfeiting Western Allied support and sponsorship for the remaining phases of their war effort. . . . We in the West had a perfect right to divest ourselves of responsibility for further Soviet military operations conducted in the spirit of, and with the implications of, the Soviet denial of support for the Warsaw uprising.[46]

But Roosevelt seemed incapable of breaking with Stalin. Undoubtedly his singleness of purpose in winning the war, without Allied disruption, ruled against it. Nor was he, with his optimist's mind, able to accept complete disillusion with the alliance he had helped to create. Yet the situation did not demand a black-or-white solution. Roosevelt did not begin to exercise the full octave of escalation that he commanded short of a final break. This unsophisticated approach in Big Three politics was his tragic shortcoming until he died at the moment of victory over the common enemy.

As for Churchill, he knew how to apply the pressure against Stalin, but he could not do it alone. He could, and did, thunder the Western world's outrage at the Soviet behavior: "They did not mean to let the spirit of Poland rise again at Warsaw."[47]

On January 17, 1945, the Red Army captured the Polish capital. As Stalin had assured Roosevelt and Churchill, the Soviets did "crush the Germans at Warsaw and liberate it for the Poles." But Poles who were in the city when the Red Army liberated it were lying dead in the rubble.

When Soviet Foreign Minister V. M. Molotov visited President Roosevelt in May 1942, he pressed for a prompt second front in France. Having refused to discuss Soviet territorial claims until the war ended, FDR felt he needed to do something to bolster Soviet morale. Molotov went home with the promise of a second front in 1942. It came in 1944. *Courtesy of the Franklin D. Roosevelt Library.*

Roosevelt and Churchill met in January 1943 at Casablanca, French Morocco, to discuss strategy. Still worried about Soviet morale, they announced a policy of "unconditional surrender" against the Axis at this press conference behind Roosevelt's villa. The declaration weighted the scales for a longer war, with a continuing Soviet advance across Europe. *Courtesy of the Franklin D. Roosevelt Library.*

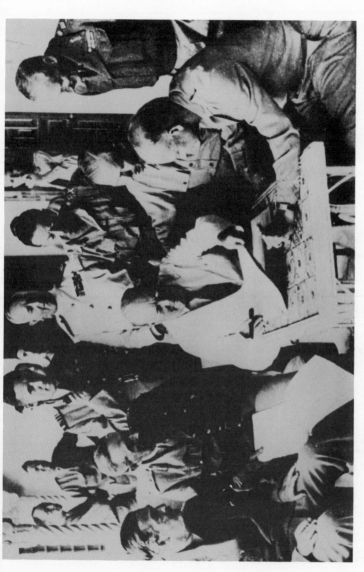

In May 1943 Churchill, surrounded by British colleagues, met in Algiers with U.S. generals Marshall and Eisenhower (right of Churchill). There he pushed his Mediterranean strategy, including action in Yugoslavia. Later he pressed for a full-scale invasion to occupy Hungary and Austria ahead of the Soviets. The U.S. generals opposed this as an unnecessary diversion from the second front. Left of Churchill are Foreign Minister Anthony Eden and General Sir Alan Brooke. Standing between Churchill and Marshall is General Sir Harold Alexander, while General Sir Bernard Montgomery looks over Marshall's shoulder. *Courtesy of the National Archives and Records Center.*

It was at Tehran in 1943, rather than at Yalta in 1945, that Roosevelt and Churchill acquiesced in Stalin's annexation of half of prewar Poland. Because of the Polish vote in the United States, Roosevelt wanted his position kept secret until after the 1944 elections. Behind Roosevelt is British General Sir Alan Brooke; behind Churchill is Admiral D. Leahy, chief of staff to the president. *Courtesy of the National Archives and Records Center.*

Roosevelt, Churchill, and Stalin at a banquet during the Tehran Conference (November 27 to December 1, 1943). Churchill pushed for Western Allied invasion at the head of the Adriatic Sea toward Budapest and Vienna (to beat the Soviets there). Stalin argued instead for a landing in southern France to support the second front scheduled for 1944. The U.S. military agreed. Seated at Stalin's left is A. H. Birse, Churchill's interpreter. *Courtesy of tbe Imperial War Museum.*

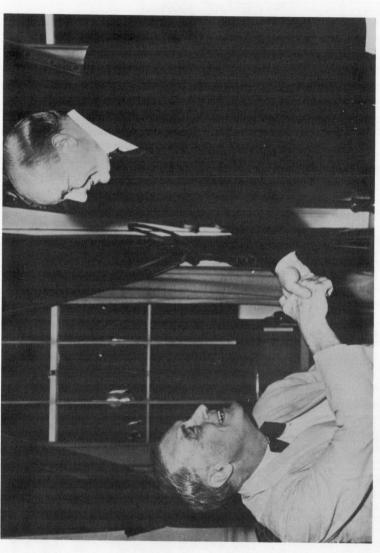

Stanislaw Mikolajczyk, premier of the Polish government-in-exile, visited Roosevelt in June 1944. His purpose was to confirm FDR's support in dealing with Stalin on Polish frontiers and sovereignty. Armed with Roosevelt's assurance that he opposed the Curzon Line as the Polish-Soviet frontier, Mikolajczyk made two trips to Moscow to negotiate with Stalin. There he learned that Roosevelt had acquiesced in the Curzon Line at Tehran. *Courtesy of the Franklin D. Roosevelt Library.*

At Yalta, in February 1945, the Big Three agreed on a formula for deciding the makeup of the provisional Polish government, and called for free elections in liberated countries. But Stalin and Molotov succeeded in eliminating binding words from the agreements, which in turn enabled them to interpret these to the Soviet Union's benefit. Left of Churchill is Stalin's interpreter, P. N. Pavlov. Behind Roosevelt are Admiral William D. Leahy and General George C. Marshall. *Courtesy of the U.S. Army Signal Corps.*

9

Carving the Balkans

By the spring of 1944 British worries about Stalin covered more than Poland.

"I confess to growing apprehension," wrote Eden, "that Russia has vast aims and that these may include the domination of Eastern Europe and even the Mediterranean and the 'communising' of much that remains."[1]

On the southern front, with the Crimea cleared, the Red Army was 200 miles from the Romanian frontier. Soviet liaison officers in Yugoslavia were strengthening ties with Tito. In Greece the Communist partisans were attacking non-Communist guerrillas and operating their own provisional government—which soon prompted a mutiny among Greek troops in the Near East. Moscow was openly encouraging the Greek Communists, and the Soviet press was criticizing Britain's Greek policy.

Churchill now feared that a linkup between Yugoslav and Greek Communists would give Stalin his long-sought foothold in the Mediterranean even before the Red Army could arrive. Communist activity in Italy was also increasing. On May 4 Churchill asked Eden, "Are we going to acquiesce in the Communization of the Balkans and perhaps of Italy?" They should, he added, "consult the United States first," but "evidently we are approaching a showdown with the Russians about their Communist intrigues in Italy, Yugoslavia and Greece. . . . I must say, I think their attitude becomes more difficult every day."

Eden had already ordered the Foreign Office to draw up a paper on the subject, commenting: "There are unhappily increasing signs of Russia's intention to play her own hand in the Balkans regardless of our desires and interests, e.g., in Greece." He now agreed with Churchill that "the time has come for us to consider from the long-term view what is going to be the after-war effect of these developments instead of confining ourselves as hitherto to the short-term view of what will give the best dividends during the war and for the war."

"You are right," wrote Churchill.

With this exchange of notes over a two-week period Churchill and Eden opened the oyster of the Cold War. The prime minister had long feared Soviet penetration in Southeast Europe—hence his scheme to counter with a military thrust from Trieste through the famous Ljubljana Gap. But now the issue was openly discussed in London. The day after Churchill's opening shot, Eden had followed his leader's admonition to "put it to them pretty plainly." He summoned Fyodor Gusev, who had succeeded Ivan Maisky as Soviet ambassador to London. In a frank discussion, Eden suggested the two governments agree that "Roumanian affairs would be in the main the concern of the Soviet Government while Greek affairs would be in the main our concern. . . . "[2]

Here, centuries of European political intrigue were speaking. Trading in such power spheres was Britain's way of keeping Stalin out of the Mediterranean, its lifeline of empire. This was a system that Americans professed to loathe—as a seedbed of future wars—except in their own power spheres in Latin America and the Pacific. Hull and Roosevelt had opposed the concept at the Moscow and Tehran conferences.

Now the Soviet ambassador, without comment to Eden, simply referred the idea to Moscow. On May 18 he was back with a response: Had Britain consulted the United States in this, and had the United States agreed?

"If so, the Soviet Government would be ready to give . . . a final affirmative answer."[3]

The Soviet punctilio was embarrassingly correct. It was more embarrassing for Eden than for Churchill, who had said in his initial note to the foreign minister on May 4: "We should of course have to consult the United States first." It now fell on Eden to approach the Americans on the issue.

"I could not imagine," he mused, fortifying himself, "that they would in any way dissent."[4]

Churchill was still more sanguine. Roosevelt, he believed, "would like the idea. . . . "[5]

Accordingly, on May 24 Eden cabled Ambassador Halifax in Washington to seek U.S. approval. Facing possible U.S. objections, he told Halifax, "We have no desire to carve up the Balkans into spheres of influence. . . . " This understanding would apply "only to war conditions" and not afterward. Eden said nothing of his earlier talks with Gusev, and in discussing the subject in his memoirs he does not mention that it was the Soviets who inquired about the U.S. position.[6]

Five days later Halifax carried Eden's message to Hull. The old eagle, shocked at such blatant trading in whole nations, answered on the spot. After such encroachment on the internal affairs of other countries, where would it stop? Such "zones of influence," he believed, would undercut the authority of the international security organization (United Nations) that he and Roosevelt were planning.

Next day, probably before Halifax sent back Hull's response, Churchill fired a cable on the subject directly to Roosevelt. Using words similar to Eden's, he described the plan and declared, "I hope you may feel able to give this proposal your blessing."[7] But he openly disclosed that the British had suggested the idea to the Soviets, who had then asked about the U.S. attitude.

When Roosevelt bucked this message to Hull for a draft reply, the reception was frigid. Eden had been caught bargaining with the Soviets behind Uncle Sam's back. Worse, while Hull and his staff were drafting a response, Churchill cabled Halifax a reply to Hull's original objections:

There is no question of spheres of influence. We all have to act together, but someone must be playing the hand. It seems reasonable that the Russians should deal with the Roumanians and Bulgarians, upon whom their armies are impinging, and that we should deal with the Greeks. . . . The same is true of Yugoslavia.[8]

So now four countries—almost the whole Balkans—were part of the deal. When Halifax handed this cable to Hull, the old war-horse fairly reared.

"It therefore seemed more urgent even than before to oppose the arrangement," he later wrote.[9]

The reply Hull drafted was sent by Roosevelt on June 10. Such an agreement, he said, "would certainly result in the persistence of differences between you and the Soviets and in the division of the Balkan region into spheres of influence. . . . We believe efforts should preferably be made to establish consultative machinery to dispel misunderstandings. . . ."[10]

At this, Churchill was clearly distressed. Hull's reliance on the "international security organization" and Roosevelt's call for "consultative machinery" were to Churchill the height of naiveté. On receipt of Roosevelt's cable, he shot back an urgent reply:

I am much concerned to receive your message. Action is paralyzed if everybody is to consult everybody else about everything before it is taken. . . . Somebody must have the power to act. A consultative Committee would be a mere obstruction. . . .

In the recent Greek crisis precipitated by the Communists, the British had been able to restore order by unilateral action, which Roosevelt himself had approved in laudatory telegrams. With a consultative committee "the only result would have been chaos or impotence." As for Romania:

It seems to me, considering the Russians are about to invade Roumania in great force . . . it would be a good thing to follow the Soviet leadership, considering that neither you nor we have any troops there at all and that they will probably do what they like anyhow.

In short, "I propose that we agree that the arrangements . . . may have a trial of three months. . . ."[11]

To these persuasive points Roosevelt reluctantly agreed on June 12, but failed to notify Hull, who drafted a stern rebuttal to Churchill for Roosevelt's signature.

Meanwhile, the tragicomic plot was spiraling. London had notified Moscow of Roosevelt's limited approval. And the Foreign Office had offered the excuse in Washington that Eden's suggestion to Gusev "arose out of a chance remark" and blamed the Soviets for escalating it into a "formal proposal."

Thus, when Roosevelt sent Hull's draft to Churchill on June 22, it made the most of Eden's embarrassment.

I should tell you frankly that we were disturbed that your people took this matter up with us only after it had been put up to the Russians and they had inquired whether we were agreeable. Your Foreign Office apparently sensed this and has now explained that the proposal "arose out of a chance remark" which was converted by the Soviet Government into a formal proposal. However, I hope matters of this importance can be prevented from developing in such a manner in the future.[12]

Such scolding was unprecedented between the two heads of state. But the English bulldog had no intention of backing off. "I cannot admit that I have done anything wrong in this matter," Churchill replied next day, gallantly shielding Eden. The Big Three could not work together if every suggestion to one had to be submitted simultaneously to another. "A recent example of this is the message you have sent quite properly to U.J. [Uncle Joe] about your conversations with the Poles, of which as yet I have heard nothing from you."

It was now Roosevelt's turn to be embarrassed. "It appears," he answered sheepishly on June 26, "that both of us have inadvertently taken unilateral action in a direction that we both now agree to have been expedient for the time being." And he promptly sent Churchill a copy of the message he had sent Stalin.

Roosevelt's chagrin was compounded when the U.S. ambassador to the Greek government-in-exile revealed to the press that Roosevelt had agreed to a three-month trial of the British proposal. And on June 26 Hull got that information, for the first time, from the same ambassador. The white-thatched sage of Tennessee was now near to bursting. In his memoirs he underlined his vexation with a one-sentence paragraph: "The President did not inform the State Department of this action."[13] But it was neither the first nor the last time a president played secretary of state without informing the secretary of state.

On June 30, responding to Eden's notice of Roosevelt's approval, Gusev raised questions about the U.S. position and declared the Soviets would ask Washington directly for its views. The new Soviet ambassador, Andrei Gro-

myko, did so in a memorandum to Hull next day. In London, Churchill
was flabbergasted.

"Does this mean," he wrote to Eden on July 10, "that all we had settled
with the Russians now goes down through the pedantic interference of the
United States . . . ? If so, it will be a great disaster."

"I fear that it is just what it does mean," answered Eden.[14]

Four days later the exasperated Churchill went directly to Stalin. Roosevelt
had agreed to a three-month trial. "Now however I see that you find some
difficulty in this. I would ask whether you should not tell us that the plan
may be allowed to have its chance for three months. . . . However, if you tell
me it is hopeless I shall not take it amiss."

Stalin answered promptly on July 15: "One thing is clear to me, that the
U.S. Government has certain doubts about this matter, and we shall do well
to return to the matter when we get the U.S. reply."[15]

On the same day, Hull responded to Gromyko with a message approved
by Roosevelt. Confirming the three-month arrangement, he then launched
into a long tirade against these or any other spheres of influence. The reply
was so ambiguous that it enabled Stalin to delay any agreement and completely mystified the British.

"Does this mean," Churchill asked Eden on August 1, "that the Americans
have agreed to the three months' trial, or is it all thrown into the pool again?"

"I don't know," answered Eden sadly.[16]

The truth was that Stalin had nothing to gain from a British disavowal in
Romania, where his Red Army would soon be in complete control. And he
had everything to lose by disavowing Greece, which was still up for grabs.
On August 4 eight Russian officers fooled the British, landed at a resistance
airstrip in northern Greece, and proceeded to meet with Communist guerrillas.

The same morning Churchill's doctor, Sir Charles Wilson, visited him in
his bedroom at 10 Downing Street. At a time when Allied troops were
overrunning France, the prime minister lay in bed, despondent. "In truth,"
Wilson told himself, "he is less certain of things now than he was in 1940,
when the world was tumbling about his ears." The good doctor tried to
cheer him: "the Third Army had crossed the Seine."

Churchill grunted, then roared.

"Good God, can't you see that the Russians are spreading across Europe
like a tide; they have invaded Poland, and there is nothing to prevent them
marching into Turkey and Greece!"[17]

By late summer Churchill was distraught. Wrote Wilson: "Winston never
talks of Hitler these days. . . . He dreams of the Red Army spreading like a
cancer from one country to another. It has become an obsession, and he
seems to think of little else."[18]

In fact, by late September 1944 the Red Army was sweeping through
Poland and entering Czechoslovakia. Moscow had declared war on Bulgaria,

clearly to preempt British influence, and the Red Army had engulfed that country. Romania, too, had fallen, and the Red Army had crossed the Hungarian frontier. For lack of the "spheres of influence" agreement that Churchill had tried to engineer with Stalin in the spring, Greece and Yugoslavia could be seized by the Red Army at any time. And Churchill's main solution to the threat of Russian inundation—a Western Allied landing near Trieste and a thrust toward Vienna—had been blocked by the U.S. strategists. One evening at 10 Downing Street, as the prime minister was retiring, he vented his bitterness to Sir Charles Wilson.

"Stalin will get what he wants," Churchill growled as he climbed into bed. "The Americans have seen to that."

Then, as if he suddenly meant to solve the problem, he rose again and began walking the floor. He needed to speak directly with Stalin again; he could talk with Stalin "as one human being to another." He got back in bed but his excitement mounted. As Sir Charles described it, "his eyes popped and his words tumbled over each other. . . . "

"If we three come together," the old bulldog declared, sitting up in bed, "everything is possible—absolutely everything."

But Roosevelt had already opposed any Big Three meeting before the U.S. election in November. Churchill could not wait. "The Red Army," he growled, "would not stand still awaiting the result of the election."

To his doctor, the prime minister suddenly announced one morning, "I am going to Moscow."[19]

On September 29 he broke the news to Roosevelt. His stated purposes were calculated to win over the president, who might not take kindly to a Churchill-Stalin tête-à-tête: first, to pin down Stalin's promised attack on the Japanese; second, an "amicable settlement" on Poland; and third, matters concerning Yugoslavia and Greece.

Next day Roosevelt's reply acknowledged that Churchill was making the trip but did not extend approval. On October 3 Churchill pressed for it: "Anthony and I start Saturday and hope in two or three days to reach U.J. We should like you to send a message to him saying that you approve of our mission and that Averell will be available to take part in the discussions." Then he showed part of his hand: "Of course the bulk of our business will be about the Poles, but you and I think so much alike about this that I do not need any special guidance as to your views."[20]

Roosevelt, even then beginning to lose his usual vigor, wrote an agreeable reply to Churchill that, in effect, gave him carte blanche to speak for the West. On the morning of October 3 Harry Hopkins, worried about the liberties Churchill might take in Moscow, discovered Roosevelt's reply in the Map Room at the White House; at that moment it was being transmitted by cable to Churchill in London. On his own authority Hopkins stopped the transmission. Then he summoned Charles Bohlen from the State Department and asked him to draft new proposed cables to Churchill and Stalin.

Hurrying to Roosevelt's bedroom, Hopkins found him shaving in the bathroom and told him why he had stopped the cable. Roosevelt, convinced that a mistake had been made, approved Bohlen's drafts and cabled them to Europe on October 4.[21]

To Stalin, Roosevelt wrote that he had hoped no important meeting would be held without him, but that he understood Churchill's wish.

[I]n this global war there is literally no question, either military or political, in which the United States is not interested. . . . It is my firm conviction that the solution to still unsolved questions can be found only by the three of us together. . . . I choose to consider your forthcoming talks with Mr. Churchill merely as preliminary to a conference of the three of us. . . .

He was proposing that Averell Harriman join the meetings, but "Of course Mr. Harriman could not commit this government relative to any important matters. . . . " And in his covering message to Harriman, Roosevelt added:

I can tell you quite frankly, but for you only and not to be communicated under any circumstances to the British or the Russians, that I would have much preferred to have the next conference between the three of us. . . . I should hope that this bilateral conference be nothing more than a preliminary exploration. . . .

He retained "complete freedom of action," Roosevelt concluded; Harriman would keep him advised during the talks and "come home immediately when the discussions are over. . . . "

To Churchill, the president was cordial but firm:

The questions which you will discuss there are ones which are, of course, of real interest to the United States. . . . I have therefore instructed Harriman to stand by and to participate as my observer. . . . Averell will not be in a position to commit the United States—I could not permit anyone to commit me in advance. . . .

He was prepared for a postelection Big Three meeting "for which your meeting with Uncle Joe should be a useful prelude, and I have so informed Uncle Joe."[22]

This rebuff seemed to demolish any real need for Churchill to visit Moscow. The Soviets were clearly mystified, as Stalin told Roosevelt in his reply on October 8. "I was somewhat puzzled by your message of October 5. I had imagined that Mr. Churchill was coming to Moscow in keeping with an agreement reached with you at Quebec. It appears, however, that my supposition is at variance with reality." Then he blamed the British for proposing the meeting without stating the purpose. "I shall keep you informed, according as I clear things up with Mr. Churchill."[23]

In London the prime minister was trying to make the best of the situation.

On October 5 he responded cheerfully to Roosevelt without acknowledging the president's admonitions.

I am very glad that Averell should sit in at all the principal conferences, but you would not, I am sure, wish this to preclude private tête à tête between me and U.J. or Anthony and Molotov, as it is often under such conditions that the best progress is made.[24]

Even Harriman, responding from Moscow, took exception to Roosevelt's instructions:

The Prime Minister might be able to come to a definite understanding with Stalin, namely, the Polish situation. It seems clear that the longer the situation drifts the more difficult a solution becomes. I assume that you will have no objection if the Prime Minister can work something out with Stalin. . . .[25]

On both these points from Churchill and Harriman, the president chose to finesse the issue without reply. Churchill, who was already exasperated with U.S. interference on "spheres of influence" the previous spring, determined to go it alone. In his memoirs he omits mentioning that he had asked Roosevelt to wire his approval to Stalin, and he puts the best color on Roosevelt's reaction to the Moscow meeting: "The President liked our plan of going to Moscow" and "The President then sent his fullest assurances of approval and goodwill."[26]

The truth is that Roosevelt understandably disliked this meeting held without him. More important, he did not grasp the overriding need of getting a Polish settlement while the Red Army was still stopped on the Vistula, and while the West still had some bargaining leverage. Undoubtedly his disavowal weakened Churchill and strengthened Stalin in this meeting, as in others. Harriman wrote later:

I was quite unhappy with the President's attitude. So far as Poland, at least, was concerned, I felt that Hopkins and the President should have encouraged Churchill to go ahead and settle the matter with Stalin, if he could. The clock was ticking and I felt the opportunity was slipping away.[27]

In any case, Churchill and Eden reached Moscow on October 9. That night they met with Stalin and Molotov in the Kremlin, without Harriman. After some discussion on Poland, Churchill came to his main point: "Let us settle about our affairs in the Balkans." He then proposed to Stalin a formula for early postwar British and Soviet influence there.[28]

"So far as Britain and Russia are concerned," he ventured, "how would it do for you to have ninety percent predominance in Rumania, for us to have ninety percent of the say in Greece, and go fifty-fifty about Yugoslavia?"

As this was being translated, Churchill enlarged on it by writing the percentages on a scrap of paper and including reference to Bulgaria and Hungary, with a 50–50 split for the latter. Calling it a "naughty document," he pushed the paper across the table to Stalin, adding that "the Americans would be shocked if they saw" how crudely he had written it.

After a pause, Stalin made a large check mark on the paper with his blue pencil and sent it back across the table. A further silence, and Churchill spoke. Apparently he felt sheepish in having so easily disposed of several countries and many millions of people. "Let us burn the paper."

"No," answered Stalin, "you keep it."

Then Churchill and Stalin fell to detailed discussion—not only about the countries already mentioned but also about Turkey and the Dardanelles, and the futures of Germany and Italy. Here Churchill insisted he "would like the Soviet Union to soft-pedal the Communists in Italy and not to stir them up." He seemed to tie this to the Italian vote in the United States, implying that American occupation troops could not be expected to withdraw after the war if there were "trouble in Italy." Stalin seemed to get the point. Claiming that he could not control Palmiro Togliatti, the head of the Italian Communist Party, he nonetheless added that Togliatti "would not start an adventure in Italy."

As for the Balkan nations, Stalin and Churchill agreed that Molotov and Eden should refine the percentages. Accordingly, next afternoon Eden found himself haggling with Molotov over the numbers.

Molotov: "If Hungary was 75/25, then Bulgaria should be 75/25 and Yugoslavia 60/40."

Eden: "Hungary 75/25; Bulgaria 80/20; Yugoslavia 50/50."

Molotov: "If the figure for Bulgaria had to be amended then Yugoslavia would also . . . have to be changed."

Eden: "With regard to Hungary we had made a concession."

Molotov: "Hungary bordered on Russia and not on Britain."

And so it went. Uncomfortable at being forced to bargain like a peddler over the fate of nations, Eden said he was "not interested in figures."

The talks ended that night unresolved. But next afternoon Molotov, undoubtedly having consulted with Stalin, proposed "80/20 for Hungary and Bulgaria, and 50/50 for Yugoslavia." Eden promptly agreed.

The bargaining finished, Churchill now had to face the Americans. To Harriman in Moscow he revealed the details of the "percent agreement" bit by bit over the next few days.

On October 10 Harriman was present at lunch when Churchill and Stalin finished drafting a message to Roosevelt about their agreement. When Harriman observed that Roosevelt wanted all major questions decided by the Big Three, Stalin said he was "glad to hear this" and shook Harriman's hand behind Churchill's back.[29]

The message therefore did not even imply that any "spheres of influence" had been determined. On October 12 Harriman visited Churchill, who read

Churchill's proposed thrust to reach Hungary and Austria before the Red Army, 1943-1944. This was impractical as long as German forces held northern Italy.

Approximate Western Allied front in Italy, last week in August, 1944. Allies advanced less than 100 miles on the eastern coast by end of year. This was due largely to weakening the force in favor of invasion of southern France on August 15, as advocated by Americans.

Approximate Red Army front line, last week of August, 1944. By end of year the Soviets had taken all of Bulgaria, Romania and most of Hungary, while Yugoslav Partisans had driven enemy from most of their country.

90/10 Ratio numbers show "percentages of predominance" in each Balkan country and Hungary, as negotiated by Churchill and Eden versus Stalin and Molotov at Moscow in October 1944. The first figure is the Soviet percentage. With Tito's triumph in Yugoslavia the 50/50 ratio became meaningless, and Churchill only saved Greece.

Ruthenia, easternmost province of Czechoslovakia, was annexed by Soviet Union in June 1945.

Churchill vs. Stalin in Southeast Europe

him a letter he proposed sending to Stalin to confirm the percentage agreement. Harriman responded that he was sure Roosevelt and Secretary of State Hull would repudiate the letter. After conferring with Eden, Churchill decided not to send the note to Stalin. Thus the Balkan deal remained a gentlemen's agreement—a handshake between two master realists.

It has been claimed that the percentage agreement was a dead letter from the start. At the next Big Three meeting at Yalta, four months later, the agreement was never mentioned. But secret deals are not negated by the public silence of the participants. For different reasons, each of the Big Three preferred to let it lie.

From Harriman, who reported in Washington after the Moscow meeting, Roosevelt learned of the verbal agreement between Churchill and Stalin. By his silence he distanced himself from it while appreciating its benefits in terms of Greek independence.

Churchill never mentioned it publicly until his memoirs on this period were published years later, but at the time of the Moscow meeting he was already asserting his gain in the deal by occupying Greece with British troops. In the next few months the British acquiesced in the harsh Soviet measures imposed on Bulgaria, Romania, and Hungary; more than once Churchill had to remind his colleagues that Britain was not in a strong position to object. "As long as the Russians leave us a free hand in Greece," Churchill wrote Eden as early as November 7, "we cannot do more than be spectators in Roumania."[30]

As for Stalin, he never mentioned the agreement publicly, and years later, after Churchill revealed it in his memoirs, a Soviet diplomat's reminiscences claimed that Stalin had never agreed to the proposal.[31] Actually, Stalin fulfilled his part of the bargain by withdrawing support for the Greek Communists. So far as the 50–50 split in Yugoslavia was concerned, he had already urged Tito to accept the return of King Peter, though he did suggest "you can slip a knife into his back at a suitable moment."[32] At the October meeting in Moscow, Stalin had even suggested to Churchill a British invasion of Yugoslavia via Trieste. And as the war ended, it was Tito, not Stalin, who punished the Četniks and other Western-oriented elements in Yugoslavia. Technically, Uncle Joe could still say, as he once boasted, "I always keep my word."

So in the end, the only country saved by Churchill's last-minute "percent agreement" was Greece. Without Roosevelt's support, the prime minister had to abandon the rest. From June to October 1944 he had tried to salvage Yugoslavia, and possibly Hungary as well, with his proposed invasion from the Adriatic and with firm diplomatic initiatives. If both had been carried through with the full participation of Washington, he could have succeeded. Without the military factor, but with active U.S. leadership in the diplomatic offensive, the issue is not so certain, since Stalin would hold the advantage by occupying the ground.

Yet Stalin respected Roosevelt and the U.S. power he represented. The tragedy is that this power was not thrown into the balance. After Roosevelt, when the United States would meet such issues with a firm stance, the Soviets showed they would give way. But by then, too many issues had already been forfeited. The sum of the forfeits was the fate of Eastern Europe.

10

The Agony of Poland

Throughout 1944, as the Red Army pushed across Central Europe and the Polish Home Army played out its tragic act of martyrdom, another struggle for Poland was being waged in London, Washington, and Moscow. Even before the Soviets entered the lands claimed by Poland in January 1944, Moscow's Union of Polish Patriots had formed a Polish National Council; according to Soviet leaflets air-dropped on Poland, it planned to form a "new Polish Government."

Stalin's strategy was out in the open. Fully alarmed, the London Poles responded quickly to assert their claims and secure Allied help. Premier Mikolajczyk, tough and unyielding, published a declaration to the Western Allies and broadcast a speech to Poland. His message: Now that the Red Army had entered Polish territory, the underground would cooperate with it if the Soviet Union resumed diplomatic relations with the London government-in-exile.[1]

The significance of this declaration may have gone over the heads of Poland's allies at first. The Americans seem to have given it little notice. In London, Eden called the Polish statements "fair" and, with surprising naiveté, asked the Soviet ambassador in London to help "ensure that the Russian reaction to the Polish statement was as favorable as possible. . . . "[2]

But Stalin, who understood every movement in the sparring with the London Poles, was adamant. On January 7 he wrote to Churchill, "[I]f we are to judge by the latest declaration of the Polish emigré Government and by other statements by Polish leaders, we will see that there are no grounds for thinking that these circles can be made to see reason. They are incorrigible."[3]

After midnight on January 11, Molotov summoned Ambassador Harriman to the Kremlin. Making him wait 15 minutes while a message was completed, Molotov handed it to him with the words, "as everyone else is talking about Poland it would be wrong for us to remain silent."

The Soviet statement was a counterattack. The Polish message was "incorrect" in assuming that the Red Army entered Polish territory. This was Soviet territory. The Soviet-Polish frontier was the Curzon Line, and Poland should be expanded westward to include "ancient Polish lands which long ago were seized by Germany." Finally:

The emigrant Polish Government, separated from its people, has shown itself incapable of establishing friendly relations with the Soviet Union. It has also shown itself to be incapable of organizing the active struggle against the German invaders in Poland itself.[4]

Before Roosevelt could react to this shot, the London Poles did so. Their first draft, shown to Eden, was uncompromising. When he tried to reason with them, they were in what he called a "suicide mind." But though Eden was discouraged, the Poles went back and drafted a softer statement that was released to the press on January 14. Shunning further public argument, it asked the British and U.S. governments to participate in settling the issue.

This, of course, put Roosevelt in the position he wanted to avoid, since any compromise would antagonize Polish-American voters. In response, Hull simply wired Harriman to urge the Soviets to try and reach an agreement with the Poles. The United States "would be glad to extend its good offices. . . ."[5]

But the Soviets had already rejected any talks with the Polish government in a curt response that Eden told the Soviet ambassador was "like a blow in the face." When Harriman gave Hull's message to the Soviets on the afternoon of January 18, Molotov answered on the spot. He was no longer talking about eliminating certain offensive cabinet members from the London Polish government; "[T]he time had now come for the formation of a new government of 'honest' men, untainted by Fascism and well-disposed toward the Soviet Union." The offer of American good offices was declined. Shocked at this turn of the screw, Harriman saw his fears confirmed.

"I believe the Soviet Government," he wrote Hull, "intends to stand pat in the expectation that with their encouragement a new Polish Government friendly disposed toward the Soviet Union can be developed."[6]

On the same day Churchill returned to London after convalescing from an illness in French Morocco. Two days later he held a stormy session with Mikolajczyk to present the Tehran proposal. In a tart mood, Churchill came straight to the issue: "The British government takes the view that Poland must be strong, independent and free—from the Curzon Line to the Oder."[7]

Then he elaborated on this westward shift of Poland by assuring Mikolajczyk that Poles, Russians, and Germans would be resettled according to the new frontiers. Mikolajczyk promptly objected to "this unilateral partition of Poland." Churchill reminded him that Britain had gone to war to defend Poland's independence, not its frontiers.

"You must understand this, Mr. Mikolajczyk," he added, curtly, "Great Britain and the United States will not go to war to defend the eastern frontiers of Poland."

While Mikolajczyk was recovering from this blast, Churchill offered his solution. If the London Poles agreed to the Curzon Line as a basis for negotiation, he believed Stalin would deal with them as the official Polish government. Speed was essential, as the Red Army was advancing daily in Poland and Stalin could set up his own Polish government.

"If you do not act quickly," Churchill concluded, "I cannot be responsible for anything that might take place."

The Polish premier was unmoved, and on January 28 Churchill reported on the talk to "my friend and comrade," Marshal Stalin. A few days later Roosevelt wired Stalin his reaction to Molotov's statement of January 18. Both Churchill and Roosevelt argued against trying to force a change of faces in the Polish cabinet, as though this were still the issue. And both the British and the U.S. ambassadors followed these messages by conversations with Stalin. Clark Kerr reported to Churchill that Stalin was furious that the Polish underground would cooperate with the Red Army only if Moscow recognized the London government.

"If the movement opposed the Russian troops and partisans, it would be attacked," Stalin had said; "if it did not, it would receive assistance."[8]

This report prompted Churchill and Eden to call another meeting with the Polish leaders at Chequers, the country residence of British prime ministers, on February 6.[9] There Churchill urged Mikolajczyk to agree swiftly with Stalin and accept the Curzon Line; otherwise, "the Soviets having occupied the whole of your country will impose their will." For the first time Churchill revealed the Soviet demand for Königsberg and the northern part of East Prussia.

Unruffled, Mikolajczyk said this revealed "the Russian scale of demands was increasing and would increase. They started asking for the Curzon Line, then for a change in the Polish Government, and now for half of East Prussia."

"Poland had taken many wrong turns in her history," warned Churchill, "and . . . a refusal now might be the most fatal and disastrous of all."

Mikolajczyk insisted he could go no further "without abandoning Poland's moral right and losing the support of his people." If the Polish government refused, Churchill concluded, he would make a separate agreement himself with Stalin.

For weeks the wrangling continued among Mikolajczyk, Churchill, Roosevelt, and Stalin. The Poles opposed the Curzon Line and especially refused to concede the heavily Polish cities of Lwów and Vilno (Vilnius). They insisted on all of East Prussia. Refusing to support them in this, Churchill nonetheless asked Stalin to recognize the London Polish government or at least negotiate with it. He knew that time worked against the Poles; the more of Poland the Red Army seized from the Germans, the stronger Stalin's bargaining position became.

Stalin, in fact, not only kept accusing the London Poles, refusing to recognize or deal with them, but also kept putting off negotiations with his allies. On March 3 he wrote to Roosevelt that "the solution of the question regarding Polish-Soviet relations has not ripened yet."[10] As for Roosevelt, who had secretly committed himself to the Curzon Line at Tehran, he kept putting off Mikolajczyk's request for a meeting with him in Washington. Like Churchill, however, he tried to mediate between Mikolajczyk and Stalin, chiefly through Harriman in Moscow.

Through March, Churchill's patience with the Poles wore thin and his exchanges with Stalin grew sharp. On March 3 Stalin wrote that raising the question of Polish control of Vilno and Lwów "is an affront to the Soviet Union." To Clark Kerr he warned of "the danger of the Polish question making a rift" between himself and Churchill.[11] By now the prime minister's impatience with the Poles was expanding to include the Soviets.

"Personally," he felt like telling them, "I fight tyranny whatever uniform it wears or slogans it utters."[12]

On March 19 the British ambassador escalated the conflict. The Soviet Union, Clark Kerr told Molotov, should postpone the eastern frontier issue until "the armistice conference." If the Soviets rejected this proposal (according to the Soviet version of the conversation), it "might give rise to difficulties in Anglo-Soviet relations, cast a shadow on the carrying out of the military operations agreed at Tehran and complicate the prosecution of the war by the United Nations as a whole."[13] This astonishing statement seemed to threaten that the Western Allies might withhold supplies from the Soviet Union and even reconsider the second front. It was so construed by Stalin.

On March 21 Churchill told Stalin of his forthcoming speech on Poland to the House of Commons.[14] He would say that talks with the Soviets had broken down; that "we now consider all questions of territorial change must await the armistice or peace conference of the victorious Powers; . . . in the meantime we can recognize no forcible transferences of territory."

Finally, in what could be inferred as confirmation of Clark Kerr's apparent threat: "[L]et me express the earnest hope that the breakdown which has occurred between us about Poland will not have any effect upon our cooperation in other spheres where the maintenance of our common action is of the greatest consequence."

The result of this unrealistic pressure by Churchill, apparently made without Roosevelt's knowledge and certainly without his concurrence, brought a predictable reaction from Moscow. In a hotly worded wire on March 23,

Stalin wrote that the British communications "bristled with threats against the Soviet Union." The reference to "forcible transferences" implied that the Curzon Line was "unlawful and the struggle for it . . . unjust." It was, Stalin declared, "a gratuitous insult to the Soviet Union." At Tehran the three leaders had agreed on the Curzon Line. "Does this mean that you no longer recognize what we agreed on in Tehran and are ready to violate the Tehran agreement?" Then Stalin loosed his clincher:

To be sure, you are free to make any statement you like in the House of Commons— that is your business. But should you make a statement of this nature I shall consider that you have committed an unjust and unfriendly act in relation to the Soviet Union.

This angry exchange came as close as any to a wartime rift between Britain and the Soviet Union. For weeks their relations were icy; Clark Kerr had difficulty getting a Kremlin appointment. Churchill had pushed Stalin far enough, and would not let the Poles split the alliance. As he told Mikolajczyk, he stopped his Polish discussion with Stalin because "instead of bringing about a rapprochement, it was rendering the situation more acute."[15]

Mikolajczyk put it more strongly to his people: "Churchill got mixed up in a row with Stalin. . . . "[16] Later in his memoirs he wrote that Churchill had said, "Stalin's last message was very rude."[17] When Churchill finally did speak in Commons on the Polish question, his remarks contained no offensive references to the Soviet Union.

By May, Churchill was shifting the initiative to the United States by urging Roosevelt to ask Mikolajczyk to Washington. The Polish premier was invited on condition that he would make no speeches in the United States that could impact the election.

Mikolajczyk had four meetings with Roosevelt between June 7 and 14, at the moment when the Western Allies were establishing their beachhead in Normandy. Each man was clearly primed to impress the other. Roosevelt told Mikolajczyk that he was against the Curzon Line and would help Poland keep Lwów and East Prussia, including Königsberg (this was contrary to his confidential conversation with Stalin at Tehran). According to Mikolajczyk's later recollection, Roosevelt told him, "Stalin is a realist. . . . But one thing I am certain. Stalin is not an imperialist."

Mikolajczyk said to himself, "Here is the perfect idealist, but his faith in Stalin is tragically misplaced."[18]

Roosevelt's main message was that he wanted to play the role of moderator between Poland and the Soviet Union; that Mikolajczyk should visit Stalin in Moscow and talk with him "man to man"; and that he, Roosevelt, would urge Stalin to extend an invitation. Reassured, Mikolajczyk described his U.S. trip in positive terms to Eden in London. But the British foreign minister wrote in a personal note:

The President will do nothing for the Poles, any more than Mr. Hull did at Moscow or the President himself did at Tehran. The poor Poles are sadly deluding themselves if they place any faith in these vague and generous promises.[19]

Five days after his last meeting with Mikolajczyk, Roosevelt wrote Stalin a summary of the meetings, urging him to invite the Polish premier to Moscow. Churchill twice proposed the same, and after a halfhearted invitation from Stalin, Mikolajczyk left London for Moscow late in July. With him were Tadeusz Romer, his foreign minister, and Stanislaw Grabski, head of the London-based Polish Citizens Council—both moderates in dealing with the Russians.

But now Stalin's price, besides acceptance of the Curzon Line, was a drastic alteration of the Polish government. And Stalin's method, now that he controlled much of Poland itself, was to summon leaders of his Lublin Committee to Moscow for talks with Mikolajczyk on a coalition government. Their offer: a Communist as president; Mikolajczyk as premier; and, out of 18 cabinet posts, 14 would be held by Communists and 4 from other parties. Outraged, Mikolajczyk snapped back:

"What you're asking me to do is sell out the Polish people. You're asking me to become a swine."[20]

Back in London, Mikolajczyk worked out with his cabinet a proposal of its own. The London government would be "reconstructed" with equal strength to the five main Polish parties, including the Communists. As for the eastern frontier, the Polish position was unchanged. But to prove his desire for an agreement, Mikolajczyk dismissed General Sosnokowski, commander of Polish armed forces and the most outspoken foe of the Soviets.

Copies of the Polish proposal had been forwarded to the Big Three on August 29. The Americans "favored" it and the British "endorsed" it. The Soviets kept quiet.

Scarcely a week after the Warsaw surrender in early October, Churchill and Eden were in Moscow to thrash out differences with Stalin over the Balkans and Poland. Churchill wired Mikolajczyk to come to Moscow. "I am sure that this is the only way in which we can break the present deadlock. . . . " Eden added that "this [was] the last chance for the Polish government to reach an agreement with the Soviet Union."[21]

Again joined by Grabski and Romer, Mikolajczyk flew to Moscow. On October 13 they met at Spiridonovka Palace with the British and Russians. Harriman was present as a U.S. observer. Seated with them at a table, Mikolajczyk described his proposal point by point. In the subsequent argument, Stalin upped the ante still higher. He now referred to the Lublin Committee as a government—a rival of the London group. But most of the quarrel was over the eastern frontier, and here Churchill sided with Stalin.[22]

Mikolajczyk: "I did not imagine that today we were to undertake a new partition of Poland."

Stalin: " . . . [O]n your part you want to carry out a partition of the Ukraine and of White Ruthenia [Byelorussia]."

Molotov added that the Big Three had agreed on the Curzon Line at Tehran. He looked straight at Churchill and Harriman. "I can quite well remember that President Roosevelt said that he fully agreed to the Curzon Line. . . . "

Dumbfounded, Mikolajczyk recalled his talk with Roosevelt, who had told him he opposed the Curzon Line. Mikolajczyk, too, looked at Churchill and Harriman. The latter was studying the floor. The Poles were astounded.

Churchill then asked Mikolajczyk to accept the Curzon as a de facto line pending the peace treaty. Stalin, standing and pacing as he spoke, disagreed and demanded a final decision now. Churchill threw up his hands, rolled his eyes to the ceiling, and coughed.

Later Mikolajczyk gave Harriman a letter declaring his shock at Molotov's statement and recalling Roosevelt's assurances. "I would be most grateful to you, Mr. Ambassador, if you could help to clear this misunderstanding on a subject of such vital importance to Poland." Harriman told him the Soviets had misinterpreted Roosevelt.[23]

Late on October 13 Churchill and Eden saw Stalin and Molotov again and met the arriving Lublin Poles, Boleslaw Bierut and Edward Osóbka-Morawski. Churchill thought they were so subservient to the Soviets that "even their masters evidently felt they were overdoing it." Eden thought the Lubliners were "creepy," and in an off moment whispered to Churchill, "The rat and the weasel."

Bierut opened the talk by saying, "We are here to demand on behalf of Poland that Lwow shall belong to Russia." Churchill looked at Stalin, who seemed to be suppressing a smile.[24]

Next morning the British and the London Poles met without the Soviets or Harriman. Churchill had arranged a tête-à-tête with Stalin at 4:00 in the afternoon and wanted an agreement to take with him. The Curzon Line must be agreed to, he insisted. If the London Poles had accepted it at the beginning of the year, they would not have had to deal now with the Lublin Poles. Even now he believed that if the Curzon Line were accepted, Stalin would retreat on the Lublin Poles, whom he was probably using as a bargaining lever. When Mikolajczyk persisted against the Curzon Line, Churchill lost his patience and his temper.

"I wash my hands of it," he roared; "as far as I am concerned we shall give the business up. Because of quarrels between Poles we are not going to wreck the peace of Europe. . . . You will start another war in which 25 million lives will be lost. But you don't care."

"I know that our fate was sealed at Tehran," retorted Mikolajczyk.

Churchill shouted back: "It was saved in Tehran."

Mikolajczyk protested that he could not "give away half of Poland."

Churchill replied, "Twenty-five years ago we reconstituted Poland . . . now again we are preserving you from disappearance, but you will not play. You are absolutely crazy."

When Mikolajczyk persisted, Churchill thundered back: "Unless you accept the frontier you are out of business forever. The Russians will sweep through your country and your people will be liquidated. You are on the verge of annihilation."

More bickering, during which Churchill stepped out to draft a proposal, leaving Eden to explain: "Churchill intends to offer Stalin the Curzon Line in exchange for his concessions in matters of the Lublin Committee. . . . "

Churchill returned with his draft, but Mikolajczyk again rejected the Curzon Line.[25] The meeting recessed, to be continued at Churchill's villa in Moscow, without Eden. Churchill's attitude was, if possible, still more savage—in the words of the Polish record, "a very violent manner." When Mikolajczyk still opposed the Curzon Line, Churchill was enraged.

"You are no Government if you are incapable of taking any decision," he charged. "You are a callous people who want to wreck Europe. I shall leave you to your own troubles. . . . It is a criminal attempt to wreck . . . agreement between the Allies. It is cowardice on your part."

Mikolajczyk, keeping a remarkable calm in the face of these towering insults, suggested that Churchill could make the presentation to Stalin as his own proposal, to which the Polish government "would confine itself to a purely formal protest." He was clearly trying to reach a solution; this was as far as he could go without causing the breakup of his London cabinet.

"I am not going to worry Stalin," barked Churchill. "If you want to conquer Russia we shall leave you to do it. I feel as if I were in a lunatic asylum. I don't know whether the British Government will continue to recognize you."

Now it was Mikolajczyk's turn to lash out. When Churchill talked of personally guaranteeing Poland's independence through his British ambassador, Mikolajczyk was contemptuous.

"Mr. Churchill, I once asked you for permission to parachute into Poland and rejoin the underground, which is at this very hour fighting the Germans. You refused to grant me that permission. Now I ask it again."

Churchill was amazed: "Why?"

"Because I prefer to die fighting for the independence of my country, than to be hanged later by the Russians in full view of your British ambassador."

Deeply hurt, Churchill wheeled and stomped out of the room. But he returned a few moments later and put his arm across the shoulders of Mikolajczyk, who apologized.[26] At 4:20 word came that Stalin would receive Churchill, who rushed out, "hardly bidding anyone goodbye."

Churchill's meeting with Stalin in the Kremlin was almost pointless without Polish approval of the Curzon Line. "Had this been settled," Churchill later wrote, "he would have been quite willing that Mikolajczyk should head the new Government." At one point they exchanged personal observations.

"Mikolajczyk is a peasant and very obstinate," ventured Churchill.

"I am a peasant, too," replied Stalin, pretending to bait Churchill, who did not disappoint him.

"You can be as obstinate as any of them."[27]

Drafts of an agreement were worked and reworked for the next two days, but each time foundered on the Curzon Line. Stalin at one point agreed to a 50–50 cabinet split between the London and Lublin Poles, and then corrected himself to what Churchill called a "worse" percentage. But since the eastern frontier was unresolved, there was no point in pursuing the makeup of the government, and the London Poles never met with the Lublin Poles in Moscow.

Mikolajczyk did meet with Stalin in a last fruitless conference. So did Churchill and Eden. Mikolajczyk declared he would return to London and urge his colleagues to accept the Curzon Line if Poland retained Lwów. Yet Stalin had not agreed to this. As Eden wrote home on October 16, "after endless hours of the stiffest negotiations I have ever known, it looks as though Lwow will wreck all our efforts."[28]

Back in London, the bitter discussions continued among the Poles and between them and the British. Hoping to get Roosevelt to break the deadlock, Mikolajczyk wired him on October 26, reminding him of his personal assurance the previous June in Washington about the Curzon Line and Lwów, and asking him to intervene directly with Stalin.

Scarcely 12 days before the U.S. election, this was hardly welcomed by Roosevelt. He delayed answering it until after the election.

Meanwhile, the London Poles were placing their last hopes on Roosevelt's support. Mikolajczyk had told Churchill he expected to be back in Moscow in 48 hours, but after 12 days in London the Polish government had not reached a decision on Stalin's Curzon Line demand. On October 31 the Poles asked the British for support on the western territories to be taken from Germany, and for a guarantee of Poland's "independence and integrity." Two days later the British replied that they supported the western territorial demands and would give "a guarantee jointly with the Soviet Government."[29] On November 6 the London Poles asked the same question of Washington and added another: "Is the U.S. Government willing to promise economic aid. . . . ?"[30]

Meanwhile, Churchill had fought another angry skirmish with the London Poles on November 2.[31] He began by scolding them for vacillating for two weeks, when Mikolajczyk had said he would return to Moscow in two days.

"Why should Poland alone among the United Nations make territorial sacrifices . . . ?" demanded Mikolajczyk.

"Well, if so," countered Churchill, suppressing his rage, "let the Lublin Poles remain in control of Polish affairs, which you are unwilling to take from them. Dirty, filthy brutes, Quisling Poles will lead your country. You can continue to stay here, but Russia will refuse to speak to you any more."

When Mikolajczyk persisted against the Curzon Line, Churchill was relentless. "I shall be obliged to tell Stalin that the Polish Government is unable to take any decision. . . . What might be Poland's prospects in the future? Think only of the terrible massacre which awaits your underground movement."

After what the Polish record calls "a rather chaotic discussion," Churchill gave an ultimatum.

"I give you 48 hours' time," he shouted. "If I have had no answer from you within this space of time I shall send a telegram to Stalin and let come what may."

Mikolajczyk then revealed the real reason for Polish hesitancy—"Roosevelt's attitude toward Poland. . . . As this is a matter of primary importance for Poland no final decision can be taken by the Polish Government until this point has been clarified."

"I told you that I shall wait another 48 hours."

Mikolajczyk answered that if he could not wait for the U.S. reply, "then I must warn you that the answer requested by you from us can be but negative."

Next day the Polish cabinet met and rejected the Moscow demands. At last the London Poles had made a decision; whether Churchill sent his wire to Stalin is not known. Still, Mikolajczyk hoped for a favorable reply from Roosevelt, and put Ambassador Ciechanowski to work on it in Washington.

On November 17, ten days after the election, Roosevelt finally sent his answer to Mikolajczyk with Harriman, who was passing through London on his way back to Moscow from Washington. The strongest statement in the message was that if the Polish, Soviet, and British governments reached an agreement about Polish frontiers, the United States "would offer no objection." And in answer to Ciechanowski's plea for a guarantee, Roosevelt refused. The Poles had waited for nothing.

After Harriman handed the message to Mikolajczyk in his study on November 22, he added that Roosevelt had ordered him to ask Stalin, when he reached Moscow, one last time to give Lwów to Poland. However, Harriman held little hope of change, and passed to Mikolajczyk a further observation from Roosevelt: Changes were fast taking place in Poland as the Red Army penetrated the country, and a Polish-Russian agreement "should be solved promptly, in Poland's best interests." Issues left unsettled would be addressed by the Big Three at their next meeting but, in confidence, this "would not take place before the end of January." And even then a question such as the independence of the Polish government "had to be solved between Poland and Russia, without any possibility of intervention from the highest Anglo-Saxon authorities. . . . "[32] Thus Roosevelt was undercutting Churchill's efforts.

Mikolajczyk was crushed. After consulting his cabinet, he took Harriman and John G. Winant, the U.S. ambassador to Britain, to lunch next day. There was no point, he said, in Harriman's talking to Stalin about Lwów, because the Polish cabinet would not even accept the rest of the Curzon Line. His own Peasant Party would do so, but not the other parties. In this situation, Mikolajczyk saw no chance of carrying out his program, and had decided to resign.[33]

Next day, November 24, Mikolajczyk gave up his post. When he saw Churchill four days later, he begged him to "continue supporting the Polish nation."

"Don't worry," Churchill answered, with a significance that may have escaped Mikolajczyk. "I'll never forget Poland."[34]

On November 30 a new Polish government-in-exile was formed, headed by Tomasz Arciszewski, a Socialist leader who had escaped from Poland early in 1944. On December 31 the Lublin Committee decreed that it was the provisional government of Poland. On January 4, 1945, without consulting the Western Allies, the Soviet Union recognized the Lublin government.

Thus did Stalin complete his strategy in putting down the Polish government-in-exile and setting up his own puppet regime. Starting with his formation of the Union of Polish Patriots in 1941, he had stretched the campaign over three years because he did not want to arouse Western opposition before his Red Army could occupy the ground and enforce his position.

Stalin had played his cards superbly, but the game was made easy for him by U.S. weakness. This in turn was born of naiveté in European politics and sophistication in U.S. politics. Roosevelt did not recognize Stalin's craving for control of Poland, just as he did not recognize the same craving for the Balkans. Roosevelt did recognize the emotional ties of Polish-American voters to the "old" Poland—its frontiers and its government. This could have impelled him to strenuous opposition of Stalin's aims. But, believing that the wartime alliance must be held together at all costs, he chose to support Stalin secretly and to mislead both the Polish leaders and the Polish-American voters.

This simplistic approach ignored the first fact of the alliance—desperate necessity. In his life-and-death struggle against Hitler, Stalin needed allies, and he had nowhere else to go for them. And so far as fears of a separate peace are concerned, this was a small factor by the time the Polish issue came into the open with the Katyn Forest discovery in April 1943. Roosevelt apparently did not recognize these facts of life that should have enabled him to stand up to Stalin in defense of Poland.

Still more shocking was his position, or lack of one, after the 1944 elections, when his excuse for inaction had vanished. Then, with the Polish government asking for a simple guarantee of Polish independence, apart from the Curzon Line issue, he still refused.

As for the British, Churchill was willing to give such a guarantee, in joint agreement with the Soviet Union. But without U.S. participation the cause was lost. Stalin was able to keep a free hand, as he had done in the Balkans.

As in other confrontations over Eastern Europe, the British leaders knew how to treat with Stalin. But they could accomplish nothing alone. By abstaining, the Americans were, without actual intention, supporting the Soviets.

Sadly, though the Poles understood Stalin only too well, they were too emotionally charged to see their own interest. As Churchill had urged, they should have used the Curzon Line as a bargaining lever to get Soviet recognition of their government-in-exile—and done so before the Red Army overran Poland. Had they been willing to give up their eastern frontier, they could have relieved Roosevelt of his concern for Polish-American voters. That even this would not have worked, however, is indicated by Roosevelt's refusal to stand for Polish independence in November 1944. In the end the hapless Poles got neither their eastern frontier nor their freedom.

11

Last Battle of the Crimea

The day after Stalin recognized the Lublin government, Churchill fired a heated cable to him:

Naturally I and my War Cabinet colleagues are distressed at the course events are taking. I am quite clear that much the best thing is for us three to meet together and talk all these matters over, not only as isolated problems but in relation to the whole world situation both of the war and the transition to peace.[1]

And so the long-heralded second Big Three meeting, postponed by Roosevelt until after the U.S. elections, was scheduled for early February 1945 at the old palaces of the czars at Yalta, in the Crimea. Poland was, Churchill later wrote, "the most urgent reason for the Yalta Conference. . . ."[2] In the minds of many the fate of unhappy Poland threatened the unity of Allied arms.

Most fearful of all were the Poles themselves. On January 22–less than two weeks before the Yalta conference—Ambassador Ciechanowski called on Joseph Grew, acting secretary of state. With him he brought new proposals for Roosevelt to take to Yalta. The Polish government was now willing to discuss frontiers "provided it involved compensation in the north and west for territories lost in the east." If the Soviets would not negotiate, the Polish government proposed a "Military Allied Commission" to oversee Poland until the first elections (this is the first suggestion of an idea that might have been the only hope of free Polish elections). And the Polish government trusted that at Yalta the U.S. government would not join in decisions on Poland without "the participation and consent" of the Polish government and would not recognize a "puppet government."[3]

Late in January, Mikolajczyk sent to Roosevelt and Churchill an urgent message that included variations on the issue of the Polish government. One of these was a Presidential Council "composed of widely known leaders who would consult with all Polish elements in creating a provisional government until the elections."[4]

While these appeals were being sent to the United States, the Department of State prepared a "Suggested United States Policy Regarding Poland." It included:

1. No recognition of the Lublin government. "It would appear that what prestige it may have is based, to a considerable extent, on that of the Red Army and the NKVD, the Soviet secret police."

2. See that the Polish Peasant Party and Mikolajczyk "are given an opportunity to take a leading role in any internal arrangements."

3. Sponsor United Nations supervision of elections.

4. Support the Curzon Line but include the province of Lwów in Poland.

5. Confine Polish compensation in the north and west to "the bulk of East Prussia," a "small strip of Pomerania," and "Upper Silesia." Although this would mean a smaller Poland than envisioned by the Soviets or even Churchill, it would minimize the transfer of populations and German irredentist pressure and "make for a viable Polish state." The Soviet motive for extreme territorial demands at the expense of Germany might be to get its own dominion as far west as possible, and by spawning German irredentist agitation, to force Poland into Soviet arms for protection, perhaps as a "full-fledged Soviet satellite."[5]

These were realistic appraisals and sound policy proposals. They were made by foreign service officers who were well informed, professional, and sophisticated. The proposals did, however, lack a position of strength for bargaining or enforcement, since the Red Army now occupied nearly all of Poland and had reached the Oder River, well inside Germany.

Roosevelt, though easily the most idealistic of the Big Three leaders, understood this as a practical politician. At a small White House meeting in preparation for Yalta on January 11, attended by a few senators and State Department officials, he recalled the situation at Tehran: "[T]he occupying forces had the power in the areas where their arms were present and each knew that the others could not force things to an issue." In a memo on the meeting apparently written by Joseph Grew, Roosevelt was further quoted on the present situation:

He stated that the Russians had the power in Eastern Europe, that it was obviously impossible to have a break with them and that, therefore, the only practicable course was to use what influence we had to ameliorate the situation.

Yet the Western Allies did have leverage with Stalin—at this point, the supply of war machines without which, as Stalin himself had acknowledged in a toast at Tehran, "we would lose this war." When Senator Arthur Vandenberg raised the question of U.S. economic power at the White House meeting, Roosevelt replied, "[O]ur economic position did not constitute a bargaining weapon of any strength because its only present impact was on Lend-Lease, which to cut down would hurt us as much as it would hurt the Russians."[6]

Thus, as Roosevelt prepared for Yalta, he seems to have been relying not on U.S. bargaining power but on his personal powers of persuasion. That these had slipped considerably since Tehran was obvious to many observers outside his own circle. As early as the second Quebec conference in September 1944, British officials noticed with dismay his failing health. Churchill called him "very frail," and the prime minister's secretary, Jock Colville, commented, "I heard him say nothing impressive or even memorable and his eyes seemed glazed."[7]

By February 1945 the change was still more evident. After the Malta conference, Eden said Roosevelt gave "the impression of failing powers," and after Yalta, "The President looked old and ill, had lost his powers of concentration and had been a hopelessly incompetent chairman."[8]

Yet the policies expressed by Roosevelt at Yalta were little different from those at Tehran and in his three-and-a-half years of correspondence with Stalin and Churchill. He continued to deal in high principles at the expense of practical bargaining; he shunned the exercise, or even the hint, of power; instead he seemed to believe that issues would be solved by reason, not pressure. His main objective was to secure Soviet participation in the postwar United Nations organization, while the objective of Marshall and the military staff was to assure Soviet participation in the war against Japan. Compared with these goals, the makeup of the Polish government seemed less important—a fit subject for good staff work by the foreign ministers.

Thus, in dealing with European power politicians Roosevelt was not much better than his predecessor in that endeavor, Woodrow Wilson. Many have explained Roosevelt's Yalta posture as the behavior of a sick man only two months away from death. Certainly this was an important factor. But Averell Harriman, who knew all the actors in the drama as well as anyone in the world, later wrote:

"I suppose that if FDR had been in better health, he might have held out longer and got his way on a number of detailed points. But I can't believe that it would have made a great difference on, say, the Polish question."[9]

In any case, as Roosevelt proceeded to Yalta, he ignored the State Department's "Suggested United States Policy Regarding Poland." Nor did he show any personal interest in British views. Eden had asked for more time to discuss the issues at the preliminary Malta conference between the British and the Americans, but Roosevelt refused, in the belief that Stalin would suspect they were conspiring against him. Eden complained to Harry Hopkins that they were "going into a decisive conference and had so far neither agreed what we would discuss nor how to handle matters with a Bear who would certainly know his mind."[10] The Polish question never came up at the Malta conference.

The subject was, however, discussed by the two foreign ministers at a preliminary meeting on board H.M.S. *Sirius* in Valetta Harbor on the morning of February 1. Stettinius and Eden agreed that their governments could not recognize the Lublin regime. Eden advanced Mikolajczyk's proposal for a Presidential Council. As a result of the meeting, each proposed the Presidential Council idea to his head of state. As to frontiers, Eden was ready to give up Lwów, while Stettinius favored Poland's claim. Both opposed too much acquisition in the west as involving a painful transfer of large populations. And since Roosevelt had been reticent on Poland at Tehran, Eden told Stettinius it was his government's turn "to take up the burden on this issue."

What about the possibility of "the Russians refusing to play"? "A deadlock would be bad but . . . a simple recognition of the Lublin Provisional Government would be even worse." Eden was ready to face the consequence: "[I]f the Russians did not agree to our approach to the Polish problem we will simply have to say that we have reached a deadlock and did not reach an agreement in the matter."[11] He wrote to Churchill in this context: "The danger is that Poland will now be insulated from the outside world and to all intents and purposes run by the Russians behind a Lublin screen."[12]

The Yalta conference opened on February 4, but the Polish issue did not arise until the third plenary session on February 6, in Livadia Palace. In the meeting room the three delegations sat about a large circular table. Roosevelt, seated in his wheelchair, had his back to the huge fireplace, with Stettinius on his right and Charles Bohlen, as interpreter, on his left. Churchill and the British contingent sat further to the left, while Stalin and the Soviets were at the opposite side of the table.

Roosevelt opened the Polish discussion by agreeing outright to the Curzon Line. He suggested that the Soviets concede Lwów but "would not insist on it." Churchill agreed: "[I]f the mighty Soviet Union could make some gesture to the much weaker country, such as the relinquishment of Lwów, this act of magnanimity would be acclaimed and admired."[13]

On this subject Stalin was adamant. It was not the Soviet Union but Lord Curzon and Georges Clemenceau who created the Curzon Line: "[S]hould we be less Russian than Curzon and Clemenceau?"

Thus ended the issue of the eastern Polish frontier. The larger question, as Roosevelt put it, was "a permanent government for Poland." U.S. opinion, he said, opposed recognition of the Lublin government, which "represents a small portion of the Polish people."[14] He proposed a presidential committee of prominent Poles from all five major parties to govern Poland until elections could be held (this is one instance in which Roosevelt advanced someone else's idea—in this case, Mikolajczyk's).

Churchill agreed that the most important issue was "the sovereignty and independence of Poland." It was for this that the British had gone to war, "at a time when that decision was most risky, and it had almost cost them their life in the world [an obvious reference to the Soviet Union's staying out of the war at that risky time]."[15] "Never could I be content," he declared, "with any solution that would not leave Poland as a free and independent state."

There was, Churchill went on, disagreement among the three powers meeting here as to the character of that government. "There will be great criticism against us all if we let them divide us when we have such great tasks and common hopes. Can we not make a government here in Poland?"

Stalin responded with a diatribe. They could not create a Polish government at Yalta without the Poles. They had tried in Moscow to set up a Polish government with the London and Lublin Poles. "Mikolajczyk returned to London and was kicked out of the government." Stalin was willing to try again here. "I am prepared to call the Warsaw Poles here or better to see them in Moscow."

In support of the Lublin Poles, Stalin pointed out that they were maintaining good order behind the Red Army's lines. On the other hand, the resistance forces or "so-called underground" connected with the London government had killed 212 Soviet soldiers and raided Red Army supply bases for arms. "If they attack the Red Army any more they will be shot."

Roosevelt called for adjournment, but Churchill got in a last word: "Anyone who attacks the Red Army should be punished but I cannot feel that the Lublin government has any right to represent the Polish nation."

It thus appeared on February 6 that the Allies were deadlocked over the Polish government. But that evening Roosevelt wrote Stalin a letter that had been drafted by Charles Bohlen. Expressing his concern over the division between them, Roosevelt proposed inviting several Poles to Yalta to establish a provisional government. Besides Bierut and Osóbka-Morawski of the Lublin government, the group could include two or three from among five others Roosevelt named.

Harriman took Bohlen's draft to Churchill and Eden that night. "It was on the right lines," observed Eden, "but not stiff enough." The British suggested two amendments that Roosevelt accepted. They involved two additional passages: "I have to make it clear to you that we cannot recognize the Lublin Government as now composed," and the provisional government "should no doubt include some Polish leaders from abroad such as Mr. Mikolajczyk, Mr. Grabski and Mr. Romer. . . ."[16]

These insertions seem to have strengthened the letter, but in fact they may have suggested to Stalin and Molotov an opening in the U.S. position. The term "Lublin Government as now composed," and the mention of three names to be included without specifying any ministerial posts, may have pointed the way to cosmetic alterations that would leave the Communists in control.

Next afternoon Stalin announced that he was trying to reach the Lublin

Poles in response to Roosevelt's letter. Regarding the others suggested by the president, he did not know their addresses. "I am afraid we have not sufficient time."[17]

However, Molotov had drafted an agreement, which was soon presented. Read aloud by Molotov, it proposed to agree on Poland's frontiers, hold early elections, and "add to the Provisional Polish Government some democratic leaders from Polish émigré circles." Molotov said there was not time to summon the Poles to Yalta; the precise character of the provisional government would be fashioned by Molotov, Harriman, and Clark Kerr, who would then report to the Big Three. Since the committee included the two Western Allied ambassadors to Moscow, and not the foreign ministers, it was obvious that they were supposed to meet in Moscow. Concluded Molotov, "I think these proposals meet the President's wishes."

At this point Churchill took his turn, whereupon Roosevelt passed a note to Stettinius: "Now we are in for 1/2 hour of it."[18] Churchill's concern was over the western frontier proposed in Molotov's draft, which included everything to the Oder River and, in the south, the Western Neisse River. This was moving Poland farther into Germany than Churchill believed was practical. "I do not wish to stuff the Polish goose until it dies of German indigestion."[19] After some discussion on this point, the three leaders agreed to "sleep on" Molotov's proposal.

Next morning, February 8, Roosevelt sent a counterproposal to the Soviet and British delegations. It approved the Polish frontiers, except "there would appear to be little justification to the extension of the western boundary of Poland up to the Western Neisse River." As for the issue of the provisional Polish government, Roosevelt proposed that Molotov, Harriman, and Clark Kerr invite Polish leaders to Moscow to form a Polish Government of National Unity—a modification of his February 6 proposal.[20]

The British also circulated a proposal that differed from Roosevelt's in giving a description of the character of the government: "a fully representative Provisional Polish Government based upon all the democratic and anti-Fascist forces in Poland and including democratic leaders from abroad."[21]

At the outset of the plenary session on February 8, Churchill supported Roosevelt's plan.[22] Molotov rejected it and favored simply enlarging the Polish National Council (Lublin government), on the grounds that it was "closely connected with the great events of the liberation of Poland" and "enjoys great prestige and popularity in the country."

"The Poles," he claimed solemnly, "would never agree to any solution which would greatly change the Provisional Government."

In a moment Roosevelt countered, "I should like to keep the Presidential committee."

"It would be better to avoid the presidential committee and enlarge the National Council," replied Molotov.

At this rather sharp exchange, Churchill stepped in. "Of course we are at the crucial point of this great conference," he observed in his stentorian tones. "This is the question for which the world is waiting." If they separated still recognizing different Polish governments, it would "stamp the conference as a failure." His information indicated that the Lublin government did not represent "the vast majority" in Poland. "If we were to brush away the London government and lend all our weight to the Lublin government there would be a world outcry." The army of 150,000 Poles would consider this "a betrayal."

"The proposals of Mr. Molotov," he concluded, "do not go nearly far enough. If we give up the Poles in London it should be for a new start on both sides, more or less on equal terms."

Stalin now put in with his own speech. Concerning the Lublin leaders, "I can assure you that these people are really very popular." The Poles were astounded that the London government was not taking part in the liberation. "Members of the provisional government they see there, but where are the London Poles?" In France the Big Three dealt with de Gaulle, who was not elected. "Why not deal with an enlarged Polish provisional government? We cannot demand more of Poland than of France."

In this impasse, Roosevelt proposed that the issue be referred to the foreign ministers, which was done.

At noon on February 9, the foreign ministers met at Livadia Palace.[23] Stettinius began by dropping Roosevelt's Presidential Committee. In his new proposal he incorporated the language of the last British proposal concerning a "fully representative government," but preceded this by proposing that "the present Polish Provisional Government be reorganized into" such a government. The U.S. formula then called for Molotov, Harriman, and Clark Kerr to "consult in the first instance in Moscow with members of the present Provisional Government and other democratic leaders from within Poland and from abroad" to "reorganize the present government."

The difference between this and the British proposal was crucial. The British would start afresh; the Americans would reorganize the Lublin government—a drastic step toward the Russian position.

Eden spoke out, his words aimed more at Stettinius than at Molotov: "[H]ardly anyone in Great Britain believed that the Lublin Government was representative of Poland." He would have thought this view "was widely held in the rest of Europe and in the United States of America." This was why the British proposal "had avoided all mention of adding to the Lublin Government and had stressed that a new start was necessary."

Molotov then countered by insisting that only the Lublin government or an enlargement of it could protect the rear of the Red Army and that, anyway, the main consideration was free elections, and these could be held in a month or two.

Unmoved, Eden spelled out the Western Allies' basic fear—that "if the elections were controlled by the Lublin Government they would not be free elections or represent the will of the Polish people."

Stettinius, evidently modifying his previous position, supported Eden. And so the wrangling continued. Molotov advised "forming the new Government on the basis of the Lublin Government." Stettinius preferred "an entirely new Government."

Molotov: "[A] serious situation would arise if a period should be created in which there were no Government in Poland."

Stettinius: "[T]he present Polish Government would continue until the new Government was formed."

Molotov: "[T]he Poles would know that negotiations were proceeding on a change in government and that the present government would not endure. This would create a situation which might well cause difficulties for the Red Army."

In straining to make this point, Molotov was, in effect, admitting that the Lublin government was not so popular after all.

Finally the foreign ministers agreed to disagree. At 4:00 that afternoon Stettinius reported to the plenary meeting that "the three Foreign Ministers thus far had not reached an agreement. . . ."[24] Molotov, who had gone over the Stettinius proposal with Stalin, suggested a key change. Instead of "reorganized into a fully representative government based on all democratic forces . . . ," Molotov proposed "reorganized on a wider democratic basis with the inclusion of democratic leaders. . . ." This was a dilution of the all-inclusive wording by Stettinius.

Molotov had other changes, including one concerning the U.S.–British insistence on the ambassadors of the three major powers observing and reporting on the Polish elections—this "would be offensive to the Poles. . . ." Molotov concluded that "with these slight amendments Mr. Stettinius' proposal made this morning was acceptable."

Churchill was not so sure the changes were "slight." He cautioned that in this "general atmosphere of agreement, we should not put our feet in the stirrups and ride off." Roosevelt suggested a half-hour intermission to study Molotov's changes. The others agreed, but Churchill continued.

"I mean more than that. I do not feel that we should hurry away from the Crimea leaving these vital problems unsolved or reach hasty decisions. These are among the most important days that any of us shall live."

After the half-hour intermission, Roosevelt cheerfully announced, "We are nearer than we have ever been before." It was "only a matter of drafting." Eden later commented, "He was deluding himself."[25] But Churchill resumed the offensive, and the question of Poland was referred to the foreign ministers, who were meeting that night in Yusupov Palace.

By that time Eden had received a stern message from the British War Cabinet, which had reviewed earlier drafts telegraphed to London. They were, ran the message, unsatisfactory. Armed with this support for his own view, Eden went into the foreign ministers' meeting and declared, "[I]f we cannot get something like [the British] text of three days ago there seems no chance of the British Government approving a formula." He did, however, present a "revised formula," which he handed to Molotov. The key sentence was "This Government should be based upon the Provisional Government now functioning in Poland and upon other democratic Polish leaders from within Poland and from abroad."[26]

Molotov, standing on protocol, insisted that the three ministers were there only to consider amendments to the U.S. draft, not to accept entirely new proposals. In the hot argument that followed, Eden told Molotov, "I would far rather go back without a text than be a party to the sort of thing [the Russians] wanted. . . ."

Finally it was agreed that the British draft was simply a modification of the U.S. formula. This opened a long but calmer discussion leading to agreement on a text. The key sentence was "The provisional government now functioning in Poland should be reorganized on a broader democratic basis with the inclusion of democratic leaders from Poland itself and from those living abroad."

This was a far cry from the British version and an adroit bit of surgery on the U.S. version. Instead of the provisional government being "reorganized into a fully representative government based on all democratic forces," it was to be "reorganized on a broader democratic basis with the inclusion of democratic leaders." Each version mentioned leaders both in Poland and abroad, but the real issue was whether there would be a fresh start in forming a Polish government or whether the Lublin government would simply be "enlarged," as Molotov and Stalin had originally offered. Now it was difficult to see much difference between "enlarged" and "reorganized with the inclusion of."

Gone now was Churchill's demand for "a new start on both sides, more or less on equal terms." Gone was the insistence of both Churchill and Eden that Britain would never agree to a formula tilting the scales to the Lublin government at the expense of the London government. As for Roosevelt and the Americans, the quest for the "right words," which seemed of primary importance to Roosevelt, had been satisfied. Eden later commented bitterly, "For the moment the outward appearances had been preserved. . . ."[27]

The situation was the same for the other major question on Poland—free elections. The issue had been raised in a broader context in a proposed Declaration on Liberated Europe, which had been drafted in Washington by State Department officials concerned about the future of nations liberated by the Red Army, particularly in view of Soviet actions in Poland and Bulgaria. Roosevelt also saw it as an instrument of U.S. public opinion in assuring the goals of the war, especially among East European ethnic voters.

To meet Roosevelt's desires, the declaration had been amended within the

U.S. delegation at Yalta. Stettinius presented it to the sixth plenary session on February 9.[28] Consisting of four brief paragraphs, the proposed declaration was essentially a reiteration of Allied war aims first enunciated in the Atlantic Charter of 1941, later subscribed to by the Soviet Union, and repeated in the Four-Power Declaration and other Allied pronouncements. Recognizing the chaotic conditions that were already following in the wake of war, the declaration pledged the Big Three to establish order, rebuild economic life, relieve distress, and "enable the liberated peoples to destroy the last vestiges of Nazism and Fascism and to create democratic institutions of their own choice."

In particular the declaration pledged the three powers "to form interim governmental authorities broadly representative of all democratic elements in the population and pledged to the earliest possible establishment through free elections of governments responsive to the will of the people; and to facilitate where necessary the holding of such elections."

The Soviet response to the draft was positive. During a discussion on elections in Poland, Stalin referred to the draft of the declaration that he had before him and said, "On the whole I approve it."

Roosevelt then called specific attention to the paragraph about forming representative governments pledged to free elections.

"We accept that paragraph . . . ," answered Stalin.

A few moments later Molotov offered an addition: "and support will be given to the political leaders of those countries who have taken an active part in the struggle against the German invaders." Stalin then observed that "with this slight amendment" he "found the Declaration acceptable."

"I like the thought," added Roosevelt. "Let the Foreign Ministers look at the language."

That evening Stettinius conferred with his staff and with Roosevelt on the Molotov amendment. At the foreign ministers' meeting in Yusupov Palace late that night, Stettinius opposed the Soviet addition. It looked, he said, "like too much interference in the affairs of these countries and involved taking decisions on who had collaborated with the enemy, which should be left to the peoples of these countries themselves."[29]

Anthony Eden agreed. Next day, at a noon meeting of the foreign ministers, Stettinius refused to accept Molotov's amendment. "To do so," he said, "would cause untold difficulties in United States domestic affairs."

Molotov conceded that "it should be dropped."[30] With two other unrelated amendments the declaration was adopted next day by the three heads of state without further discussions.

It had occupied very little time in the deliberations. Stettinius had introduced it simply by distributing copies around the table. Most participants in the conference who have written their memoirs scarcely mention it, or omit any notice of it. The Soviet version of the Yalta proceedings published in 1965 even omits any reference to the Molotov amendment on giving political support to those who had struggled against the Germans.

But Roosevelt had won Stalin's agreement to foster free elections, which would at least make it more difficult to impose his will on Eastern Europe. Yet the declaration did not specify machinery for assuring such elections. This question had already been approached in the debate on Poland when the British and Americans had called for the "observing and reporting" of elections by the Big Three ambassadors in Poland. Churchill took the lead in arguing this point at the sixth plenary session on February 9. The Americans and British did not know what was going on inside Poland. He had to assure the House of Commons that the election would be free.

"For instance, would Mikolajczyk be allowed to take part in these elections?"

"Mikolajczyk is a representative of the Peasant Party," answered Stalin. "The Peasant Party is not Fascist and will take part in the elections."

After further discussion Roosevelt chimed in: "I want the election in Poland to be the first one beyond question. It should be like Caesar's wife. I did not know her but they said she was pure."

"They said that about her," quipped Stalin, "but in fact she had her sins."[31]

If this was a subtle disclaimer on the elections, Roosevelt ignored it: "I don't want the Poles to be able to question the Polish elections. The matter is not only one of principle but of practical politics."

By this time it was becoming clear that both Churchill and Roosevelt were as concerned about appearances as they were about actualities—Churchill worrying about the House of Commons, Roosevelt about his Polish vote.

But the issue was unresolved, and Molotov continued to oppose "observing and reporting" by the ambassadors. At the foreign ministers' meeting at noon on February 10, Stettinius opened by giving way on this point. The president was, he said, "so anxious to reach agreement that he was willing to make this concession."[32] Eden made it known that he did not agree. But Roosevelt's capitulation on the ambassadors' observing the elections made it difficult for the British to carry the point alone.

The last working meeting of the Big Three was scheduled for 4:00 P.M. at Livadia Palace. Eden had reported the one remaining impasse to Churchill. The two of them met with Stalin and Molotov privately at Yusupov Palace just before the main meeting. Churchill raised the issue of the ambassadors as election observers. He would be asked in Parliament about the elections.

"I must be able to say that I knew what was happening."

"After the new Polish Government is recognized," replied Stalin, "it would be open to you to send an Ambassador to Warsaw."

"Would he be free to move about the country?"

"As far as the Red Army is concerned, there will be no interference with his movements . . . but you will have to make your own arrangements with the Polish Government."

They then agreed to add a sentence referring to the "Ambassadors by whose reports the respective Governments will be kept informed about the situation in Poland." Nothing about observing elections.

"This," Churchill later wrote, "was the best I could get."[33]

Late for the plenary session because of his meeting with Stalin, Churchill stepped to Roosevelt's side: "I believe that I have succeeded in retrieving the situation."[34]

At the opening of the session, Eden read the agreed draft. At this point Roosevelt handed a copy to Admiral William D. Leahy, his chief of staff, who read it with fresh eyes. He handed it back to Roosevelt. "Mr. President," he said, "this is so elastic that the Russians can stretch it all the way from Yalta to Washington without technically breaking it."

"I know, Bill—I know it. But it's the best I can do for Poland at this time."[35]

The only objection to the draft was from Churchill, who pointed out that there was no mention of Polish frontiers. In the east the Curzon Line (Russian version) had been accepted, but both Churchill and Roosevelt had objected to the western frontier going as far as the western Neisse River. In the end a sentence was added citing the Curzon Line in the east (no mention of Lwów) and "substantial accessions of territory in the north and west," with final delineation reserved for the postwar peace conference.

This appeared to be the only Polish issue on which the Allies had not agreed. But if the other Polish questions on the composition of the government and the safeguarding of elections had been agreed upon, it was in words only, for the public communiqué. Stalin and Molotov had protected their control. No mention had been made of the proportion of non-Communists in the new cabinet, or how the key posts would be filled, or the name of the new president or premier. This had all been left to Molotov and the Western ambassadors meeting in Moscow with Polish leaders. There was a mention of "free and unfettered elections as soon as possible on the basis of universal suffrage and secret ballot." But there was no mention of Allied machinery for assuring this.

Defending the Yalta statement, Stettinius later wrote, "The agreement on Poland was, under the circumstances, a concession by Marshal Stalin to the Prime Minister and the President."[36] The professional diplomats most familiar with Moscow did not agree. "Altogether our foreign policy seems a sad wreck," Eden wrote in his diary.[37] Discussing the outcome while still at Yalta, Harriman and Bohlen agreed there was "trouble ahead."

Harriman believed Roosevelt and Churchill should have insisted on bringing the Poles to Yalta and forming a provisional government then and there, rather than leaving it to others meeting in Moscow. "We had established nothing more than the machinery for renegotiation," he later wrote. And the crucial wording of the agreement—"reorganized on a broader democratic basis with the inclusion of democratic leaders from Poland itself and from Poles abroad"—was far too vague a guideline. "I was gravely concerned because unless you knew whom you were talking about, that could be fudged."[38]

Bohlen believed Roosevelt "did everything he could to help the Poles," but "The Red Army gave Stalin the power he needed to carry out his wishes, regardless of his promises at Yalta." Bohlen's conclusion: "Stalin held all the cards and played them well. Eventually, we had to throw in our hand."[39]

Yet the "game" did not have to be played to a finish at Yalta. As Eden had pointed out beforehand, it would have been better to have no agreement than to yield to Stalin on Poland. The necessity of reaching agreement is the fallacy that impelled Roosevelt and Churchill to settle at any cost. Surely, failure to agree is far less disastrous than agreeing to a sham.

What would have happened if, among all the issues resolved at Yalta, the Big Three had announced disagreement on Poland? For a few more weeks a dying Third Reich would have won a propaganda issue. But far more important, the Western Allies would have had a much larger incentive to win the race for Berlin. For by occupying most of the designated Soviet zone of Germany, they would have gained a bargaining lever to match Stalin's occupation of Poland. Then the provisional Polish government could have been fairly structured, and machinery could have been created to assure free elections.

Whether Roosevelt or even Truman would have seized this opportunity is questionable. But failure to do so would have been more difficult after U.S. public opinion had time to crystallize on the Polish issue.

As for the British leaders, they opposed the Polish agreement at Yalta, but could not hold out alone. Eden preferred no agreement on Poland. Churchill reluctantly accepted it, but was stricken with remorse as the declaration on Poland was read at the final plenary session on February 11.

It would, he growled, "be very heavily attacked in England. It will be said we have yielded completely on the frontiers and the whole matter to Russia."

"Is it in earnest?" asked Stalin, apparently questioning Churchill's sincerity. "I doubt it."

"I assure you it is," snapped Churchill. "The London Poles will raise a dreadful outcry."

"But the other Poles will predominate."

"I hope you're right. We're not going back on it. It's not a question of numbers of Poles but of the cause for which Britain drew the sword. They will say you have completely swept away the only constitutional government of Poland. However, I will defend it to the best of my ability."[40]

At this point Roosevelt could not resist a final word. He had (according to the Soviet transcript) "ten times as many Poles in the United States as Churchill had in Britain, but . . . would nevertheless back the Declaration on Poland in every way."[41] It was as though he were saying to himself, "The American election is over, and I will never see another."

As for the Poles themselves, they denounced the Crimean agreement as a betrayal. In London the Polish government-in-exile declared publicly that it had not been consulted on the Yalta declaration on Poland, that it did not recognize the decision and would not be bound by it. The Poles could not know that Yalta was only the culmination of more than three years of consistent U.S. policy. Beginning in December 1941–when the British were arguing that Stalin's bargaining position would never be weaker—Hull and Roosevelt had opposed territorial settlements with the Soviet Union until the postwar peace table. As the Red Army's progress strengthened Stalin's position, the lofty U.S. position began to erode. As early as March 1943 Roosevelt seemed ready, in conversation with Eden, to accept the Curzon Line. At the Tehran conference he did accept it in secret conversation with Stalin. Mikolajczyk learned of this in October 1944, but still hoped that Roosevelt would actively insist on Polish independence. Even after the U.S. elections in November, Roosevelt refused. Yalta merely confirmed openly what the Polish leaders had, belatedly, feared.

After the Yalta meeting General Wladyslaw Anders, whose Polish troops had distinguished themselves in battles from Italy to France, was devastated. His British superior officer in Italy had to plead to keep him from withdrawing his troops from the line. On February 21 Anders met with Churchill in London.

"You are not satisfied with the Yalta conference," Churchill began abruptly.

"It is not enough to say that I am dissatisfied," Anders retorted. "I consider that a great calamity has occurred."[42]

On February 27 Churchill defended the Polish decision in the House of Commons. Afterward, nursing a large brandy, he told a colleague that Britain could do no more for Poland.

"Not only are the Russians very powerful, but they are on the spot; even the massed majesty of the British empire would not avail to turn them off that spot."[43]

12

"Who Will Take Berlin?"

By September 1944 the Western Allied armies were, in Eisenhower's words, "crowding up against the borders of Germany." But though heavy fighting still lay ahead in breaching the Siegfried Line and crossing the Rhine, it was certainly time to plan the death blow of the Third Reich.

Since August, Montgomery had been urging on Eisenhower a strong thrust through the Ruhr Valley to northern Germany, with all other efforts to be secondary. More cautious, Eisenhower believed in a "broad front" strategy. On September 4 the great port of Antwerp fell, assuring an adequate supply at the northern front. The same day Montgomery pressed his argument further with Ike: "I consider we have now reached a stage where one really powerful and full-blooded thrust towards Berlin is likely to get there and thus end the German war." In the argument that followed, Eisenhower still pushed for a wider front with the Ruhr and Saar industrial basins as immediate goals. But after that he seemed to come closer to Montgomery's plan in a message on September 15:

Clearly Berlin is the main prize, and the prize in defense of which the enemy is likely to concentrate the bulk of his forces. There is no doubt whatsoever, in my mind, that we should concentrate all our energies and resources on a rapid thrust to Berlin.

Montgomery was quick to agree. "I consider that as time is so very important, we have got to decide what is necessary to go to Berlin and finish the war. . . . "[1]

At this point Berlin was strictly a military objective—the checkmate in the game of war. The Germans might, of course, surrender before their country was completely overrun. But the "unconditional surrender" demanded by the Allies, together with Hitler's fanatical resistance to the end, made Berlin the Allies' ultimate military target.

The German capital had already been largely removed as a political prize between East and West. Since January 1944 the European Advisory Commission, created at the Council of Foreign Ministers' meeting in Moscow, had been drawing the zones of occupation for postwar Germany. Consultation with the heads of state had produced substantial agreement by June 1. The Soviet zone would extend westward to a line running from near Lübeck on the Baltic Sea south to roughly the northern border of Bavaria. Within that area, Berlin itself would be divided into separate zones. The division, already supported by the Soviets, was accepted by Roosevelt and Churchill in September at the second Quebec conference, where they also resolved differences over the British and U.S. zones. The boundaries remained to be ratified at Yalta, where a French zone was created from the Western area.

According to a later statement by Eisenhower, as early as January 1944 he secretly flew to Washington and vainly argued with Roosevelt against isolating Berlin inside the Soviet zone. A year later, when his forces were poised along the Rhine, Eisenhower claims that he protested to both Roosevelt and Churchill against fixing the occupation zones prematurely. Neither his war memoirs nor his collected papers confirm such objections. In any case, once the final decision on occupation zones was made at Yalta, as Eisenhower later said, "all of my movements, all of my planning, had to take into consideration where we were going to be situated after the war."[2]

The approach was typical of Eisenhower, who played the good soldier in obedience to superiors. Like Marshall, he prided himself on taking only military decisions—within the political framework established for him by civilian leadership. Lack of direction by that leadership sometimes forced political criteria into his decisions, but for him it was an uncomfortable and unsure role.

Certainly Eisenhower was an accomplished politician in the diplomatic sense; here the British were among his greatest admirers. Churchill praised him for achieving a pinnacle of unity in Allied arms: "At no time has the principle of alliance between noble races been carried and maintained at so high a pitch."[3] Montgomery, who repeatedly clashed with Eisenhower, later wrote, "I know of no other person who could have welded the Allied forces into such a fine fighting machine in the way he did. . . . "[4]

But on the question of the strictly military decisions to which Eisenhower tried to limit himself, British comment was often in the nature of damning with faint praise. General (later Field Marshal) Sir Alan Brooke: "As Supreme Commander what he may have lacked in military ability he greatly made up for by the charm of his personality."[5] And Montgomery: "I would not class Ike as a great soldier. . . . But he was a great Supreme Commander—a military statesman."[6]

If Marshall had only limited experience in battlefield command, Eisenhower had none at all—a point that British observers have not missed. Montgomery's definitive biographer, Nigel Hamilton, has faulted Eisenhower for mistakes in campaigns from Tunis to Germany. Yet it is awkward to criticize success. If Eisenhower's military strategy can be faulted, it is in too little daring and too much caution. Here his lack of field experience may have shaped his conservatism—made him less willing to take chances.

Again like Marshall, Eisenhower was devoted to logistics; perhaps he was right in fearing that a deep thrust into enemy territory could outrun its fuel and ammunition. In this he agreed with such strategists as George Marshall and Joseph Stalin, and disagreed with such others as George Patton and Bernard Montgomery.

As he prepared for the final assault on Germany, Eisenhower's natural caution was affected further by a political fact: Berlin was already consigned to the Soviet zone and its administration split among the Allies. Did it matter who took Berlin?

In the weeks following the dialogue between Eisenhower and Montgomery, the plot thickened in the Berlin drama. German strength in repulsing the Arnhem bridgehead in September and launching the Battle of the Bulge in December proved that, as Eisenhower had told Churchill, the Germans were "not licked." Even if Eisenhower approved Montgomery's thrust for Berlin, it could not begin until the Western Allies had successfully crossed the Rhine. Caution still ruled in the West, as it did in the East.

There the Red Army remained along the Vistula for five months while it straightened out its flanks to the north and south, repaired its supply lines, and brought up materiel for the next offensive. Stalin had set January 20, 1945, as the starting date for the new advance to the Oder River, less than 50 miles from Berlin.

On January 3, during the Battle of the Bulge, Churchill was at Eisenhower's headquarters in Reims. The Allies had already attacked General von Rundstedt's extended salient from the south, and on that day Montgomery struck it from the north. From this moment, according to Eisenhower, "all danger from the great German thrust had disappeared." But three days later Churchill sent an anxious message to Stalin:

The battle in the west is very heavy. . . . It is Eisenhower's great desire and need to know in outline what you plan to do. . . . I shall be grateful if you can tell me whether we can count on a major Russian offensive on the Vistula front, or elsewhere during January. . . . I regard the matter as urgent.

Stalin replied promptly:

In view of our Allies' position on the Western Front, GHQ of the Supreme Command have decided to complete preparations at a rapid rate and, regardless of weather, to launch large-scale offensive operations along the entire Central Front not later than the second half of January.[7]

Accordingly, Konev's First Ukrainian Front attacked from bridgeheads across the Vistula on January 12, and Zhukov's First Byelorussian Front two days later. By February 1 the Red Army had reached the Oder in one of the most powerful drives of the war. Afterward the Soviets claimed that with this pressure they had relieved Eisenhower's predicament and saved the Allies in the Battle of the Bulge. Actually, Hitler had ordered the withdrawal of Rundstedt's forces back through the Allied pincers on January 8, four days before the Soviet offensive began.

The main effect of Stalin's stepped-up onslaught was to place the Red Army on the Oder when the Big Three met at Yalta on February 4. The Red Army now occupied nearly all of Poland, including part of the German provinces that the Allies were handing to her in compensation for territory taken by the Soviets in the east. Britain and the United States had little bargaining leverage left to demand the machinery for an independent Poland.

As for the rest of Northern Europe, Stalin was now 50 miles from Berlin, while the Western Allies had not yet crossed the Rhine—some 300 miles to the west. Could the Soviets be contained within their assigned German occupation zone, or would they roll on past Denmark to the North Sea? And with such hegemony over Europe, would Stalin find any advantage in withdrawing to the assigned Soviet zone?

Marshal V. I. Chuikov, one of Zhukov's army commanders, claims that the drive from the Oder to Berlin was planned as far back as November 1944, as a second phase of the offensive that began on the Vistula; that Berlin could have been taken in February, perhaps during the Yalta conference; and that Stalin halted the drive at the Oder for political reasons, probably to keep from alarming Churchill and Roosevelt.

Other Soviet generals, such as Zhukov and S. M. Shtemenko, chief of the General Staff, refute this. They argue that the flanks of the huge salient won by Zhukov and Konev were threatened by gathering German forces, and that Stalin had to redirect Zhukov to assist Marshal Rokossovsky in driving northward through East Pomerania to the Baltic Sea. Both Rokossovsky and Konev confirm this need to clean up the flanks before proceeding to Berlin. It was characteristic of Stalin's conduct of the war to proceed from assured strength and take few risks, even if this meant allowing the enemy time to improve defenses.[8]

Barring risks, would Stalin have preferred to go on and take Berlin in February? It would have given him more leverage in the Yalta debates, but considering Roosevelt's cooperative attitude, he already had a great deal. Had he intended to push beyond Berlin and beyond the Soviet zone, he might have set off alarm bells among the Americans—bells that were already ringing in Churchill's ears. It was in February 1945 that Churchill, viewing the utter destruction of Germany, asked, "What will lie between the white snows of Russia and the white cliffs of Dover?"[9]

Stalin seemed to prefer keeping U.S. goodwill at this juncture. At his first tête-á-tête with Roosevelt at Yalta on February 4, he told the president he was "certain that the Americans would get to Manila before the Russians got to Berlin. . . . "[10]

At this point the Western Allies, having recovered from the Battle of the Bulge, resumed the offensive. By early March the northern forces had reached the Rhine; by March 22 the Allies were across it at three points. Within three weeks Montgomery and General Omar Bradley had closed a pincers around the Ruhr industrial center and trapped 350,000 German troops, the largest single haul in the European war.

But already the Western Allies were rushing eastward on an even larger mission—to overrun Germany, link with the Red Army, and end the war. On March 27 Montgomery wired the British chief of staff: "My intention is to drive hard for the line of the Elbe . . . thence via the *autobahn* to Berlin, I hope."[11]

The same day Bradley and Eisenhower were lunching at Reims, putting what Bradley called "the final touches" on the plan to split the Reich. Oddly, Eisenhower had now changed his mind about the importance of Berlin. It was too far to be taken from supply bases that were still west of the Rhine. Instead he favored a powerful thrust by Bradley due east to the industrial complex of Leipzig and Dresden to meet the Russians. After all, the Red Army, with a bridgehead across the Oder, was now only 35 miles from Berlin, and all of eastern Germany had been designated in the Soviet oc-cupation zone. Berlin "was not the logical or the most desirable objective for the forces of the Western Allies."

But as Eisenhower believed, a more southerly drive linking with the Soviets would probably split Germany sooner, would overrun its last industrial center, and would enable the Allies to deal with another threat—intelligence reports that the Nazis were planning to make a last stand in the Alpine fastnesses of Upper Bavaria and Austria.

This decision not to drive for Berlin quickly became a fierce and long-drawn cause célèbre. The logic of Eisenhower's arguments has been heatedly debated by British and U.S. partisans, starting with Montgomery and Brad-ley. Besides logic, personal interest was certainly involved. Montgomery argued that the Allied leaders had agreed at their Malta meeting on a single main thrust through the Ruhr and northern Germany; as the Allied com-mander on the northern flank, he was in the position to command this main thrust and eventually to target Berlin.

The rivalry, and indeed rancor, between Montgomery and Bradley is clearly depicted in the latter's second book, *A General's Life*. From the moment his forces made the first bridgehead across the Rhine by capturing the Re-magen Bridge, Bradley was determined to exploit it until his own offensive became the main Western thrust and Montgomery's effort would be "massively upstaged."

"This was not my usual straightforward way of doing business," he wrote, "but the circumstances compelled me to resort to a little duplicity."[12]

Thus, at the March 27 luncheon at Reims, Bradley promoted his plan for a major thrust across the middle of Germany and was delighted to find Eisenhower completely receptive. The change of strategy meant that the U.S. Ninth Army, previously "lent" to Montgomery, would be returned to Bradley; that Bradley would command the main Allied offensive to link with the Russians and end the war; and that Montgomery would be relegated to a supporting role on Bradley's northern flank. But this could be justified only if Berlin were removed as the ultimate Allied objective.

Was Eisenhower, as well as Bradley, influenced by this personal factor? By this time his relations with Montgomery were strained, and he was annoyed at the lopsided publicity given to Montgomery in the British press and even some U.S. newspapers. Eisenhower's leading biographer, Stephen E. Ambrose, while fully supporting Eisenhower's arguments against Berlin, also states: "Eisenhower wanted Bradley to lead the last campaign. Had Bradley been on the northern flank, Eisenhower might well have sent him to Berlin."[13]

During the luncheon with Bradley, Eisenhower received a cable from Marshall that suggested the possibility of an eastward drive even more southerly than the one Eisenhower and Bradley were discussing. This seemed to clinch the decision, and Ike's mind was set. That afternoon he flew to Paris for a press conference.

"Who do you think will be in Berlin first," asked a reporter, "the Russians or us?"

"Well," answered Eisenhower, "I think mileage alone ought to make them do it."[14]

Back in Reims the next day, he sent a message to Moscow. The addressee: Joseph Stalin.

For a theater commander to open direct liaison with an Allied head of state was, to say the least, unusual. Eisenhower later explained that, as experience had shown, it was Stalin who made the top military decisions, and addressing anyone else would simply cause delay.

In any case, Eisenhower's message—transmitted through the U.S. military mission in Moscow—told Stalin that "in late April or even earlier" his next move "will be to divide the enemy's remaining forces by joining hands with your forces" along the axis of Erfurt, Leipzig, and Dresden. "Could you, therefore, tell me your intentions. . . . "[15]

Before Eisenhower's message reached Stalin, it kindled a political firestorm in the Western camp. In March 1945 there was plenty of reason for Berlin to become a political pawn. The Soviets were breaking the Yalta agreements almost before the ink was dry. In Romania, Andrei Vishinsky had forced the king to install a pro-Soviet government—in clear violation of the Declaration on Liberated Europe. In Moscow, the committee designated to create a unified government of Poland was paralyzed by Molotov's insistence that it be dominated by Soviet stooges—a contradiction of the Yalta agreement on the Polish question. In Poland itself, the NKVD had tricked 16 top leaders of the Polish underground into attending a meeting at which they were arrested on trumped-up treason charges—again, a flagrant violation of the Yalta agreement for a free and independent Poland.

In fact, in all the East European countries occupied by the Red Army, the press was censored, the governments controlled, property confiscated, citizens arbitrarily arrested, and Britons and Americans—businessmen, correspondents, and officials—either forbidden entry or subjected to outrageous restrictions. No amount of protest availed; where Stalin had the power, he used it.

In these circumstances, Churchill's desire to seize as much of Eastern Europe as possible now proved painfully correct. His hopes to liberate Budapest and Vienna were now lost—the former fell to the Red Army on February 12; the latter would fall on April 13. There remained two Central European capitals—Berlin and Prague—for the taking.

As for Berlin, it was destined for a four-power occupation within the Soviet zone of Germany, but no schedule for starting the occupation plan had been agreed among the Big Three, since at Yalta they could not know when the war would end. If the Western Allies captured most of the future Soviet zone, including Berlin, they could delay their withdrawal until the Soviets adhered to the other Yalta agreements. This might be considered a small lever for securing the independence of all of Eastern Europe, but it was about the only one they had left.

These factors now spurred Churchill to eloquent protest of Eisenhower's plan. The British Chiefs of Staff had objected strenuously to the Joint Chiefs of Staff in Washington—Eisenhower was exceeding his authority, and his strategy was wrong. They "could not exclude the possibility that Stalin intended to take Berlin himself, and to keep the Allies out of it as long as possible."

On the night of March 30 Churchill contacted Eisenhower via the scrambler telephone. He protested sending the main Allied thrust toward Leipzig. He argued heatedly for the importance of Berlin. And he demanded the facts on which Ike had based his decision. In a telegram, Eisenhower explained his strategy.

"I propose," he declared, "to drive eastward to join hands with the Russians or to attain the general line of the Elbe."[16]

On March 31 the prime minister fired back his answer: "I do not know why it would be an advantage not to cross the Elbe . . . why should we not cross the Elbe and advance as far eastward as possible?" The Soviets were already about to take Vienna. "If we deliberately leave Berlin to them, even if it should be in our grasp, the double event may strengthen their conviction, already apparent, that they have done everything." Berlin, he continued, was as significant as ever. "The fall of Berlin would have a profound psychological effect on German resistance in every part of the Reich. While Berlin holds out great masses of Germans will feel it their duty to go down fighting."[17]

Then, to assure that the Americans got his message, Churchill wired Roosevelt next day:

I say quite frankly that Berlin remains of high strategic importance. Nothing will exert a psychological effect of despair upon all German forces of resistance equal to that of the fall of Berlin. It will be the supreme signal of defeat to the German people.

Churchill then repeated his argument against letting the Soviets take both Vienna and Berlin:

[M]ay this not lead them into a mood which will raise grave and formidable difficulties in the future? I therefore consider that from a political standpoint we should march as far east into Germany as possible, and that should Berlin be in our grasp we should certainly take it.[18]

As early as the first Quebec conference in August 1943, Roosevelt had asked for plans to get U.S. and British troops into Berlin as soon as the Soviets, in case Germany collapsed. But now his reply, apparently drafted by Marshall, supported Eisenhower. At this stage Ike was mounting his own defenses.

To Montgomery he explained his strategy, adding that Berlin "has become, so far as I am concerned, nothing but a geographical location, and I have never been interested in these. My purpose is to destroy the enemy's forces and his powers to resist."

To Marshall, who had forwarded the British protest: "Berlin itself is no longer a particularly important objective. Its usefulness to the German has been largely destroyed and even his government is preparing to move to another area."

To the Combined Chiefs of Staff: "Berlin as a strategic area is discounted as it is now largely destroyed . . . moreover it is so near to the Russian front that once they start moving again they will reach it in a matter of days."

And again to Churchill, with some conciliation: There was little difference in their two strategies. Regarding the "political importance" of taking Berlin, "I clearly see your point in this matter." While not agreeing to Berlin as a primary objective, Eisenhower promised that if Germany suddenly collapsed, "we would rush forward . . . and Berlin would be included in our important targets."[19]

At this point the British, led by Churchill, wound down the crisis. But in his final message on the subject to Eisenhower on April 2, Churchill insisted, "I deem it highly important that we should shake hands with the Russians as far to the east as possible."[20]

Across Europe, Stalin was making new plans. Through March his attitude toward his allies, in contrast with the closing cordiality at Yalta, was savage. When the Germans had tried to negotiate the surrender of the army in Italy to the Western Allies, Stalin's worst suspicions had been aroused. No assurances by Roosevelt and Churchill would avail. The Western Allies, cried Stalin, were trying to close a separate peace with Hitler and let the Soviets fight on alone. Even if a surrender were not official, the broad-front breakthrough of the Americans and British across the Rhine proved that the Germans were encouraging them and transferring all their strength to the east. At the rate the Western Allies were advancing, they might reach Berlin. Stalin summoned Marshal Georgi K. Zhukov, who left the front at the Oder and reached Moscow on March 29. That night he met with Stalin in his Kremlin office.

"The German front in the west has collapsed for good," Stalin began without preliminaries, "and probably the Hitlerites don't want to take any measures to halt the advance of the Allied forces. In the meantime they are reinforcing their groups on all the major directions against us."

While Zhukov studied the intelligence map, Stalin asked when the Red Army "could be ready for the offensive." Zhukov's answer: his own front would be ready in two weeks. Konev's, to the south, probably the same. But Rokossovsky was still mopping up in the Baltic and would not be ready by then.

"Well then," snapped Stalin, "we shall have to begin the operation without waiting for Rokossovsky.'" Then Stalin showed Zhukov an intelligence report about the German surrender overtures to the Western Allies and the "possibility of the Hitlerites letting the Allied forces through to Berlin."

"I believe Roosevelt will not violate the Yalta agreement," said Stalin, referring to the occupation zones, "but as for Churchill, he can do anything."[21]

Stalin then summoned Konev, who arrived in Moscow two days later. The same day, March 31, Eisenhower's original cable of March 28 was delivered to the Kremlin by Harriman, accompanied by the British ambassador, Clark Kerr, and the U.S. and British military representatives.

Stalin's response to the message they brought was positive and friendly— in surprising contrast with his angry demeanor in previous days. Eisenhower's proposal was a good one. "It would succeed in cutting Germany in half." And he emphasized that the Germans were expected to "make their last stand" in western Czechoslovakia and Bavaria. "The direction of the Western attack," he added, was favorable for "a link-up with the Red Army."[22]

Back of Stalin's cordiality was his new plan to turn the tables on the Western Allies. Next day his answer to Eisenhower was enthusiastic. He agreed "that the place for the joining up of your forces and the Soviet forces should be the area Erfurt, Leipzig, Dresden." The "main blow of the Soviet forces should be delivered in that direction." And that blow would begin "approximately the second half of May."

Unlike Eisenhower's message, Stalin's specifically mentioned the German capital: "Berlin has lost its former strategic importance. The Soviet High Command therefore plans to allot secondary forces in the direction of Berlin."[23]

The significance of this message is that Stalin immediately proceeded to do the opposite. Next day he met in his study with Zhukov, Konev, and other military leaders. He showed them an intelligence report on Western Allied plans to drive for Berlin. It has been suggested that this was a garbled version of Eisenhower's message, or a skeptical staff analysis of it. Whether genuine or contrived, it was used effectively by Stalin in spurring his generals toward Berlin.

"Well," he demanded, "who is going to take Berlin, we or the Allies?"

With his military chiefs he completed his plans for an enormous Soviet offensive to be launched on Berlin. And this "main blow" would begin not in mid-May but within two weeks—on April 16.

No doubt Stalin intended to fool Eisenhower, and with him the other two partners in the Big Three. He agreed to meet Ike at Leipzig and Dresden, but instead he would turn his main force on Berlin. And as a double precaution, in case the Western Allies were trying to play the same game on him, he would make them think they had plenty of time—Uncle Joe would not strike westward for six weeks. In fact, he would strike in two weeks.

There has been some historical speculation that Eisenhower was, in fact, joining with his superiors in trying to mislead Stalin by his March 28 cable, and also that Stalin disbelieved him. All the evidence shows that Eisenhower made this decision and sent this message on his own, and was absolutely sincere. As for Stalin, he told his comrades at the April 1 meeting that Eisenhower, on the basis of his message, was "a man who was true to his obligations." Still, there was considerable room for doubt, as Stalin's intelligence report suggested.

To speed his commanders to Berlin, he introduced a very bourgeois element—competition. Under the original plan Zhukov was to take Berlin, with Rokossovsky and Konev protecting his flanks. The dividing line on the planning map between Konev's and Zhukov's forces passed south of Berlin, leaving no chance for Konev to join in taking the capital. Stalin now crossed out part of the dividing line—the section beyond Lübben, some 50 miles southeast of Berlin. According to Konev, Stalin said nothing, but the general noticed the gesture and concluded that beyond Lübben he might swing toward Berlin. According to Zhukov, Stalin told Konev that if Zhukov's frontal attack were delayed, Konev's army group was to "be in readiness to strike at Berlin with its tank armies from the south." In any case, Stalin later told his general staff, "Let the one who is first to break in take Berlin."

Now Konev, no less than Zhukov, was fired with what he called the "ardent desire" to capture Berlin. To make the race even more competitive, Stalin shifted two armies from Rokossovsky to Konev. On April 3, after their plans were approved by Stalin, Zhukov and Konev hurried out of Moscow—their planes taking off within two minutes of each other—to prepare the final attack.[24]

In the west another attack was already launched. Receiving Stalin's answer of April 1, Eisenhower next day ordered his army group commanders to attack—the main thrust being on the Kassel-Leipzig axis to "make a junction with the Soviet forces in that area." Bradley's army group was to deliver this powerful blow. Both Montgomery and Bradley were to "seize any opportunity of capturing a bridgehead over the river Elbe and be prepared to conduct operations beyond the river Elbe."[25]

Once again the race was on. Bradley, while mopping up in the Ruhr pocket with part of his forces, pressed for the Elbe. In the north, Montgomery was already planning beyond the Elbe. To Eisenhower he wrote on April 6 that his forces would drive to Lübeck on the Baltic, thus cutting off the Danish Peninsula, and then southeastward toward Berlin. As for Berlin's strategic value, he disagreed with Eisenhower. "I consider that Berlin has definite value as an objective and I have no doubt whatever that the Russians think the same. . . . " Then, with better insight than Ike's, he added, "but they may well pretend that this is not the case!!"

Eisenhower, now revealing some impatience, answered him on April 8:

I am quite ready to admit that it has political and psychological significance but of far greater importance will be the location of the remaining German forces in relation to Berlin. It is on them that I am going to concentrate my attention. Naturally, if I get an opportunity to capture Berlin cheaply, I will take it.

And to Marshall, as a rejoinder to further British–U.S. dialogue about Berlin, he wrote on April 7:

I regard it as militarily unsound at this stage of the proceedings to make Berlin a major objective, particularly in view of the fact that it is only thirty-five miles from the Russian lines. I am the first to admit that a war is waged in pursuance of political aims, and if the Combined Chiefs of Staff should decide that the Allied effort to take Berlin outweighs purely military considerations in the theater, I would cheerfully readjust my plans and my thinking so as to carry out such an operation. I urgently believe, however, that the capture of Berlin should be left as something that we would do if feasible and practicable. . . . [26]

Even as Eisenhower wrote, Lieutenant General William H. Simpson's U.S. Ninth Army was fast fulfilling these terms. In 19 days from the crossing of the Rhine on March 24, the Ninth covered 226 miles—an average of 12 miles a day. On April 11 advance units of the Ninth reached the Elbe south of Magdeburg, 75 miles west of Berlin. They were not as close as the Soviets, but were within five or six days' drive at their current rate.

That night Eisenhower and Bradley were visiting Patton in his command post at Hersfeld, south of Kassel. Eisenhower proposed to Patton that he stop his forces at a certain point, explaining:

From a tactical point of view, it was highly inadvisable for the American Army to take Berlin, and he hoped political influence would not cause him to take the city. It had no tactical or strategical value, and would place upon American forces the burden of caring for thousands and thousands of Germans, displaced persons, Allied prisoners of war, etc.

Patton, who was as distrustful of the Soviets as the British were, disagreed: "Ike, I don't see how you figure that one. We had better take Berlin and quick, and on to the Oder."[27]

Next day other units of Simpson's Ninth Army reached the Elbe at Tangemunde, 53 miles from Berlin. Within three days, according to General Simpson, seven divisions were on the Elbe. By April 13 they had two bridgeheads across the river. Notified by Simpson, Bradley phoned Eisenhower. "At that time," Bradley wrote later, "we could probably have pushed on to Berlin had we been willing to take the casualties Berlin would have cost us." In the agitated conversation, Eisenhower seemed to be reopening the Berlin question—at least in his own mind. He asked Bradley what "it might cost us to break through from the Elbe to Berlin." Bradley's answer: 100,000 casualties.

"A pretty stiff price to pay for a prestige objective," he added, "especially when we've got to fall back and let the other fellow take over."[28]

Bradley's cost estimate may have been high. He later stated that he considered the truly costly part was in Berlin itself, not en route. But according to him, the terrain west of Berlin was still soaked and full of rivers, lakes, and canals, while east of Berlin the Soviets would operate on dry ground. Eisenhower had another concern that may have been given him by Bradley. He wrote to Marshall: "While true that we have seized a small bridgehead over the Elbe, it must be remembered that only our spearheads are up to that river; our center of gravity is well back of there."[29]

Supporting this view many years later was General S. L. A. Marshall, who was an officer at the bridgehead south of Magdeburg at the time. The Army corps that had reached the river, he wrote, "was spread out over 150 miles with its rear dangling in air and the Germans besetting it on front and both flanks." At the bridgehead there was "a real fire-fight." The 50 miles to Berlin were not "soft miles," but "long, hard miles and troops do run out of wind." The corps commander concluded that "at best the Corps might get a few motorized patrols into western Berlin by the time the Red Army had taken the main body of the city."[30]

On the other hand, General Simpson of the U.S. Ninth Army believed he could go on immediately to take Berlin. Although German counterattacks had forced him to abandon one of his two bridgeheads, he had been able to expand the other to some 30 square miles. At the main bridgehead south of Magdeburg, opposition was intense at first, but Simpson called the German units "scratch outfits at best" and the resistance "only a crust." His supply lines were in good shape and improving daily. "The U.S. Ninth Army had ample supplies to drive and capture Berlin." As for the Ninth itself, Simpson believed "morale and combat effectiveness were extremely high." The force at the river "was in excellent posture to continue on to Berlin." After reviewing the intelligence and logistic situation and conferring with his two corps commanders, Simpson concluded, "There was no question in my mind but what we could do it and do it economically with little loss."[31]

Supporting Simpson's view was Major General James M. Gavin, whose crack 82nd Airborne Division had been placed in readiness to drop on Berlin. He later argued that much of Eisenhower's concern could have been resolved by ordering a reconnaissance in force to Berlin—a normal step in such circumstances.[32]

But whether Simpson's views had been forwarded to Bradley or, if so, Bradley had simply downgraded them, is not clear. In any case, possibly confirmed in his decision by Bradley's opinion, Eisenhower on April 14 notified the Combined Chiefs of Staff that he would "stop on the Elbe and clean up my flanks." Next day he ordered Bradley to go on the defensive at the Elbe River and its southward extension, the Mulde. "Present bridgeheads over the Elbe will be secured but offensive operations beyond the Elbe will be undertaken only on later orders."[33] He ordered Montgomery to drive on Lübeck on the Baltic, and Lieutenant General Jacob L. Devers to press down the Danube Valley to meet the Russians, who had already captured Vienna on April 13.

When Bradley relayed this order to Simpson on April 15, the Ninth Army commander was dumbfounded. To one of his generals he said, woodenly, "This is the end of the war for us."[34]

By this time the Soviet buildup on the eastern front had generated German radio broadcasts that the Red Army would soon drive on Berlin. On April 15, noting this in Moscow, Ambassador Harriman asked Stalin about it. The generalissimo answered that there would be an offensive. "However, the main blow of this attack would be aimed toward Dresden, not Berlin"—as he had already told Eisenhower.

Before dawn next morning, the Red Army launched its main blow— toward Berlin. More than 700,000 troops under Marshal Zhukov were aimed directly at Berlin. More than 400,000 more under Marshal Konev supported his left flank. According to Konev, only two of his armies were aimed at

Dresden. Seven armies were part of the Berlin operation. As Konev put it, his task "was to advance south of Berlin and contribute to its capture, to split the German front in two, and to link up with the Americans."

Preceded by a stupendous artillery barrage, the offensive rolled toward Berlin—Konev at first making faster headway than Zhukov. About April 17 Stalin ordered Konev to forget the dividing line with Zhukov: "Turn your tank armies toward Berlin."[35]

On April 17 and 18 Eisenhower met with Churchill in London. The prime minister again urged a drive on Berlin, and again Ike turned him down.

By April 21 Zhukov's forces were on the outskirts of Berlin, meeting fierce opposition. The same day Eisenhower sent another message to Moscow: "[W]e shall not advance in any strength in the center for some weeks at least." Meanwhile, he would clean up his flanks—to the Danish Peninsula in the north and the Danube Valley in the south. And he authorized the U.S. military mission in Moscow to tell the Soviets "as occasion demands" that he had decided to "halt the advance in the center for the time being" at the line of the Elbe and Mulde rivers.[36]

Even at this late date Eisenhower had never reported that he intended to halt for good at the Elbe. He had kept open the Berlin option, never flatly foreclosing it. Possibly this was to avoid more violent arguments from his critics. But in the end, on the day the Soviets reached Berlin's outskirts, he notified them he would not go beyond the Elbe for several weeks—tantamount to saying "Berlin is yours."

Why did Eisenhower reject this second chance to target Berlin? Any desire he might have had to let Bradley and the Americans lead the final assault was already being fulfilled, and the glory would have been enhanced by joining the Soviets in Berlin.

From the personal standpoint, having denied Montgomery's chance to take Berlin on grounds that it was no longer important, Eisenhower would have been doubly embarrassed had the Americans now done so. The psychological factor may have been compelling. But Eisenhower voiced worthier reasons— different reasons at different times. At the outset of his drive on Leipzig, he declared that the important goal was to split the German forces and destroy them. Later he pointed out that the Soviets were much closer to Berlin, and anyhow, it was in their assigned zone. He agreed with Bradley that if it would require 100,000 casualties to take Berlin, it wasn't worth it. He told Patton that it would pose a huge burden on the Americans in caring for "thousands and thousands." Years later in an interview he added still another:

It didn't seem to be good sense to try, both of us, to throw in forces toward Berlin and get mixed up—two armies that couldn't talk the same language, couldn't even communicate with each other. It would have been a terrible mess.[37]

Yet all of Eisenhower's reasons can be challenged. Neither the Soviets nor the British thought Berlin had lost its military importance. By April 15, the day Ike gave his stop order at the Elbe, the Soviets were only a day's march closer to Berlin than the Americans, and they faced by far the largest proportion of enemy forces; their offensive took 16 days to complete the capture of Berlin on May 2.

No one has claimed it would have taken the Americans that long to reach Berlin and, if not to capture it, at least to join in its capture. Although Berlin was inside the future Soviet zone, it was scheduled for a four-power occupation. If, as Eisenhower and Bradley argued, there was a link between the wartime fighting and the postwar occupation, what about the Americans being on hand to assert their right to their own Berlin zone?

As for casualties (killed, wounded, captured, missing), these were a serious consideration. Bradley's estimate of 100,000 seems high, and Eisenhower's estimate in a later interview was between 10,000 and 30,000. Yet what about Soviet casualties in a battle unaided by their allies? The killed alone have been estimated at between 100,000 and 150,000. Could the fighting have been stopped sooner if the Americans and British had played their part in the battle for Berlin—especially since the Germans had showed they would much rather surrender to the Western Allies than to the Red Army?

There was still one more reason, voiced by Marshall rather than Eisenhower. In a taped interview years later, he said:

I do not think we should have gone into Berlin at that time . . . all this time we were trying to do business with Russia. . . . They had played a great part in the fighting—the wearing down of the German strength . . . they were exceedingly sensitive . . . looking all the time for something that would indicate that the British and Americans were preparing to go off alone and to settle the thing in a way to their . . . satisfaction and to the disadvantage of the Russians. . . . But we were trying very hard to find that basis of negotiation to go along with the Russian government.[38]

This, more than concern for casualties, more than worry about taking care of displaced persons, more than any of the other reasons, was evidently Marshall's rationale and perhaps the real basis for Eisenhower's decision on Berlin. And for all his insistence on making a military decision, this was in reality a political decision.

To Eisenhower's credit, it is clear that, except for Churchill, his superiors did not touch the issue. Eisenhower wrote Marshall that he would gladly change his strategy if the Combined Chiefs of Staff changed his objectives, but they never made any such change. As for the U.S. Joint Chiefs, they did not, according to Admiral Leahy, even discuss the issue of Berlin. The published record does not show that top State Department officials voiced any views on the capture of Berlin. True, Roosevelt and Churchill had discussed and disagreed over the question in early April, but no instructions were sent to Ike. Thus Eisenhower, a theater commander, was left by his superiors to make military decisions on an issue that, in the last stages of a coalition war, had taken on a political character.

Churchill saw this clearly, and tried to get a political decision made on a political level. The U.S. leaders did not recognize this, and left the decision to Eisenhower. Thus a failure to consider Berlin the main target was primarily the fault of U.S. leadership in Washington, and only secondarily the fault of Eisenhower.

As for Eisenhower, he prided himself as a soldier achieving by military means the objectives set forth by his political superiors. He believed that military leaders should not usurp political decisions. Yet from Africa through Italy to France, Eisenhower made numerous political decisions in his dealings with various governments. In Germany, at the very time he was avoiding Berlin by a punctilious abhorrence of political factors, he was basing other decisions to the north and south on the same political factors. Regarding Montgomery's dash to Lübeck, he wrote to Marshall, "the holding of it would prevent Russian occupation of any part of the Danish peninsula."[39] And in ordering Patton's southern drive toward Austria, as Eisenhower later pointed out, "the division of Germany had already been decided and zones of occupation delineated. This was not true of Austria and I was anxious to get as much of the latter country as possible."[40]

And so, lacking direction from Washington, and protesting that he was observing military judgment, Eisenhower made another political decision. In essence it was the same kind of decision the Americans, from Roosevelt to Hull to Marshall, had been making throughout the war. We must get along with the Soviets because we want them to come into the war against Japan and join the United Nations. They could not see, with Churchill and Eden, that such a policy would lose Eastern Europe and threaten Western Europe.

Could the Western Allies have taken Berlin? General Simpson flatly stated later: "I am convinced that the U.S. Ninth Army could have captured Berlin well ahead of the Russians if it had not been stopped at the Elbe. . . ."[41] Probably if Simpson had been ordered to advance instead of halt on April 15, the Ninth could have reached Berlin ahead of the Soviets. But whether the Germans had intended to fight the Americans or surrender to them, the Soviets would have found it easier to take the city. The most likely result is that the Americans, while not capturing Berlin alone, would have participated in its capture. Rather than meeting at an obscure town along the Elbe on April 25, G.I. Joe and Ivan—and perhaps the British Tommy—would have met on the ruins of Berlin.

Would this have been worth the trouble? At this time the Soviets were using all the leverage of the Red Army to impose their government on Poland, to deny Western diplomats and journalists access to conquered countries, to control or arrest political opponents in those countries. Britain and the United States had almost no leverage left, but the occupation of most of the future Soviet zone and all or part of Berlin would have given them some. Churchill understood, and pushed mightily for this. The U.S. attitude was expressed by General Bradley:

"As soldiers we looked naïvely on this British inclination to complicate the war with political foresight and nonmilitary objectives."[42]

As for Stalin, he acquired a profound appreciation of Eisenhower, as he did of any ally who did not oppose him. According to Nikita Khrushchev's memoirs, "Stalin said that if it hadn't been for Eisenhower, we wouldn't have succeeded in capturing Berlin."[43]

13

"On to Czechoslovakia!"

As the Red Army approached Czechoslovakia in the late summer of 1944, President Eduard Beneš had reason to question his wisdom in pinning his national strategy on friendship with Stalin. From August to October, Slovak guerrilla fighters had risen and held large areas of their mountain homeland against the Germans. But help from the Red Army, pounding on the Carpathian Mountains, was too little and too late—and much of it was limited to the Communist partisans. With meager help from the Western Allies as well, the Slovak uprising was allowed to die in the fashion of the Warsaw Rising.

More blatant was the Soviet policy as the Red Army entered Ruthenia, the easternmost part of Czechoslovakia. Seized by Hungary during the war, Ruthenia (also known by other names, such as Carpathian Ukraine) had been discussed by Beneš and Stalin in 1943. Beneš had previously told the Soviet minister to the Czechoslovak government-in-exile that Ruthenia "can only belong either to Czechoslovakia or to Russia."[1] But according to Beneš's secretary, Edward Taborsky, when Beneš had brought this up at the 1943 Moscow meeting, Stalin had immediately responded: "Subcarpathian Russia will be returned to Czechoslovakia."[2] However, Stalin later reminded Beneš, "[Y]ou yourself told me in Moscow that you were prepared to cede the Subcarpathian Ruthenia to the Soviet Union."[3]

To assure the transfer of liberated areas to Czechoslovak civil administration, Beneš had drafted, and the Soviets had signed, an agreement in May 1944. But no sooner had the Red Army penetrated to the Ruthenian capital in October 1944 than the process of seizure began.

Capturing all communications, the Soviets began broadcasting pleas from Ruthenians "to live in one body with the Ukrainian people." Mayors of towns

were forced to sign petitions asking to join the Soviet Ukraine. Communist
agents assumed control, openly supported by the Red Army. The Czechoslovak delegation sent in to assume civil control was confined to a small part
of Ruthenia, and its only communication with the London government was
filtered through the Red Army and Moscow. Known anti-Communists were
taken away by the Soviet secret police. The Soviets drafted Ruthenians into
the Red Army, sometimes by force.

Efforts of the Czechoslovak delegation to recruit men for a Czechoslovak
army were blocked by Soviet army officers and NKVD agents—posters were
seized, those posting them were detained, the printer of the posters was
arrested. Communist-dominated National Committees sprang up in various
sectors and met at Mukacevo on November 26. The Red Army prohibited
the Czechoslovak delegation, except the Communist members, from attending. The National Committees formed a National Council that called for
annexation by the Soviet Union, proclaimed itself the only civil authority
in Ruthenia and ordered the Czechoslovak delegation to leave.[4]

There followed a charade between Beneš, who protested without directly
accusing the Soviet Union, and Moscow, which blamed everything on "a
spontaneous expression of the free will of a people feeling close affinity with
the Ukrainian nation." The Soviet Foreign Office reminded Beneš, ironically,
"As we have promised you and as it is stipulated in the Soviet-Czechoslovak
treaty we are not entitled and we do not wish to interfere in your internal
affairs."[5] An exchange of letters between Stalin and Beneš carried on the
danse macabre.

Stalin: The fact that the Soviet Union has not forbidden Subcarpathian Ukrainians
    to express their will does not mean that the Soviet government has the intention
    to break the agreement between our countries and thus unilaterally solve the
    question of the Subcarpathian Ukraine. Such an opinion would be offending
    the Soviet Government.

Beneš: I assure you most emphatically, Mr. Chairman, that neither I personally nor
    the Czechoslovak government has for a moment suspected that the Soviet Gov-
    ernment desired to solve the question of the Subcarpathian Ukraine unilaterally
    or had the intention of violating the agreement between our two states. . . . I
    therefore beg you to believe my words.[6]

The end result of this pas de deux was that Ruthenia was annexed by the
Soviet Union. The agreement was signed on June 29, 1945. A few months
later Beneš wrote:

As far back as 1918 President Masaryk and I regarded Czechoslovakia as only a trustee
of that land [Ruthenia], and we were willing to relinquish the trusteeship to the
Ukraine as soon as the Ukrainian people were nationally united. This occurred when
Eastern Galicia [southeast Poland] became a part of the Ukraine, and thereby of the
Soviet Union.[7]

If this is so, Beneš had not mentioned it to his colleagues, including the delegation sent to administer Ruthenia, when the question was at issue. In fact, when journalist C. L. Sulzberger had asked him early in 1943 whether he would be willing to give up Ruthenia to the Soviet Union, Beneš had replied, "Certainly not."[8]

Still another shock was in store for the Czechoslovaks when the Red Army set foot on their soil, starting in October 1944. With the invasion of Ruthenia, and continuing with the advance through Slovakia, the Red Army acted like a conquering horde. Some 7,000 Slovaks were arrested and deported to the Soviet Union, and many never returned.[9] Czechoslovak factories and matériel that had been under German control, which included anything of importance in the country, were seized by the Soviets as "war booty." This meant that, as one Czechoslovak official said, his country's "industrial wealth was pillaged for the second time within seven years, first by the Nazis and now by the Soviets."[10]

Less official but more devastating was the behavior of the Red Army soldiers. Pillage and rapine were the order of the day. They took what they wanted—cameras, silver, silks, and especially watches—from anybody, at any time. They confiscated houses and hotels and proceeded to ruin them. They raped the women—up to half of them in some villages. In Brno, the hospitals received over 2,000 women who had been raped. In Prague, 500 Soviet soldiers with a written order from the local commandant entered a hospital and for two hours raped 40 ill or injured German women. They left a scene of horror, with five of the women dead. As one Czech writer put it, "[T]he Russian St. George came, killed the dragon and liberated the imprisoned princess, but then he got drunk, looted the castle and raped the princess."[11]

The terror was the same wherever the Red Army moved—in enemy countries such as Romania and Hungary, in Germany and Austria, in tortured Poland, and in friendly Czechoslovakia and Yugoslavia. Stalin himself took the attitude that a soldier who had fought the Germans all the way from Stalingrad deserved to "have fun with a woman." In 1944, when Milovan Djilas complained of Red Army excesses in Yugoslavia to Soviet officers, Stalin heard of it and showed bitter hostility to Djilas when he next visited Moscow.

President Beneš must have had dark misgivings as he prepared to return to his "liberated" homeland in January 1945. The Red Army was 50 miles inside Slovakia, while the Western Allies had not crossed the Rhine. If Beneš were to preside at the rebirth of the Czechoslovak nation, he would have to continue dealing with the Soviets. Despite Stalin's broken promises in Ruthenia and Slovakia, Beneš would have to suppress his outrage and maintain his diplomatic posture. This was something that, by disposition and training, he was prepared to do.

Contacting the Kremlin to arrange the trip, he made plans to go via Moscow with a delegation from Czechoslovakia's government-in-exile. Before leaving Britain on March 11, he had lunch with Winston Churchill at his country home.

"I heard that you have some fears of what the Soviets and the Red Army might do to your country," ventured Churchill.

Beneš allowed that he had "certain worries, not fears." And he went on, "I did all that was possible. I concluded a treaty with Moscow. I pursued democratic domestic policy—I could do no more. I hope it will be possible to keep matters under control."[12]

Reaching Moscow on March 17, Beneš met again with Stalin and Molotov. This time the atmosphere had hardened. The war was all but won. Nothing of consequence stood in the way of Soviet occupation of all Eastern Europe. To Molotov, Beneš agreed to confirm in writing his willingness to cede Ruthenia. From Molotov he won a concession on the "war booty" issue; the Soviets would take only the industrial assets that the Germans had brought to Czechoslovakia. From Stalin, at a state banquet, he received an unexpected apology for the Red Army's behavior:

As every Army, the Red Army has also committed acts of wantonness. . . . it is necessary to realize that they came from Stalingrad to the vicinity of Berlin. The war is not finished yet, and some of them presume they can still be killed. . . . You know, in this army are many people, and just those who are uneducated consider themselves heroes and are misusing this honor. . . . it is essential to comprehend that the army is not composed of angels. Grasp this and forgive them.[13]

Turning to the future, Stalin acknowledged that many had suspected the Soviet Union wished to bolshevize Europe. He looked at Beneš and added, "[Y]ou were justified in sharing this suspicion." However, the Soviet policy had been reoriented. The various Communist parties would become nationalist parties supporting the interests of their own countries. "I give the assurance that we will never interfere in the internal affairs of our allies."[14]

If this was intended to make more palatable the coalition government to be proposed by the Czechoslovak Communists in Moscow, it had the desired effect. The main event in the Beneš visit was the series of meetings between representatives of the parties in the London government and the Communist exiles, both of London and of Moscow. Members of the Slovak underground, especially the Communists, had been flown to Moscow for the meetings.

From these sessions Beneš held himself aloof; as he told Averell Harriman, he had necessarily used personal control in London, but now, with the return of popular government to Czechoslovakia, he was "adopting the constitutional attitude of the President, ready to receive the proposals of the party leaders . . ."[15]

Stalin had, in fact, counseled Klement Gottwald, the leader of the Czechoslovak Communists, to accept Beneš and come to an agreement with him.[16] When the Czechoslovak leaders met, the Communists were ready. As one of them, Rudolph Slansky, later said, "We asked them what sort of program they have, they told us, none."[17] The Communists then presented a 32-page program. It included the establishment of National Committees to wield local and regional authority. It did not include a constitutional bill of rights. When the London representatives suggested this, the Communists, according to a participant, "smiled and immediately inserted the clause on constitutional freedom."

Oddly, the program also did not include any reference to the nationalization of industry (one could see here the restraining hand of Stalin). The London delegation, in which two Socialist parties were represented, took the lead in adding a section on nationalization of important industries.[18] Beyond these amendments, the Communist program was adopted with little change.

Far more important was the issue of power. Originally Beneš had wanted to leave the formation of a new government until the liberation, when homeland Czechoslovaks could participate. The Moscow Communists had insisted on formation of the cabinet beforehand; in this way they could return to Czechoslovakia as officials of the government. Beneš acquiesced in thus forming a National Front, or coalition government, in Moscow.[19]

Beneš had left London expecting, as he told Harriman in Moscow, that the Communists would have about a quarter of the 16 cabinet positions. When the discussions were over, the Communists had 8 out of 25. More to the point, they held two of the five vice premierships; the Ministry of Interior, which had the police and intelligence-gathering power; the Ministry of Information, with obvious propaganda and indoctrination control; and the Ministries of Agriculture and Social Welfare, which enabled them to gain credit for material rewards, such as land reform and social benefits.

Not counted in the eight were others who, though not nominal Communists, had worked with them hand in glove. One was General Ludvik Svoboda, head of the Czechoslovak Brigade, whom the Soviets had built up as a national hero; as minister of defense he controlled the army. Another was Zdenek Fierlinger, the longtime Czechoslovak ambassador to Moscow. A left-wing member of his country's Social Democratic Party, Fierlinger had served the Soviets so faithfully that many London Czechoslovak leaders came to consider him a traitor. They had urged Beneš to fire him, but the president feared such an act would antagonize the Soviets. Later, in a rare display of language, Beneš confided to one of his associates, "Fierlinger is a swine." But in Moscow in March 1945, along with acceptance of the rest of the cabinet proposed in the meetings, Beneš approved of Fierlinger as premier. Bruce Lockhart, Beneš's close friend, wrote, "Fierlinger would never, never have been his choice if his [Beneš's] hands had been free." One of

Beneš's associates later observed that the Communists "never tired of stressing how unselfish it was on their part that they did not claim that function for a Communist."[20]

One of the key posts was left unchanged—the minister of foreign affairs remained the veteran diplomat Jan Masaryk, who had no party affiliation. Even here, however, the Communists secured the position of under secretary of foreign affairs—presumably to monitor Masaryk.

This was the complexion of the new government that Beneš would take with him to Czechoslovakia. Three pre–1945 right-wing parties, including the important Agrarian Party, were outlawed for collaborating with the Nazi occupation forces. Fierlinger suppressed the right wing of his Social Democratic Party and would work hand in glove with the Communists. The center of the political spectrum had shifted to the left, and the Communists and their collaborators held nearly all the key cabinet posts exercising domestic power. Beneš had adopted a statesman's stance above the power struggle. The result was that the London officials lost their traditional leadership in dealing with the Communists in Moscow.

For his part, Beneš was still playing the diplomat's game of saving what he could. He knew the Soviets were masters in the use of power. He could not count on the support of the Western allies. Taborsky later wrote that Beneš knew he could not form a government without Communist participation. "He was afraid that such a procedure would have meant civil war with overwhelming odds in favor of the communists."[21]

Other participants went further. An associate of Beneš wrote that in Moscow the Communists threatened, "[I]f the program is not accepted the London government will not be permitted to return to Czechoslovakia." Fierlinger later said that, "had not these claims of the Moscow group been accepted, there would have been no train to take the delegation home."[22]

Still Beneš played the optimist. He believed the Communist leaders, especially Gottwald, were Czechoslovaks first and Communists second. And he had faith in the Czechoslovak electorate. A few days before his departure from Moscow, he seemed "as buoyant as ever" to Harriman.

Beneš and the entire Czechoslovak group left Moscow by train on March 31, 1945, and four days later reached the temporary capital of their country, Kosice, in eastern Slovakia. The president was received with delirious acclaim, as he was elsewhere as soon as other parts of Czechoslovakia were liberated. On April 4 he announced the new government and emphasized that he was to be "a constitutional president"—that is, he would stay above party politics and factional debate. Next day, when the new national program was announced, he dramatized his statesmanlike posture by leaving the assembly as the program was presented.[23]

Such niceties were not observed, however, by the Soviet officials in Kosice, who were headed by the new Soviet ambassador, Valerian Zorin. Controlling all communications, they prevented Beneš from keeping in touch with his associates still in London. When he made a public radio broadcast, the range (unknown to him) was no more than 25 miles from Kosice. Any newly arriving Czechoslovak officials had to pass through three checkpoints manned by Red Army soldiers before they could see Beneš. Wrote one department head in the Finance Ministry, "When we reached Kosice my first experience in my own homeland was to be arrested."[24]

Meanwhile, the U.S. Department of State had recognized the importance of getting its representatives into Czechoslovakia promptly. In February 1945 the acting secretary of state, Joseph Grew, had cabled the U.S. chargé to the Czechoslovaks in London: "When the Czechoslovak government transfers itself into Czechoslovak territory, our mission should be prepared to send key personnel to take up their functions at the capital as soon as possible."[25] Beneš had urged that diplomats of various countries reach Czechoslovakia as early as possible, attaching "great value, among other considerations, to the moral effect of their presence."

Accordingly, on February 9 the Czechoslovak government notified the Soviet government of plans for the diplomatic corps to proceed to Kosice with the Czechoslovak officials, and forwarded a list of the diplomats of various countries early in March. But on March 28 the Soviet chargé handed the Czechoslovak government a message stating that, due to "the military situation in the district of Kosice" and "difficulties in accommodation," it was necessary "to postpone the arrival of the Diplomatic Corps in Czechoslovakia for some time." He added verbally that the Soviet authorities in Bucharest had been ordered to "refuse a transit permit across Romania for the Diplomatic Corps."[26]

Outraged, the U.S. Department of State reduced the number of people in the U.S. delegation to four in order to ascertain, as Washington wired Harriman, "if the Soviet authorities are using the situation in Kosice as a nominal excuse for their refusal to admit the representatives of friendly governments during the initial stages of political reconstruction. . . . "[27] When Washington learned from Harriman that the Soviet ambassador had arrived in Kosice with Beneš, and that civil authority was in the hands of the Communist-led Slovak National Council, American ire was complete.

As Molotov arrived in Washington on his way to the United Nations conference, Stettinius confronted him on the issue. Molotov blamed "the military situation," and assured Stettinius that the U.S. mission would "be able to proceed shortly." Grew cabled the U.S. embassy in Moscow on April 26: Tell the Soviet government that, since Ambassador Zorin accompanied Beneš to Kosice, "We expect that our mission will be accorded the same facilities provided to Soviet missions in Western Europe." He continued:

Unless our mission is given permission to proceed immediately and be provided with facilities equal to other missions in Czechoslovakia we must take the view that the Soviet government is interfering with the right of this Government to carry on normal diplomatic relations with the Czechoslovak Government and the objective of concerted action in the liberated areas agreed on at the Crimean Conference is not being carried out by the Soviet Government with respect to Czechoslovakia.[28]

Still the Soviets dragged their feet. When the U.S. embassy group finally was permitted into Czechoslovakia on May 29, nearly two months after the Soviet ambassador had arrived, none of the Czechoslovak correspondents were permitted to interview or photograph the Americans, and the Soviet censor delayed the news story on the event for five days.[29]

During those two months, as the Red Army advanced through Czechoslovakia, Communist workers followed in its tracks. Their entrenchment in key positions and their organizational activity were especially frenzied in the first weeks, before outside witnesses could arrive.[30] The Soviets arrested anyone the Communists claimed had been a Nazi collaborator. War booty that was useless to the Red Army was turned over to the Communist Party. This included reichsmarks held in banks, and equipment needed for propaganda, such as linotypes, newsprint, and typewriters with the Latin alphabet, which were used to start Communist newspapers. As in Ruthenia, the Czechoslovak delegation for civil administration was restricted in its travel. So were campaigners for the Slovak Democratic Party. On the other hand, Communist operators were allowed to spread out freely and organize National Committees, which they then dominated.

Lacking access to regular communications, the non-Communist political leaders used a clandestine radio transmitter to send reports to London. Said one of their dispatches: "The presence of the NKVD increases the self-confidence of their agitators and backs up their threats, which are plentiful." Claiming to be partisans from the mountains, "revolutionary guards" appeared in the villages—ostensibly to prevent German sabotage but actually to support Communist agitators.

Soviet seizure of Ruthenia created fear of a similar takeover in other provinces. In Slovakia the Communists were advocating that their homeland follow the path of Ruthenia as a Soviet republic. Since the Communists were the only civilians who had any influence with the Red Army in mitigating its rapacity, they were often given more power by the public. People who had learned to live with the Nazis now decided they must live with the Communists, the Red Army, and the NKVD.[31]

Thus far the fate of Czechoslovakia was being determined by aggressive Soviet policy and by Beneš's need to accommodate the Communists under threat of losing everything if he did not. Beneš wanted above all to keep Moscow's support for *his* government and give it no reason to create its own puppet government.

This was a vain hope from the beginning, since to Moscow a "friendly" Czechoslovak government meant a Soviet-controlled Czechoslovak government. The National Front government that to Beneš was a solution for reviving Czechoslovak democracy was to Stalin a holding pattern to keep up appearances for the time being with the Western democracies.

As the war neared its end toward the close of April 1945, one other factor loomed as a counterforce to the second fall of Czechoslovakia. This was the spectacular advance of the Western armies across Germany to the very gates of Bohemia. If the U.S. army could take Prague, the Communists would be denied the moral advantage as liberators and the psychological advantage of the Red Army's presence in the very seat of government.

By mid-April the Red Army had taken Bratislava, the capital of Slovakia, but continued advance was slow due to stiff German resistance in the foothills of the Western Carpathians. By April 19 the U.S. Third Army had reached the pre-Munich Czechoslovak frontier and General George Patton was asking permission to move into Czechoslovakia. The Soviets were about 130 miles from Prague; the Americans, about 90 miles.

On April 21, Eisenhower notified the Soviet High Command in Moscow of his plans for completing the conquest of Germany and Austria. Unfortunately, he did not mention Czechoslovakia. But he added: "Information as to the development of Soviet operations and any alterations in plans or timing would be helpful."[32]

Three days later the Soviets responded. Among other things, they intended to "clean out German forces from the Eastern shore of the Elbe River . . . and the Vltava (Moldau) . . . River Valley, where according to information we have, the Germans are concentrating considerable forces."[33]

This message was apparently miscontrued in one respect by Eisenhower and his staff, who thought the Soviets meant to limit their advance to the "Eastern shore" of both the Elbe and the Vltava. But the British Chiefs of Staff, apparently recognizing the significance of the word "Valley," knew the larger meaning: "This sentence meant that the Russians would take Prague."[34]

But at this point Eisenhower had a different worry. According to rumor, the Nazis were planning to entrench themselves in a "National Redoubt" in the Bavarian and Austrian Alps. He was therefore pushing Patton's Third Army south of Czechoslovakia, toward Linz, Austria.[35]

Concerning Czechoslovakia, both Churchill and Eden were fully aware of its significance. As early as April 13 Eden had initiated a dialogue with the Americans through their London embassy, urging them to "press forward into Czechoslovakia and liberate Prague."[36] On April 18 Eden, still in Washington after Roosevelt's funeral, cabled Churchill:

I am sure that you still have Prague in mind. It might do the Russians much good if the Americans were to occupy the Czech capital, when no doubt, they would be willing to invite Soviet Ambassador to join the United States and ourselves, in contrast to the behaviour the Russians have shown us. . . . [37]

The latter referred to the Russian refusal to let Western Allied missions into Vienna and into the temporary Czechoslovak capital at Kosice.

On April 26 Churchill cabled Eden asking him to speak to Stettinius. Eden, then in San Francisco for the opening of the United Nations conference, did so by handing Stettinius a formal memorandum:

In our view the liberation of Prague and as much as possible of the territory of Western Czechoslovakia by the United States troops might make the whole difference to the post-war situation in Czechoslovakia and might well influence that in nearby countries. On the other hand, if the Western Allies play no significant part in Czechoslovakia's liberation, that country may go the way of Yugoslavia.[38]

Stettinius responded that he "entirely shared" the British views and had "sent word accordingly" to President Truman.[39] Eden added that Churchill was not sure whether Eisenhower was aware of the significance of Prague, and that the "British Chiefs of Staff have been asked to draw attention of the United States Chiefs of Staff to this matter." On April 27 the British Chiefs of Staff pressured Eisenhower to take Prague.[40] And to the U.S. Chiefs of Staff they argued the "remarkable political advantages derived from liberation of Prague and as much as possible of Czechoslovakia by U.S.–U.K. forces." They asked that Eisenhower be told to "take advantage of any improvement in your logistical situation or any weakening of enemy resistance to advance into Czechoslovakia provided such action does not hamper or delay final German defeat."[41]

To these pressures the U.S. army chief of staff, George Marshall, was indifferent. On April 28 he cabled Eisenhower for his views, adding:

Personally and aside from all logistic, tactical or strategic implications I would be loath to hazard American lives for purely political purposes. Czechoslovakia will have to be cleared of German troops and we may have to cooperate with Russians in so doing.[42]

Actually, the chances of added casualties were now minimal. Patton was experiencing little or no opposition, and once the Third Army had passed over the Sudeten Mountains, it could roll over the low terrain of Bohemia. Within a few days the German High Command, discussing surrender with the Western Allied Command at Reims, urged U.S. forces to take Prague, indicating that opposition would be "insignificant."[43] The reason was that, during Allied bombings of Germany, many high-ranking German officials had sent their families to Czechoslovakia. But now, with the Red Army's reputation preceding it, Czechoslovakia was as dangerous as Germany. Eisenhower believed that German stalling on the surrender date was intended to give those families time to escape westward.[44] For the same reason, the Germans were inviting the Americans to take Prague before the Russians did. General Walter Bedell Smith, Eisenhower's chief of staff, told the U.S. ambassador to France, Jefferson Caffery, that "it could have been a comparatively simple matter for the U.S. Third Army to have penetrated deeply into Czechoslovakia and to have taken Prague."[45]

As for the American soldiers in Patton's army, far from worrying about risking their lives, they were anxious to reach a friendly country where fraternization was permitted and a capital where the generous reception would be reminiscent of Paris. General Bradley asked Patton, "Why does everyone in the Third Army want to liberate the Czechs?"

"On to Czechoslovakia—and fraternization!" shouted Patton with a knowing grin. "How in hell do you stop an army with a battle cry like that?"[46]

To Marshall's cable of April 28, Eisenhower responded the next day. The Allied drives toward the Baltic and into Austria "are straining our resources." Later, "I have in mind the possibility of operations into western Czechoslovakia, in Denmark and in Norway." While the Western Allies would operate in Scandinavia, "the Red Army is in perfect position to clean out Czechoslovakia." He added: "The Soviet General Staff contemplate operations into the Vltava [Moldau] valley, which would result in the liberation of Prague. It seems that they could certainly reach this objective before we could."

Actually, the Americans at the Czechoslovak border were closer to Prague than the Russians, who were still encountering stiff German opposition in the mountain approaches to Brno, Moravia.

Eisenhower then outlined his plans in case "a move by us in Czechoslovakia" was desirable—a move on Pilsen, Karlsbad, and possibly Budejovice—a line restricted to western Bohemia. "I shall *not*," he concluded, "attempt any move I deem militarily unwise merely to gain a political prize unless I receive specific orders from the Combined Chiefs of Staff."[47]

To promote such orders, Churchill took his argument over Eisenhower's and Marshall's heads. Next day, April 30, he cabled President Truman with almost the exact words that Eden had used to Stettinius. "Of course," he added, "such a move by Eisenhower must not interfere with his main operations against the Germans, but I think the highly important political considerations mentioned above should be brought to his attention."[48]

Truman, who had then been president for 18 days, wrote later in his memoirs, "I turned to our military leaders for their appraisals of the situation." It appears obvious that Truman's principal adviser on this issue was Marshall. From the beginning Truman's dependence on Marshall's opinions was so great that Marshall later called it "almost frightening."

At that time Marshall's attitude toward dealing with the Soviets was one of restraint. As he had counseled in a White House meeting with Truman and other leaders on the Polish question on April 23, the United States should not bring on a break with the Soviets that could cause them to delay their entry into the war against Japan.[49] He had already urged such caution on Eisenhower when the British were pressing to capture Berlin, and on

April 28 had done so in the case of Prague. Apparently he showed Truman the response from Eisenhower, since Truman used almost the identical wording in his answer to Churchill on May 1. (Truman told Churchill he had referred Churchill's suggestion to Ike, but the Eisenhower Papers do not reflect this.) Truman concluded that Eisenhower's attitude "meets with my approval."[50]

Churchill observed later, "This seemed decisive," but in fact he had not given up. As for Truman, he later wrote that although the U.S. Department of State favored taking Prague, the Chiefs of Staff agreed with Eisenhower in not "exposing our troops to unnecessary casualties." Churchill, he added, was constantly pressing for military advantage in Europe to counter the Soviets. It would have been desirable to hold great cities such as Prague, but they "were under Russian control or about to fall under her control."[51] This is true, but in the case of Prague, even more than Berlin, the reason was that the Americans allowed it to happen. Eisenhower had, in fact, wired Moscow of his latest intentions on April 30. They include:

[M]y forces will initially hold approximately along the 1937 frontiers of Czechoslovakia. . . . Later should the situation dictate, these forces may be advanced to the towns of Karlsbad, Pilsen, Budejovice. . . . I note that the Soviet forces will be undertaking the cleaning out of the eastern shores of Elbe and Vltava (Moldau) Rivers in this sector of the front.[52]

As usual, the message was transmitted by the U.S. military mission in Moscow to General Alexey I. Antonov, chief of the Red Army General Staff. On May 4 he responded with "full agreement."

In the intervening four days, the U.S. armies had invested the so-called National Redoubt—taking Berchtesgaden, Salzburg, and Innsbruck, and approaching Linz. The fear of a Nazi holdout in the Bavarian and Austrian Alps had proven groundless. At this late date Eisenhower felt he could turn to Czechoslovakia. The Fifth Corps was added to Patton's Third Army, making it, in Patton's words, "the biggest army we have had." At 7:30 on the morning of May 4, Bradley phoned Patton and said "the green light was on for the attack on Czechoslovakia." Patton phoned the Fifth Corps commander and told him to "get going."[53]

At this time the Americans were a little more than 60 miles from Prague. The Russians were in Moravia, more than 100 miles away. That afternoon Eisenhower wired Moscow: "[W]e are about to embark on a thrust into Czechoslovakia to the general line Budweis [Budejovice], Pilsen, Karlsbad, and to seize those places." Thus far the message was simply confirming what the Soviets already knew.

Later we are prepared if the situation so dictates, to advance in Czechoslovakia to the line of the Vltava (Moldau) and Elbe Rivers to clear the west banks of the Rivers in conjunction with the Soviet move to clear the east banks.[54]

Next day General Antonov made, through the U.S. military mission in Moscow, what General John R. Deane called "a violent protest ... since Eisenhower's proposed advance might have meant that American rather than Soviet forces might liberate the Czechoslovakian capital of Prague."[55]

Antonov declared that he had previously, on April 24, stated that the Soviets would clear German forces "from the valley of the Vltava River. What was meant was that the Soviet forces will clear the enemy from both banks (East and West) of the Vltava River."

He then reminded the Americans that General Eisenhower had stated the Allied forces would advance to Karlsbad, Pilsen, and Budejovice. Pursuant to this understanding, the Soviet Command "has already established the appropriate grouping of its forces and approached the fulfillment of the stated operations. . . . "

In order to avoid a possible confusion of forces, the Soviet Commander asks General Eisenhower not to move the Allied forces in Czechoslovakia East of the originally intended line, that is, Ceski-Budejovice, Pilsen, Karlsbad.

At the same time the Soviet Command, to meet the wishes of General Eisenhower, . . . stopped the advance of its own forces to the lower Elbe East of the line Wismar, Schwerin, Domitz.

We hope that General Eisenhower in turn will comply with our wishes relative to the advance of his forces in Czechoslovakia.[56]

In Moscow, General Deane saw the "fine hand of the Soviet Foreign Office" in Antonov's message. "Czechoslovakia was to be in the orbit of the Soviet Union and Czech gratitude to America for the liberation of her capital was not part of the program."[57]

Next day, Eisenhower ordered Bradley to stop at the Pilsen line, and on May 6 wired the Soviets that he would comply. "Presume Soviet Forces can advance rapidly to clear up the situation in the centre of the country."[58]

Simultaneously, a battleground meeting was occurring between General Bradley and Marshal Konev at the latter's command post near Torgau, Germany, on May 5. Bradley showed Konev the disposition of all his divisions in Germany and Austria, using a map. Konev, showing concern as his translator spoke, and pointing to Czechoslovakia on the map, asked Bradley how far he planned to go.

"Only to Pilsen," Bradley answered, "see, it's marked here with a line. We had to go in to protect our flank on the Danube."

With a slight smile, Konev said he hoped the Americans "would go no farther." According to Konev, Bradley asked "how we planned to take Prague and whether the American troops should give us assistance in taking it."

Konev said there was "no need to give us any assistance in taking Prague . . . any advance of the American troops east of the agreed line of contact with us could lead to confusion. . . . " He asked Bradley "not to do it."[59]

Bradley, following Eisenhower's orders, agreed. On the same day he told
Patton not to go beyond Pilsen. Frustrated, Patton argued that he "could go
all the way on to Prague." Bradley later acknowledged that Patton "could
probably have been in Wenzel [Wenceslas] Square within 24 hours."[60] In his
diary the disgruntled Patton wrote:

Eisenhower does not wish at this late date to have international complications. It
seems to me that as great a nation as America should let the other people worry about
the complications. Personally, I would go to the line of the Moldau River and tell
the Russians that is where I intended to stop.[61]

Later, Patton put the matter more strongly: "I was very much chagrined,
because I felt, and still feel, that we should have gone on to the Moldau
River and, if the Russians didn't like it, let them go to hell."[62]

Nor was Patton the only objector. The U.S. State Department, having
ignored the Berlin question, came alive over Prague. Secretary of State Stettinius had already advocated to Truman that Americans take Prague. On
May 5 Acting Secretary of State Joseph Grew sent a memorandum to President Truman, reminding him of Soviet "unilateral acts" in Austria and
Czechoslovakia and recommending some "hard bargaining": "We propose
that American forces advance to the Moldau River throughout its length. If
they could do so we shall then be in a position of equality in both Austria
and Czechoslovakia in dealing with the Soviet Government."[63]

Truman still chose to leave the decision to Eisenhower; whether or not
the supreme commander was ever apprised of the State Department's view
is not in the record. In a last effort, Churchill wired Eisenhower directly on
May 7:

I am hoping that your plan does not inhibit you to advance to Prague if you have
the troops and do not meet the Russians earlier. I thought you did not mean to tie
yourself down if you had the troops and the country was empty.[64]

But while Eisenhower was ignoring British pleas to take Prague, events
were catching up in Czechoslovakia. On May 5 the people of Prague rose in
revolt against the Germans. That morning the two announcers at the Prague
radio station barricaded themselves inside and began announcing the news
in Czech only, rather than in German and Czech. When German troops
tried to break in, the announcers appealed for help.[65] The same morning a
rumor flew through the city that the Americans were only seven miles away,
triggering spontaneous street demonstrations. American, British, and some
Soviet flags fluttered from most houses.[66] Although they had planned for an
uprising two days later, the Czechs now took to arms, threw up street
barricades, seized German arsenals, and attacked German troops throughout
the city. By afternoon the German commander reported, "Prague city east

of the Moldau, except for a small bridgehead round my office, practically in the hands of the insurgents. . . . Considerable casualties as we are under fire from every house."

On the outskirts of Prague the army of General A. A. Vlasov, a turncoat Russian group that had fought alongside the Germans on the eastern front, joined the insurgents in a last-ditch bid to win mercy from the advancing Red Army. The German forces, including an SS unit, struck back; the German commander called for the Luftwaffe to bomb central Prague with incendiaries: "The whole nest must burn."[67] German planes strafed the streets of Prague.

Next day, May 6, Patton's Third Army took Pilsen amid delirious celebration. Immediately, delegations from Prague arrived to beg for help against the Germans. One U.S. officer wrote in his journal:

Between the time of our arrival in Pilsen and midnight the same day a total of 14 separate missions were received and heard from Prague. They all brought in substance the same message—urgent pleas and in many cases prayers that we come on to Prague and liberate them.

But the Americans replied, "[W]e were taking orders from our own higher headquarters, and could not go beyond our present positions without appropriate instructions."[68]

At Patton's headquarters, the Americans were beside themselves. Wrote the Third Army officer quoted earlier, "Not only were we ready, but hundreds of men in the command wanted and pleaded to go on to Prague, and could not understand why we did not go on." Patton himself contacted Bradley and asked permission to take Prague: "In view of the radio report about the Patriots having taken Prague, it seems desirable to me to push on and help them."[69]

But again Bradley, acting on orders, refused. Later, at a press conference in Regensburg on May 8, a reporter asked, "Would you explain why we didn't go into Prague?" Patton's reply: "I can tell you exactly—we were told not to."[70]

In Prague the revolt continued. The Czech National Council broadcast an emotional appeal: "Brothers in the Red Army, American and English friends, we are sure that tomorrow your fighter planes will protect the skies over Prague. Tank troops, set out for Prague!"[71]

In London the remaining Czechoslovak government representative, Hubert Ripka, pleaded with British and U.S. officials for help to the Prague insurgents. On May 7 the BBC announced in its Czech-language broadcasts that Czechoslovak airmen in the Royal Air Force were preparing to bomb German targets in Prague. Ripka later wrote: "The crews were already aboard their planes when the operation was abruptly forbidden by the Inter-Allied Command."[72]

For Eduard Beneš, by this time headquartered in Bratislava, the moment was frenetic. When his secretary rushed into his study with the news that Patton had entered Czechoslovakia, the usually stoic Beneš cried out, "Thank God, thank God!" He bolted into the next room, shouting to his wife: "Hanicko, Hanicko, the Americans have entered Czechoslovakia. . . . Patton is across the border!" But he was quickly plunged into despair when the Americans failed to advance beyond Pilsen.[73]

However, the Americans did apparently make one contribution. A high-ranking German officer was escorted by four U.S. tanks and a heavily armed guard from Pilsen to Prague. There he notified the German commander that all German forces had surrendered to the Western Allies. The Germans in Prague then surrendered on May 8 to the Czech National Council.

Meanwhile, the roads from Prague westward were jammed with refugees; between 175,000 and 250,000 went through Pilsen between May 7 and May 9. "Most were Czechs trying to get away from the attentions of approaching Russian liberators," wrote the U.S. officer in charge of the roadblock east of Pilsen.[74]

The Soviets, of course, heard about the Prague uprising. According to Marshal Zhukov, the Supreme Commander ordered the Red Army "to speed up the movement of our forces toward Prague in order to help the insurgents and prevent the Hitlerites from crushing the uprising."[75] Konev states that when his troops marched into Prague early on the morning of May 9, they encountered some German resistance in certain quarters, but this is not substantiated by Czechoslovak sources. A Red Army commander later recalled, "The only resistance we met in Prague was that of separate SS units, which were quickly wiped out or taken prisoner."[76] Konev described the jubilation as his advance officer team entered the city:

Any officer who appeared was instantly taken "prisoner", embraced, kissed and tossed in the air. One by one my liaison officers were encircled and smothered with flowers, kisses and refreshments. . . . And I must frankly admit that this unprecedented expression of popular sentiment on Victory Day adversely affected all the officers in the performance of their immediate official duties.[77]

Even after these events, German units continued to fight the Soviets in Bohemia, Austria, and Germany's Southern Silesia. The envoy from the German High Command caught up with the area commander, Field Marshal Ferdinand Schoerner, in northern Bohemia, near the Silesian border. He agreed to go to the area between Pilsen and Prague and see to it that his commanders submitted. But he warned that "virtually no order would make his troops leave their comrades behind or voluntarily surrender to the Red forces." Schoerner was captured by the Americans on May 18 and turned over to the Soviets.[78] So ended the last campaign in Europe in World War II.

Was the U.S. decision not to take Prague justified? The U.S. leaders—

⇨ Eisenhower's declared objective, "along the axis of Erfurt, Leipzig and Dresden," in his message to Stalin, March 28, 1945.

━ Approximate Western and Eastern Front in mid-April, when Eisenhower halted his forces that had reached the Elbe River (west and southwest of Berlin), and Stalin launched the Red Army toward Berlin.

•━•━ Approximate north and south ends of Western Front when war war ended, May 7. The British had reached the Baltic Sea at Lübeck, cutting off any possible Soviet attempt to occupy the Danish Peninsula. Americans had entered Czechoslovakia as far as Pilsen, where Eisenhower halted them.

•••••• Approximate Eastern Front at end of war, May 7 (includes Yugoslav Partisan advance in south).

▦ Area held by German forces when war ended, May 7. Soviets dashed for Prague from the East and entered city May 9.

The Soviets Capture Berlin and Prague

Truman, Marshall, and Eisenhower—clearly thought so at the time, though Marshall later (in a 1957 interview with his biographer) said he was "not certain that the Western Allies should have made" that decision.[79] All three leaders were trying to avoid serious difficulty with the Soviets, chiefly because of Marshall's desire to get them into the Far East war as soon as possible.

As matters turned out, the Soviets did enter that war—almost exactly three months after the end of the European war, as Stalin had promised at Yalta in return for territorial gains in the Pacific. In retrospect it seems clear that, since the two atom bombings of the Japanese homeland would in themselves have brought a prompt Japanese surrender, the Soviets were simply hurrying to get into the war before they were left out completely. Both of the top U.S. observers of the Soviets in Moscow—Ambassador Averell Harriman and General John R. Deane, head of the U.S. military mission—spoke out against appeasing Stalin to assure Soviet entry into the Pacific war. It is more likely that nothing could have kept them out of that war—as soon as they could move their military strength across Siberia. In this respect and at that time, Marshall misjudged the Soviets, believing they were best influenced by one-way efforts to cooperate.

Certainly when Antonov reminded Eisenhower that the Red Army had stopped at the Elbe, per agreement, Eisenhower could have cited many instances of flagrant Soviet noncooperation—refusal to let Allied planes land near Warsaw or Vienna, recognition of a Polish and an Austrian government without consulting the Allies, refusal to let Allied diplomats into Austria and Czechoslovakia long after Soviet diplomats were there.

Equally damaging was the lack of understanding by U.S. leaders of the Czechoslovak situation—its strategic importance, and the intentions of the Soviets. The British leadership and the U.S. Department of State understood full well what the Soviets had in mind for Czechoslovakia, as for all Eastern Europe, but their pleas were ignored by men who seem, at that time and from this distance, amazingly naive. Both Marshall and Eisenhower seemed to abhor the idea of making a political decision, though at their level of leadership they were continually making political decisions.

If they were leaning over backward to avoid political leadership—certainly a proper stance for military men in a democracy—Truman was under no such restraint. And he not only rejected the best political advice coming his way but also seemed to have no understanding of the geography of Czechoslovakia or of the military situation there at the moment.

In fact, both Marshall and Truman mistakenly thought the Soviets were closer to Prague than the Americans were. Both Marshall and Truman expressed fears of unnecessary casualties when these were not really a factor.

Eisenhower, whose mission was to defeat the Germans as soon as possible, stuck to this single purpose too literally at a time when the Germans were already defeated. Certainly Eisenhower and Marshall had done a magnificent job in securing victory; certainly events and decisions were crowding in too fast at the end of the war for ordinary mortals to be omniscient in all things, at all times. Yet they were outmaneuvered by other ordinary mortals in Moscow.

Since the decisions on Prague had been left to Eisenhower, at what point did he go wrong? Probably in not suggesting that U.S. forces might go all the way to Prague in his April 21 exchange of messages with General Antonov on strategic plans. Even if he was not sure at that time that he could get there first, he had little to lose by keeping that option open. But once Antonov, in his reply, had staked the Russian claim to the Vltava Valley, Eisenhower was on weak ground—and all the more so after he had cited the Karlsbad-Pilsen-Budejovice line in his next message.

At the same time no one—not the British, the U.S. Department of State, or even Patton—faced another key fact: Moving up to the Vltava was not the same thing as taking Prague. The Vltava runs through Prague, and although Hradcany Castle (equivalent to the capitol building) is on the west bank, the center of the city and most of the population were on the east bank. The Third Army, which could have arrived by May 7, also could have marched over the bridges and taken both banks, but no American on either side of the issue ever talked about crossing the Vltava. It could have been done—probably without a drastic rift with the Soviets—but only if Eisenhower had been the first to stake out Prague as a military objective.

In any case, the error was made, and the result was a disaster for Western influence in Czechoslovakia. The Czechs themselves, who claim to have lost some 2,000 people in the Prague fighting between May 5 and 8, were dumbfounded at this U.S. abdication. Like the failure to give more than token help to the Slovak uprising in 1944, it was added evidence that the West had abandoned Czechoslovakia to the Soviets. Some called it a second Munich. As for the Soviets and the Communists, they promptly took credit for liberating Prague. Some even claimed that the Americans held back because they wanted the uprising to fail.

If the Americans had taken Prague, three benefits would have followed. First, in the capital city and most of Bohemia, the Communists would not have had the initial Red Army support that gave them such a head start against the other political parties. Second, with the U.S. presence covering a significant part of the country, rather than the mere toehold represented by the Pilsen occupation line, international visibility of the entire country would have been elevated and Soviet-led excesses would have been more exposed. Third, the psychological orientation of Bohemia would, through the confidence regained by a U.S. liberation, have been toward the West. But with Soviet seizure of Prague, Czechoslovakia's fate was sealed and the partition of Europe was complete. The West's options for preventing it had run out.

14

"Let the Sparrows Twitter!"

Within days of the Yalta agreements, the Big Three alliance began to crack. The war was nearly won, the Soviet Union was at the peak of power, and there was no longer much reason for Stalin to consider his allies' feelings. Instead, the wages of appeasement were about to be paid, as they had been in the summer of 1939. Openly and unilaterally, Stalin would now take what he wanted in defiance of Roosevelt and Churchill. He moved quickest in the Balkans, where his percent agreement with Churchill was good only until the war's end.

In Romania, where a coalition government ruled, the Soviet-supported Communist Party acted swiftly. On February 24 the National Democratic Front, an alliance of leftist parties led by the Communists, staged a large demonstration in Bucharest against the coalition government of General Nicolae Radescu. At one point the government guards fired machine guns over the heads of the crowd, giving the Communists an excuse to cry "massacre." The Communist press whipped up a vitriolic storm against Radescu.

On February 27 Andrei Vishinsky, Soviet vice commissar for foreign affairs, arrived in Bucharest. The opposite of Molotov in everything but doctrine, Vishinsky had a winning personality and a witty but often biting tongue. His handicaps in the Soviet hierarchy were that he was more Polish than Russian, and in the Revolution had been a Menshevik, though he later fought on the Bolshevik side against the Whites in the civil wars. A brilliant lawyer, he won Stalin's esteem as the prosecutor in the purge trials of 1936–1938. He could be as devious as Molotov but enjoyed a party and spoke his mind freely—sometimes too freely. Walter Bedell Smith wrote that while Vishinsky could, if he desired, "exercise a great deal of personal charm," his "outstanding characteristic is a brusque truculence."[1]

On the night of his arrival in Bucharest, Vishinsky met with King Michael and demanded that he dismiss Radescu, since he could not maintain order in the rear of the Red Army fighting the Germans in Hungary. The U.S. representative on the Allied Control Commission in Romania tried in vain to see Vishinsky next day, and sent him a note warning, "[W]e would particularly deplore the use or display of force or any political chicanery to bring any group into power."[2]

Vishinsky needed no chicanery, but the threat of force was implicit in the Red Army's occupation of Romania. On February 20 the Soviets had ordered a reduction in the Romanian police force in Bucharest, and stepped up the presence of their own soldiers and tanks.

At a meeting with King Michael at 3:30 P.M. on February 28, Vishinsky demanded his answer. The king replied that he was consulting with party leaders to pick a new prime minister. Vishinsky retorted that this was unsatisfactory. He got up, glancing at his watch.

"You have just two hours and five minutes to make it known to the public that General Radescu has been dismissed," he snapped. "By 8 o'clock you must inform the public of the name of his successor."[3]

The Romanian foreign minister, who was present, protested that the king could, under the constitution, choose a prime minister only on advice of party leaders. Vishinsky told the foreign minister not to interrupt. In a moment he stormed out of the king's study, slamming the door so hard it cracked the plaster around the frame.

Since the king's first choice was unsatisfactory to the Soviets, Vishinsky named another—Petru Groza, leader of a party in the National Democratic Front. Groza was duly appointed prime minister by the king, who then rejected Groza's proposed cabinet because it heavily favored pro-Communist elements. Vishinsky told King Michael that unless the Groza government was installed, he "could not be responsible for the continuance of Rumania as an independent state. . . ."[4]

Reinforcing Vishinsky was the arrival in Bucharest at this juncture of Soviet Marshal Rodion Malinovsky. The king considered abdicating, but after consulting with party leaders decided that he might still be able to "do something" for his people if he stayed on and "ate some humble pie." Accordingly, Groza's Communist-dominated cabinet was announced and sworn in on March 6.

Both before and after Vishinsky's arrival the U.S. and the British delegates to the Allied Control Commission for Romania had asked that the Soviet chairman consult with them, as required by the armistice agreement. The issue escalated to a verbal dual in Moscow between Molotov and Harriman. The British found the issue delicate because of their "percent agreement" and Stalin's fulfillment of his part of the bargain by keeping out of events in Greece.[5] The United States punctiliously refrained from asserting its views on a Romanian premier or cabinet.

"I could not," the U.S. representative told King Michael, "suggest any personality that would be interpreted as putting our finger into the Rumanian political broth."

"Why should you hesitate to put your finger in the broth," demanded the king, "when you know that your ally has put his hand down my throat?"[6]

The shock waves were quick to reverberate in London and Washington. On March 8 Churchill cabled Roosevelt:

The Russians have succeeded in establishing the rule of a Communist minority by force and misrepresentation. We have been hampered in our protests against these developments by the fact that, in order to have the freedom to save Greece, Eden and I at Moscow in October recognized that Russia should have a largely preponderant voice in Roumania and Bulgaria while we took the lead in Greece. Stalin adhered very strictly to this understanding. . . .

Thus, continued Churchill, it was awkward for Britain to object in Romania, and anyway, Poland was the more important ground on which to make a stand. But since there was fear of "an indiscriminate purge of Anti-Communist Roumanians," someone should ask Stalin to prevent this; "if you will show me the text of any message you feel inclined to send Stalin, I will also send one to him supporting it."[7]

But Churchill's clever effort to shift the Romanian burden to the Americans, who were not parties to the "percent agreement," was unavailing.

"I am fully determined, as I know you are," Roosevelt replied on March 11, "not to let the good decisions we reached at the Crimea slip through our hands and will certainly do everything I can to hold Stalin to their honest fulfillment."[8]

But he was letting Harriman do the talking in Moscow, and in any event, "Rumania is not a good place for a test case." Thus Western Allied action went by default. The British at least afforded Prime Minister Radescu the safety of their embassy, and the military mission there was ordered to "open fire, if necessary, to guard the fugitive." Such sanctuary was something the Americans both in Bucharest and in Washington hesitated to provide for any possible additional refugees, including the king and the queen mother.[9]

For days Harriman and Molotov jousted over Romania—Harriman pointing out that according to the Declaration on Liberated Europe, the Big Three should consult together on Romania, and Molotov responding that the Soviets interpreted the declaration otherwise. The declaration clearly called for tripartite action in the kind of circumstances prevailing in Romania; even Roosevelt, in a larger message to Stalin on the Polish issue on April 1, referred to Romania and the Declaration on Liberated Europe: "I frankly cannot understand why the recent developments in Rumania should be regarded as not falling within the terms of that agreement."[10]

In the end nothing came of the efforts by Harriman or by Roosevelt, who died 11 days after his message. Harriman thought there was little to be gained except to register protest, since the Romanian coup was probably part of Soviet "long range plans established some time ago for the Balkan and eastern European states."[11] Red Army possession had given Stalin ten points of the law.

At the first dinner of the Yalta conference on February 4, 1945, Stalin and Churchill had discussed the responsibility of the big powers, not the little ones, for maintaining the peace. But Churchill argued that the little powers should at least be allowed a voice. "The eagle suffers little birds to sing," Churchill expounded, "and is not careful what they mean thereby."[12]

At the same dinner was Vishinsky, who evidently had heard Churchill's aphorism. After the Romanian crisis a reporter asked him about the protests of Britain and the United States. His reply revealed the new Soviet attitude: "Let the sparrows twitter."

The sudden hardening of the Soviets after Yalta was evident wherever the Red Army held power. In Poland the Soviets were arresting thousands of underground officers and suspected sympathizers; many were, according to a London Polish government report, "starved, beaten and tortured. . . . There are many deaths."

In Bulgaria the coalition government, or Fatherland Front, became a tool of the Communists when they ousted the genuine leaders of the dominant Agrarian Party and installed their own supporters. There followed thousands of arrests and executions of their opponents—a reign of terror.

In Hungary the Soviets moved more slowly—the first stage of a true coalition government was prolonged, though the Soviets openly looted the country of industrial machinery and interfered repeatedly in the Hungarian government.

In all three former enemy countries—Bulgaria, Romania, and Hungary—the three-power military Allied Control Commissions established to assure order and democratic institutions were chaired by Soviets who acted unilaterally without consulting or, in most cases, even informing the British and U.S. officers. The latter were physically restricted in their movements, and the civil governments were instructed by the Soviets not to talk directly to the British and Americans.

In Hungary the chairman of the Allied Control Commission (ACC) was Marshal Kliment Y. Voroshilov, assistant chairman of the Soviet Council of People's Commissars and a close friend of Stalin from early Bolshevik days. Western observers regarded him as less than brilliant, but he was determined to assert Soviet power in Hungary. He told a Hungarian bishop, "The Western populations, Western democracies, having nothing to do with territories occupied by the Red Army." The bishop objected to a particular course of action on the ground that "the Yalta agreement wouldn't permit that."

"In Hungary," growled Voroshilov, "I am Yalta."[13]

Protests against such tactics by U.S. and British representatives, both to the Soviet ACC chairmen and to their own superiors in London and Washington, were fruitless. The British were paralyzed by the "percent agreement" and could only encourage the Americans to lead any initiative. The American representatives in turn were under orders to get along with the Soviets. On May 19 the U.S. ACC representative in Hungary, General William S. Key, wrote to his superior in Washington:

I have endeavored to maintain cordial personal relations with Marshal Voroshilov and his principal assistants. . . . I have entertained them and they me and our social relations have been increasingly amiable, but that's as far as it goes. . . . I am sure you can appreciate the tremendous demands on one's patience to continue outwardly friendly and cheerful while inwardly boiling with chagrin and frustration. . . . My natural impulse is to adopt a belligerent attitude and tell them where to get off in true Western style and tradition, but the war is over and I do not want to be responsible for starting another one.[14]

Since Key's protests were rejected or ignored, the U.S. diplomatic representative in Budapest took up his cause with Washington, pleading for a true functioning of the ACC on a three-power basis. By that time Stettinius had been succeeded as secretary of state by former Supreme Court Justice James F. Byrnes. He replied that Key should try not to discuss the question of three-power rights: "If the matter should be brought up by chance he should indicate that he is without instructions in the matter and that it is one to be settled at Government level."[15]

The change of Soviet policy had come even more swiftly in Yugoslavia. There the British had acted to assert their 50–50 agreement made with Stalin in Moscow. Dr. Ivan Subasić, premier in King Peter's government-in-exile, was put forward to join Tito's regime in a coalition government. But from the birth of the new regime in March 1945, Tito was in complete control, and Subasić resigned as foreign minister a few months later. Tito suppressed free speech, staged a one-slate election of the Soviet type, and made mass arrests of political opponents, including General Draža Mihailović.

At all of these East European debacles, Churchill and Eden were outraged. "My God," exclaimed Eden to a colleague as early as March 1, "what a mess Europe is in! What a mess!"[16]

From the first the British and U.S. diplomats—from Moscow to London and Washington—were stunned at the turnabout in Soviet attitudes and speculated over the cause. Were hard-line members of the Politburo pressing Stalin? Were the Red Army marshals, flushed with near-victory, asserting their power in the Kremlin? Was Stalin jealous of the spectacular Western advance in Germany and suspicious of German complicity?

Developments in neutral Switzerland seemed to trigger this latter reaction and support this explanation. In February 1945 German military representatives began talks with the U.S. Office of Strategic Services organization in Bern. The subject: surrender of the German forces under Field Marshal Albert von Kesselring in Italy. Relatively isolated from Germany, this command could surrender without interference from Berlin.

By March 9 the Germans were ready to discuss surrender with Field-Marshal Alexander, commander of Allied forces in Italy. At the request of the Combined Chiefs of Staff, the Soviet government was informed before any of Alexander's representatives were sent to Bern. In agreeing, Molotov said his government "would like to have officers representing the Soviet Military Command take part in these conversations."[17] But in Moscow, Harriman—supported by General Deane of the U.S. military mission—opposed Soviet participation in a strictly military surrender in a single theater. The Soviets were told that following the initial arrangements in Bern, the surrender talks would take place at Alexander's headquarters at Caserta, Italy, where the Soviets would be present but negotiations and decisionmaking would be done by Alexander.

Molotov's answer on March 16 was explosive: The U.S. refusal to allow Soviet participation was "utterly unexpected and incomprehensible." The Soviet government withdrew its agreement and "insists that the negotiations already begun in Bern be broken off." Further, the Soviet government "insists that also from now on" any separate negotiations without all three powers participating "be ruled out."

To this blast of cold Russian air, the Americans and British explained again and went ahead with their plans. Molotov's second answer on March 22: The British and Americans had been negotiating with the Germans for two weeks in Bern "behind the back of the Soviet Government which has been carrying on the main burden of the war. . . . " This was "absolutely inadmissible."

Three days later the U.S. response came from Roosevelt to Stalin, supporting the budding negotiations: "I cannot agree to suspend investigation of the possibility because of objection on the part of Mr. Molotov for some reason that is completely beyond my understanding."

Stalin's reply on March 29, much less prickly than Molotov's, emphasized that the Soviets were worried about the possibility of German troops in Italy being allowed to transfer to the eastern front; already three German divisions had been shifted to that front during the negotiations; at Yalta the Big Three had agreed to deliver coordinated blows on all three fronts. "This is being violated by Field-Marshal Alexander." Stalin closed with an admonition: "[T]he Allies should have no secrets from each other."

Considering that the first Allied message to Moscow specified negotiations in Switzerland, not Italy, the suspicion of the suspicion-prone Soviets is understandable. Even Stalin's emphasis on a coordinated three-front war can be justified. One must conclude that the initial exchanges between the Allies and the Germans, and between the Allies and the Soviets, were crudely handled. However, this was only the first misstep. The quarrel now proceeded to a dangerous escalation.

Roosevelt's answer of March 31 was mild enough, but he did dispute Stalin's facts about the transfer of three divisions—only two went to the Russian front, and the last of these had left two weeks before the surrender possibilities arose. Roosevelt stated categorically, "No negotiations for surrender have been entered into. . . . "

Stalin's answer of April 3 boosted the stakes far beyond the Italian theater. The Soviets were aware that

the negotiations have taken place and they have ended in an agreement with the Germans, on the basis of which the German commander on the Western front, Marshal Kesselring [who had been transferred there from Italy], has agreed to open the front and permit the Anglo-American troops to advance to the East, and the Anglo-Americans have promised in return to ease for the Germans the peace terms.

By this means "the Anglo-American troops get the possibility to advance into the heart of Germany almost without any resistance. . . . ":

As a result of this at the present moment the Germans on the Western front in fact have ceased the war against England and the United States. At the same time the Germans continue the war with Russia, the Ally of England and the United States.

Stalin was accusing the Western Allies of making a separate peace, and of welshing on their "unconditional surrender" agreement.

Obviously stung, Roosevelt answered next day that the Allied advance into Germany was due not to any agreement but to military action; "it is astonishing that a belief seems to have reached the Soviet Government that I have entered into an agreement with the enemy without first obtaining your full agreement." And he closed thus: "Frankly I cannot avoid a feeling of bitter resentment toward your informers, whoever they are, for such vile misrepresentations of my actions or those of my trusted subordinates."

An equally irate message was sent from Churchill to Stalin on April 6. Next day Stalin answered both Roosevelt and Churchill. To Roosevelt: "I never doubted your honesty and dependability, as well as the honesty and dependability of Mr. Churchill." To the prime minister: "I can assure you that I had and have no intention of offending anyone." To both of them he called the issue a difference of opinion. It was, as Churchill wrote to FDR, "as near as they can get to an apology." On the morning of his death on April 12, Roosevelt answered Stalin that the Bern incident "now appears to have faded into the past without having accomplished any useful purpose."

On May 2, 1945, the German forces in Italy surrendered to Alexander. It was seven weeks after the Bern incident had begun and six days before Germany surrendered to all Allied forces.

Did the Soviets blow the Bern incident out of proportion? The sensitivity of a nation just emerging from worldwide disdain, the deeply suspicious nature of the Soviets, and their headlong assertion of newfound power—all combined to escalate the Bern incident.

That it triggered the hardening of Soviet policy is hardly credible. The change in Soviet tactics came earlier; for example, the Romanian coup preceded it by two weeks. The Bern incident did, however, give some justification in the Soviets' mind for the roughshod tactics now employed. And there is ample room to believe that Stalin and Molotov used it for just this purpose.

Even more blatant than Soviet behavior in Southeast Europe was that in the most critical arena—Poland. Here in these flat expanses was the historic avenue of conquest—eastward and westward. Here the British, certainly, had spent most of their effort in resisting Soviet political pressure. Here they were most determined to make a stand. Churchill told his secretary at the end of February: "I have not the slightest intention . . . of being cheated over Poland, not even if we go to the verge of war with Russia."[18]

The test came with the first meeting in Moscow of the Tripartite Commission—Molotov, Harriman, and Clark Kerr—charged at Yalta with agreeing on a new government for Poland. The wording of the assignment had itself been fought over at Yalta and embodied what the British, at least, thought was a dubious compromise—the Warsaw provisional government set up by Stalin was to be "reorganized on a broader democratic basis with the inclusion of democratic leaders from Poland itself and from those living abroad." Who would be president or premier, what proportion of cabinet posts would go to democratic leaders, who would get the key ministries of Interior and Defense—these questions were left entirely open.

At the first meeting of the Tripartite Commission, Molotov took the same position that he and Stalin had taken at Yalta—that the provisional government would simply be enlarged. It soon became clear that Molotov intended to obstruct the West at every turn. He insisted that the Tripartite Commission should meet with the Warsaw government representatives before meeting with any other Polish leaders. He insisted further that the names of other Poles who would come to Moscow to discuss a government should be subject to veto by both the Soviets and the Warsaw government. These ideas were absent from the Yalta agreement, but British and U.S. protests were unavailing.

Meanwhile, on the excuse that Poland was the supply route for the battle zone in Germany, all Allied personnel were banned from the country. It was clear that the Soviets were trying to give the Warsaw regime all possible help, unseen by foreign eyes, in consolidating its grip on Poland. Through clandestine radio transmitters and underground couriers the London Polish government was getting the only word out of Poland—reports of mass arrests, executions, and deportations to the Soviet Union of those who opposed the

Communists. Churchill wired Roosevelt on March 10, "It suits the Soviets very well to have a long period of delay so that the process of liquidation of elements unfavourable to them or their puppets may run its full course."[19]

Seeing his fears about the Yalta compromise now confirmed, Churchill proposed to Roosevelt that the two of them intervene directly with Stalin. But Roosevelt wanted to wait "until every other possibility of bringing the Soviet Government into line has been exhausted."[20]

Other moves were also afoot. Moscow had demanded that representatives of the Warsaw provisional government be seated at the first United Nations conference in San Francisco. The Western Allies opposed this. Knowing the importance of the United Nations to Roosevelt, Stalin refused to let Molotov attend—a clear threat that the Soviet Union might not participate in the world organization. The distraught Churchill, fearing that every day meant a more entrenched puppet government in Poland, pleaded with Roosevelt for direct intervention. "Poland has lost her frontier," he cabled FDR on March 13. "Is she now to lose her freedom?"[21]

By March 27 Churchill had become "extremely concerned at the deterioration of the Russian attitude since Yalta." Surely, he exclaimed, "we must not be manoeuvered into becoming parties to imposing on Poland, and on how much more of Eastern Europe, the Russian version of democracy?" Finally, knowing Roosevelt's hopes for the United Nations, Churchill concluded, "[I]f the success of San Francisco is not to be gravely imperiled, we must both of us now make the strongest possible appeal to Stalin about Poland. . . . "[22]

Roosevelt agreed, and on April 1 he and Churchill sent lengthy cables to Stalin, calling for a solution along the lines of the Yalta agreement. Both were moderate; the stronger statement was by Roosevelt: "I do not fully understand in many respects the apparent indifferent attitude of your Government."[23]

It was soon apparent that Stalin was unmoved. At another Tripartite Commission meeting two days later, Molotov was, if anything, more difficult. Harriman reported to Washington that "we are at a breaking point." In fact, the strain was affecting his health. Visiting him in this period, C. L. Sulzberger noticed, "He looked poorly and had a tic in his right eye, a sort of wink."[24] On April 7 Stalin replied to Roosevelt and Churchill: "Matters on the Polish question have really reached a dead end." But if Britain and the United States would accept all the Russian points, then "a harmonious decision on the Polish question can be reached in a short time."[25]

Roosevelt died before he and Churchill could agree on a response. In his last days he was clearly disturbed by the truculent Soviet posture since Yalta, and some of his associates have emphasized this as a change of policy. To one friend he is said to have confided on March 23, "We can't do business with Stalin. He has broken every one of the promises he made at Yalta."[26] Yet it took six more days of fruitless negotiations after this statement, as well as Churchill's eloquent pleas, to persuade Roosevelt to throw the presidential weight into the Polish issue.

It seems clearer that, to the very end, Roosevelt believed—and wanted the world to believe—that the differences with Stalin could be resolved. In his final message to Stalin on April 12 concerning the Bern incident, he referred to "minor misunderstandings of this character." When Harriman had suggested that it was not minor and that he might want to delete the word, Roosevelt insisted on leaving it in, "as it is my desire to consider the Berne misunderstanding a minor incident."[27] When Churchill asked Roosevelt his views before making a statement on the Polish deadlock in the House of Commons, Roosevelt answered—also on his last day, April 12: "I would minimize the general Soviet problem as much as possible because these problems, in one form or another, seem to arise every day and most of them straighten out as in the case of the Bern meeting."[28]

Certainly Roosevelt was disturbed as Stalin discarded any pretense of cooperation after Yalta. But he did not change his own policy of attempting to cooperate with Stalin. There is no evidence that he realized Europe had been partitioned, or that a cold war had opened between East and West.

When Harriman notified the Soviet leaders of Roosevelt's death, both Molotov and Stalin expressed genuine sorrow, and as a gesture Molotov was released to attend the San Francisco conference. Through the four years of wartime alliance, Roosevelt had been their friend. They had achieved practically all their political goals with little resistance from him, his secretaries of state, or his military leaders. Resistance had come from the British, from some governments-in-exile and their underground fighters, from U.S. foreign service officers in the field, and from numerous second-level U.S. generals, but these elements did not set U.S. policy.

One high-level figure who early took the measure of the Soviets and tried to harden U.S. policy was Ambassador Averell Harriman; he had Roosevelt's confidence and his ear. But Roosevelt had other advisers who were closer at hand in Washington—among them Harry Hopkins, who was known by his White House colleagues as "pro-Russian." Yet while such influence tended to neutralize Harriman's, in the end the decisions and the policy were made by Roosevelt, the optimist, the idealist, by comparison with the British the amateur diplomat, whose foreign policy was shaped too much by domestic politics, who conducted international negotiations not from power but from personality. He thought Stalin was "getable," but in the end it was Roosevelt who was getable.

Through it all Stalin had played a superb hand. Dealing always from strength, he kept an appearance of reasonableness to hold Roosevelt's cordiality, gaining all that he wanted until there was no more to gain. He had fulfilled Eden's estimate: "[I]f I had to pick a team for going into a conference room, Stalin would be my first choice."[29]

Now Roosevelt was gone. If Harry Truman was an unknown quantity to the Soviets, he would not remain unknown for long. The day after Roosevelt died, the new president cabled Churchill, proposing "another go" with Stalin on the Polish question. Accordingly the Western leaders sent another message to Moscow—without success. More messages and more discussions between Churchill and Stalin, and among Molotov, Stettinius, and Eden. On April 29 Churchill cabled Stalin, deploring a future in which countries dominated by the Soviets would confront the Western nations: "It is quite obvious that their quarrel would tear the world to pieces and that all of us leading men on either side who had anything to do with that would be shamed before history."

Stalin's answer on May 5: The Western position on Poland "excludes the possibility of an agreed solution of the Polish question."[30]

Thoroughly alarmed, Churchill now pinned his hopes on a new Big Three meeting before the Americans could withdraw their troops from their positions in Germany and Austria. If the issues were not settled before "the Western World folds up its war machine," he wrote to Eden, "there are no prospects of a satisfactory solution and very little of preventing a third World War."[31]

Meanwhile, in his first days at the White House, Truman briefed himself on Roosevelt's correspondence with Stalin and Harriman. The latter, returning to Washington, personally briefed Truman on April 20. The Soviets were determined to extend their rule through Eastern Europe and, if possible, beyond. It was, warned Harriman, "a new barbarian invasion of Europe."

On April 22 and 23 Truman met with Molotov. Before the second encounter he assembled his top advisers in the Oval Office. He opened the discussion by declaring that U.S. "agreements with the Soviet Union so far had been a one-way street and that could not continue; it was now or never." He would go ahead with the United Nations conference in San Francisco, and if the Soviets did not wish to join "they could go to hell." Then he asked the advice of each on the Polish issue. The advice was split.[32]

Henry L. Stimson, secretary of war: "[W]e ought to be very careful and see whether we couldn't get ironed out on the situation without getting into a head-on collision."

James Forrestal, secretary of the navy: "[T]his was not an isolated incident but was one of a pattern of unilateral action on the part of Russia. . . . we might as well meet the issue now as later on."

Averell Harriman, ambassador to Moscow: "[T]he real issue was whether the United States was to be a party to the Soviet program for dominating Poland."

Admiral William D. Leahy, chief of staff to the President: "[T]he Yalta agreement was subject to two interpretations. . . . it was a serious matter to break with the Russians but . . . we should tell them that we stood for a free and independent Poland."

Secretary of State Edward Stettinius read aloud the pertinent wording in the Yalta
declaration: "[T]his was susceptible to only one interpretation."

General George C. Marshall, army chief of staff: The military "hoped for Soviet
participation in the war against Japan at a time when it would be useful to us.
The Russians had it within their power to delay their entry into the Far Eastern
war until we had done all the dirty work. . . . difficulties with the Russians . . .
usually straighten out." He agreed with Stimson that the "possibility of a break
with Russia was very serious."

General John R. Deane, head of the U.S. military mission in Moscow: "[T]he Soviet
Union would enter the Pacific war as soon as it was able irrespective of what
happened in other fields." He was convinced from his Moscow experiences that
"if we were afraid of the Russians we would get nowhere and . . . we should be
firm when we were right."

Despite this mixed advice, Truman was confirmed in his tough approach
to the Soviets. Molotov came to the Oval Office with Andrei Gromyko,
Soviet ambassador to the United States, and interpreter V. N. Pavlov. Also
present were several of Truman's top advisers. Shunning protocol, Truman
went immediately to the Polish question.[33]

"The United States Government," he declared, "could not agree to be a
party to the formation of a Polish Government which was not representative
of all Polish democratic elements." And in a somewhat crude reference to
"economic collaboration," he pointed out that he "could not hope to get these
measures through Congress unless there was public support for them."

Molotov's answer seemed to imply that Britain and the United States "had
attempted to impose their will" on the Soviet Union. In the exchange that
followed, Truman kept repeating his main point.

First: "[A]ll we were asking was that the Soviet Government carry out the
Crimea decisions on Poland."

And again: "[A]n agreement had been reached on Poland and . . . it only
remained for Marshal Stalin to carry it out according to his word."

Still again: "[A]n agreement had been reached on Poland and . . . it only
required carrying out by the Soviet Government."

And finally: The United States was ready to carry out all the Crimea
agreements and "only asked that the Soviet Government do the
same."

Each of these repetitions was delivered with rising force. Molotov was
now experiencing his own tactics thrown back in his face. As Charles Bohlen
described it, he "turned a little ashy. . . ."

"I have never been talked to like that in my life," Molotov protested.

"Carry out your agreements," barked Truman, "and you won't get talked
to like that."

When Molotov tried to change the subject Truman interrupted, "That
will be all, Mr. Molotov. I would appreciate it if you would transmit my
views to Marshal Stalin."

Molotov and his party retreated. Bohlen commented, "They were probably the first sharp words uttered during the war by an American President to a high Soviet official."

Molotov went on to San Francisco, where he still tried to get the General Assembly to seat the representative of the puppet Warsaw regime. There he approached Jan Masaryk, foreign minister of Czechoslovakia. A year earlier Masaryk's government had dutifully recognized the Lublin Committee as Poland's government as soon as the Soviet Union had done so. Now Molotov's note to Masaryk declared, "Czechoslovakia must vote for the Soviet proposition in regard to Poland, or else forfeit the friendship of the Soviet government." Czechoslovakia voted with the Soviets, and Masaryk told Bohlen, "You can be on your knees and this is not enough for the Russians."[34] Despite Molotov's campaigning, his motion lost and no Polish delegation was seated.

By this time a still more serious Polish issue had surfaced. About five weeks earlier, 16 Polish underground leaders had been invited to meet with Marshal Zhukov to discuss the new government of Poland. They had not been heard from since. On April 6 the London government-in-exile announced their disappearance, but the Soviets had remained silent despite inquiries from the British and Americans. On May 3, as Stettinius arrived for a dinner at the Soviet consulate in San Francisco, Molotov greeted him with "Oh, by the way, Mr. Stettinius, about those sixteen Poles; they have all been arrested by the Red Army." At this he turned and greeted Anthony Eden while Stettinius stood with a frozen smile.[35]

The Western Allies did not share Molotov's cavalier attitude on the subject. They immediately demanded facts, which the London Polish government was ready to supply.[36] Beginning March 6, Soviet authorities in Poland contacted the top underground leaders to arrange for meetings "to include them in the general current of democratic powers in independent Poland." The London government-in-exile approved the contacts, and the Western Allies provided names of four of the leaders. Preliminary meetings between underground representatives and a Soviet general established a panel of 15 delegates—the four ministers of the London Polish government who were in Poland, the chairman of the Council of National Unity, the head of the Polish Home Army, and representatives of each of the political parties except the Communist Party.

These were the surviving underground leaders who had fought the Germans, and had been in fact the key figures rallying the Poles throughout the war. Together with Mikolajczyk and ministers of the government-in-exile in London, they had been regarded by most Poles as the nucleus to lead the nation after the war.

In opening arrangements for the meetings, the Soviet general had written, "I give you my word of honour that, from the moment of your arrival at the place of the meeting, your safety will be my concern personally. You will be perfectly secure."

Some members of the delegation suspected a trap, and the decision was taken to go to London and confer with the government-in-exile. For this the Soviets agreed to provide an aircraft. Accordingly, on March 27 the three top Polish figures went, as agreed, to the headquarters of the First Byelorussian Front at a farmhouse just outside Warsaw. Next day 12 others arrived. They were put into an airplane for the flight to London. Instead they were flown to Moscow, where they were placed in Lubyanka Prison. Another Polish leader, previously arrested, was put with them, for a total of 16.

The Soviets had succeeded, through the rankest kind of duplicity, in robbing Poland of most of its top leaders—except those who were Communist or Communist-controlled (who had practically no constituency except the Soviet Union). The motive was the same as that in the Katyn Massacre—to deprive Poland of future leaders.

When the arrest was finally admitted by the Soviets on May 3, the Western Allies protested. They were told the 16 had been arrested for "diversionary activities against the Red Army." Stalin denied they had been tricked. Stettinius and Eden told Molotov on May 4 that until the Soviets gave a full explanation, "the conversations on Poland would have to be suspended."

This did not in the least concern the Soviets, who felt no need to agree with the West about Poland. Finally it was the West that had to reopen the Polish talks, despite the uncertain fate of the 16 Poles in prison. At Bohlen's suggestion and Harriman's urging, Truman asked Harry Hopkins to go to Moscow and try to break the deadlock.

As a friend of Stalin's since his first visit in 1941, Hopkins might be able to get the Soviet dictator to pay some attention to U.S. public opinion. Rising from a sickbed, Hopkins left for Moscow on May 23, accompanied by Harriman and Bohlen. They met with Stalin and Molotov in the Kremlin on the night of May 26.

Over the next ten days Hopkins met with Stalin seven times, including a state dinner, pressing for the release of the 16 leaders and for a solution to the impasse over Polish delegates to a Moscow meeting to form a government. Stalin insisted the 16 must stand trial, but for those (most of them) charged only with operating illegal radio transmitters, he would try to be lenient. On the makeup of the panel for establishing a government, he agreed to include Mikolajczyk, who had publicly humbled himself by accepting the Yalta agreements and the Curzon Line. On the rest, Hopkins consulted Mikolajczyk through Churchill in London. Three-way messages flew among Truman, Hopkins, and Churchill.

Finally agreement was reached on five non-Warsaw regime Poles from inside Poland (two of them picked by Molotov), three from London, and four from the Warsaw government. But this gave no guarantee of the complexion of the actual government to be formed.

"I cannot feel therefore," Churchill wrote to Truman, "that we can regard this as more than a milestone in a long hill we ought never to have been asked to climb."[37]

Truman, however, was elated with Hopkins's success. Even the U.S. press, which had generally maligned Hopkins as the Rasputin of the White House, now applauded him. Though wracked with terminal illness, Hopkins had performed a remarkable feat of self-sacrifice and political virtuosity. But his main accomplishments in the talks with Stalin were in areas other than Poland.

On the fate of the 16 he had little impact; they were all tried, not just for using illegal transmitters but for a whole range of alleged offenses. The familiar Soviet-type trial employed the usual abuses to extract confessions; no witnesses for the defense were permitted. Twelve were convicted and some died in prison; others returned under a 1946 amnesty to their homeland, where some were rearrested.

As for the new Polish government itself, the delegates were invited to Moscow by the Tripartite Commission on June 12. From June 17 to 21 they deliberated, with the first notice of an agreement published on June 23. Of 21 cabinet posts in the new Polish provisional government of National Unity, 14 went to the Warsaw puppet regime and 7 to other Polish groups, including the London government. Boleslaw Bierut and Edward Osobka-Morawski of the Warsaw government became president and premier, respectively. The Soviet-sponsored group also secured the posts controlling the use of force— Interior, with the state police, and Defense, with the army. Mikolajczyk was made one of two deputy premiers (the other was a Communist, Wladyslaw Gomulka) and was also named minister of agriculture. This arrangement was similar to coalition governments then being established in other East European countries in which democratic leaders were employed as window dressing while Soviet stooges held the levers of power.

However, the solution was not incompatible with the "reorganized" Warsaw government called for at Yalta, where the main damage had been done. Even Harriman supported the deal, while emphasizing that the real test would be in the forthcoming free elections.

On July 5, 1945, Britain and the United States recognized the new Polish Provisional Government of National Unity. Churchill did so with deep misgivings, and now bent his efforts to securing a final Big Three meeting while the U.S. and British armies still occupied part of the Soviet zone in Germany.

Poland was by no means the only issue. In Hungary, Romania, and Bulgaria, the Allied Control Commissions were simply tools of their Soviet chairmen, with the British and U.S. members being excluded from participation in decisions, and even restricted in their movements within the countries. In Austria the Soviets were denying Western representatives access to the Soviet zone, including Vienna, while unilaterally recognizing a new government they had helped create. In Czechoslovakia the Soviet puppets

within Beneš's coalition government were demanding that U.S. troops leave
the narrow corner they occupied. In Yugoslavia the so-called coalition government created with the inclusion of Dr. Ivan Subasić had become a farce;
Tito repudiated Britain, openly declared allegiance to Moscow, and was
trying to grab Trieste from Italy. Churchill complained to Stalin:

Our joint idea at the Kremlin in October was that the Yugoslav business should work
out around 50–50 Russian and British influence. In fact it is at present more like 90–
10, and even that poor 10 we have been subjected to violent pressure by Marshal
Tito.

And to Stalin's entire victory in Eastern Europe he made frank if unrealistic
protest:

It seems to me that a Russianized frontier running from Lübeck through Eisenach
to Trieste and down to Albania is a matter which requires a very great deal of argument
conducted between good friends.[38]

Churchill's fears about the Soviet Union were plunging him into depression. The position was, he told Eden, "more dangerous than 1939." And
Eden, tormented with night pains that repeatedly awakened him, wrote in
his diary that the Americans had "all the errors and illusions of Neville C,
substituting Russia for Germany."[39]

To President Truman, Churchill now urged speed in meeting with Stalin
while Allied troops occupied positions as far east as possible. This was the
last chance to hold some bargaining leverage in dealing with Soviet violations
of Yalta. He ordered British forces throughout Europe to stand fast and not
destroy any captured German arms. And he urged the same for U.S. forces
on Truman.

"If the situation is handled firmly before our strength is dispersed," he
wrote to the president, "Europe may be saved from another blood bath."[40]

By May 12 Churchill was in full alarm. He asked Truman about the
situation

when the British and American Armies have melted . . . when we may have a handful
of divisions, mostly French, and when Russia may choose to keep two or three
hundred on active service? . . . An iron curtain is drawn down upon their front. We
do not know what is going on behind.

And if the U.S. armies now well within the Soviet zone were to withdraw,
there would be another "enormous Muscovite advance into the centre of
Europe. . . . " He urged a meeting with the Soviets "before we weaken our
armies mortally or retire to the zones of occupation."[41]

But Truman insisted that the occupation zones be honored promptly; the
proposed Big Three meeting in Germany could not be held until mid-July,

and Allied troops were withdrawn from the Soviet zone two weeks before that. Hordes of refugees, many of whom had been fleeing for months all the way from the Baltic states, surged ahead of the Red Army.

"Soviet Russia was established in the heart of Europe," moaned Churchill. "This was a fateful milestone for mankind."[42]

Without this last bargaining chip, Churchill and Truman met Stalin at Potsdam on July 17, 1945. Since the results of the British elections could not be known until the votes of soldiers overseas came in, Churchill and Eden brought with them Clement Attlee and Ernest Bevin of the British Labour Party; on winning the election these two completed the agenda in the last days of Potsdam. Truman brought with him his new secretary of state, James F. Byrnes; both would later assert U.S. interests against the Soviets, but at Potsdam both lacked experience in dealing with Stalin and Molotov. Before the Americans left Washington, Churchill asked Ambassador Halifax to outline British fears to Byrnes:

I have the impression that the Americans take a rosier view of European prospects than we do. They seem to think that, given the settlement of a few outstanding problems, and the enunciation of general political principles and desiderata Europe can safely be left to look after itself and that it will soon settle down to peaceful and orderly development. Our view, on the contrary, is that unless we all work very hard the situation in Europe will deteriorate rapidly and dangerously.[43]

One key question at Potsdam was the western frontier of Poland, which had not been settled. The main contention was over the southern extension of the frontier with Germany, the Western powers favoring the eastern Neisse river and the Soviet Union insisting on the western Neisse. The latter would give the Poles more of Germany than they could absorb and would require the displacement of too many German families, in the minds of the British and Americans. They believed it would create more friction in the future between Germany and Poland, driving the latter into the Soviet Union's arms.

Stalin got his way on this issue, but it was largely academic because Poland was already being embraced by the Russian bear, and the partition of Germany put Soviet power even further to the west.

A more pressing issue came up at one of the early foreign ministers' meetings at Potsdam on July 20, when Byrnes and Eden pushed for three-power supervision of elections in Southeast Europe and Italy. Declared Byrnes, "The world knows we meant what we said at Yalta." Molotov was opposed.

From then on, the subject of elections continued to be argued at meetings of the foreign ministers and heads of state. At the plenary session in the late afternoon of July 20, both Churchill and Truman said their countries did not wish to "supervise" or "superintend" the elections. " 'Observe' would be a better word," offered Byrnes. Churchill agreed that the British simply wanted to know what went on.[44]

At a foreign ministers' meeting on July 22, Molotov noted that the only election that had been held in a former enemy country was in Finland. Was there, he asked, "any suspicion that this election had not been free?"

When Byrne acknowledged that "so far as we knew this election had been all right," Molotov inquired what grounds there were for suspicion. Byrnes answered, "[W]e would, frankly, always be suspicious of elections in countries where the press cannot report freely."[45]

Adding poignancy to the arguments were the steps then being taken by the Communist government in Bulgaria to hold a single-ticket election on August 26. Democratic leaders there wired the Big Three at Potsdam, urging three-power supervision.

But Stalin and Molotov were adamant. The U.S.–British proposal for three-power "observation" of elections was dropped from the agenda in mid-conference. On July 25 the U.S. delegation reported, "There seems no likelihood of reaching agreement on . . . observation of elections."[46]

Thus the part of the Yalta agreement guaranteeing democratic governments dedicated to free elections was killed at Potsdam. Stalin's argument was that the governments of Southeast Europe were democratic—at least in the Soviet sense of the word. Said Stalin at the plenary session on July 24, "If a government is not Fascist a government is democratic."[47]

Still another issue was the arbitrary Soviet use of the Allied Control Commissions in Hungary, Romania, and Bulgaria. For the first time Churchill, who had previously felt inhibited by the "percent agreement," spoke out against Soviet actions in those countries. The British mission in Bucharest, he complained, "had been penned up with a closeness approaching internment."

Stalin interrupted to ask how Churchill could cite facts "that had not been verified."

Churchill retorted that Stalin "would be very much astonished" to read the long list of difficulties met by the British mission in Romania. "An iron fence had come down around them."

"All fairy tales," quipped Stalin.[48]

In the end the question of ACC procedures was referred to a staff committee. After continued disagreement, according to the U.S. member, "it was clear that there will not be time to work out all these details during the present Conference." The group then drew up a statement that the Soviet proposals for Hungary, Romania, and Bulgaria "constitute a basis" for the future work of the ACCs, "subject to elaboration of details which will be worked out through diplomatic channels. . . ." On August 1, when Molotov tried to claim that the Soviet ACC formula "had been accepted," Secretary of State Byrnes insisted "it had not been accepted as to details."

Molotov admitted that "it had been accepted as a basis for discussion."[49]

Afterward, on this understanding, Washington set about drafting further ACC revisions for consideration.

But ACC reform was already beaten. Leaving it to subsequent diplomatic action was as deadly as it had been at Yalta. Two weeks after Potsdam, when Marshal Voroshilov returned to Hungary from a trip to Moscow and submitted a new procedure to General Key, he called it "the new Statute of ACC in Hungary." When Key tried to present a U.S. revision at an ACC meeting on August 22, Voroshilov was inflexible. The Soviet procedure, he shouted, "was the procedure agreed upon by the three governments at Potsdam." When Key pointed to the words "revision would now be undertaken" and "taking as a basis" in the Potsdam statement, Voroshilov was still immovable.[50] The marshal was saying, as he had about Yalta, "In Hungary, I am Potsdam."

Thus the pattern was the same with Potsdam as with Yalta. Stalin, outwardly amiable, held his quiet demeanor and conceded nothing of real interest to the Soviet Union. On issues where the Allies were divided, he and Molotov succeeded in creating language that was ambiguous—at least admitting of a loophole through which they could drive a tank. What the Western powers lacked in armed strength inside Eastern Europe they tried to make up by diplomacy, but even here the Soviets beat them through duplicity. As Alexander Cadogan wrote in his diary on August 1, "Joe has got most of what he wants, but then the cards were mostly in his hands. . . ."[51]

As for Stalin's attitude on keeping international agreements, this had been made clear at one point during the meetings with Hopkins in Moscow. Stalin declared, "The Soviet Union always honors its word." Dropping his voice, he added a phrase that the interpreter, V. N. Pavlov, did not translate. Charles Bohlen, interpreting for Hopkins, spoke up: "I believe there is a little more, Pavlov." And the Soviet interpreter quickly spoke the words in English: "except in case of extreme necessity."[52]

15

The Curtain Descends

In the years 1945 to 1948 Eastern Europe, from Bulgaria to East Germany, became complete Soviet satellites. Though the timetables differed, each country went through a gradual transition to disguise eventual Soviet control. The first phase: a coalition government in which the Communist Party invariably controlled the police and the army. The second phase: a phony coalition in which the Communist Party controlled the government. The third phase: a complete Soviet-type government with only one party, single-slate elections, thought control, and police terror.

It was, of course, a cat-and-mouse game, since the Soviets had already gained complete control through occupation by the Red Army during the war. Though in each country the democratic leaders believed they were influencing events in the postwar years, they were actually playing a script already written in Moscow.

In Bulgaria and Romania—the earliest independent countries invaded by the Red Army—the process moved swiftly through the three phases toward complete submission. In Albania and Yugoslavia the Communist parties controlled politics by the war's end—they simply took over as the Germans retreated to keep from being trapped by the Soviets. But in the rest of Eastern Europe, sovietization took longer.

In Hungary, the Soviets mistakenly believed that the Communist Party was popular; accordingly they permitted a free election in November 1945 that gave the Communists 17 percent of the vote and the predominant Small-holders Party 57 percent. But before the election they had forced on the Hungarians a coalition cabinet, and in its subsequent creation the Interior Ministry with its police power went to the Communists.

There followed a period of rising agitation, persecution, and finally mass arrests and "conspiracy" trials. Phony accusations wrung by NKVD methods implicated higher and higher officials until the premier, Ferenc Nagy, took refuge in Switzerland in May 1947. The second phase of the Soviet pattern, involving an artificial coalition dominated by Communists, continued until the summer of 1948, when Hungary became an outright Soviet satellite. Throughout these events the U.S. and British observers in Hungary reported their outrage to Washington and London, which responded with some equally outraged protests.

In Czechoslovakia the schedule was somewhat slower, due in part to the fame and popularity of President Eduard Beneš, both in his own country and in the Western world.

From July to December 1945, the U.S. and Soviet armies carried out a phased withdrawal from Czechoslovakia. The Red Army remained adjacent to the country in East Germany, Poland, Austria, and Hungary.

On May 26, 1946, elections were held for the Czechoslovak parliament. The voting was conducted without irregularities. However, the Czechoslovaks were reminded of the proximity of the Red Army when a number of units were scheduled to be transported across Czechoslovakia from Austria to Poland two days before the election. Foreign Minister Jan Masaryk protested to the Soviets and the movement was canceled, but the event was seen as an intimidation.

In the election, the Communists won 38 percent of the votes and confirmed their claim as the largest single party. This was due mainly to their strength in the most populous Czech portion of the country, Bohemia and Moravia, especially among factory workers, and also to their superior organizing activity.

The results brought a cabinet reshuffle, with Klement Gottwald, as head of the largest party, becoming premier. The Communists, who previously had 9 out of 26 portfolios, now had 12 out of 24, not counting Ludvik Svoboda and Zdenek Fierlinger, who consistently cooperated with them. With their power further consolidated, the Communists now moved to discredit their enemies—in Slovakia, the Slovak Democrats; in the Czech lands, the National Socialists (the party of Beneš). General Svoboda systematically purged the army of non-Communist officers. The interior minister gradually removed non-Communists from key police positions, replacing them with Communists. Fierlinger's Social Democrats voted with the Communist Party in the National Assembly, giving it a working majority.

In July 1947 the United States invited Czechoslovakia to attend a Paris conference on the Marshall Plan for European economic recovery. On July 4 and 7, the Czechoslovak cabinet—lacking a timely Soviet direction on policy—voted unanimously to accept. Two days later a Czechoslovak delegation, headed by Gottwald and including Jan Masaryk, was in Moscow on another, previously scheduled mission. Stalin told the delegation point blank that acceptance of the Marshall Plan invitation was an affront to the Soviet Union, and that Czechoslovakia would have to choose between East and West. On July 10 Gottwald telephoned Prague with this message for the cabinet, which then unanimously reversed itself.

This step effectively ended Czechoslovak independence. When Masaryk stepped off the plane back in Prague, he told his friends: "It is a new Munich. I left for Moscow as Minister of Foreign Affairs of a sovereign state. I am returning as Stalin's stooge."[1]

Late in 1947 the political tide began to turn against the Communists. On November 16 the Social Democrats, meeting in Brno, repudiated Fierlinger as secretary general and denounced the Communists. In January 1948 a nationwide poll taken by the Communists showed their voting strength had dropped to 28 percent. This confirmed the trend that had surfaced in a number of recent student elections, in which Communist support ranged from 12 to 25 percent. It was clear the Communist strength would suffer in the next elections, scheduled for May 1948.

Events now moved rapidly toward a coup d'état. In September 1947 attempts had been made to bomb Masaryk and two other non-Communist leaders; evidence linking the crime to the Communist Party had been suppressed by the Interior Ministry. To counter rising indignation over the bomb attempt, the Communists accused leaders of the National Socialists and the Slovak Democrats of treasonous acts and arrested many of the latter.

In February 1948, when it was discovered that the interior minister had replaced the last remaining non-Communist police heads in the Prague area with Communists, the anti-Communist cabinet members called for an accounting. The minister refused, Gottwald supported him, and 12 cabinet members resigned in protest.

The issue brought both Communist and non-Communist demonstrations. The Communists mobilized the "work militias" and "action committees" that they had organized among the workers. Gottwald harangued crowds of supporters in Wenceslas Square. Private businesses, including non-Communist newspapers, were closed down and their proprietors arrested. From Moscow came Valerian Zorin, former ambassador to Czechoslovakia, who arrived on February 19.

In the midst of this crisis Gottwald visited Beneš with his own new list of National Front Cabinet officers—nearly all of them either Communists or Communist supporters. Beneš at first insisted that a reshuffle of the cabinet must be done by parliamentary procedure. But finally, believing that further resistance meant civil war, he agreed to the new cabinet. "You are talking to me like Hitler!" he told Gottwald, but he nonetheless signed the announcement.[2] Gottwald shouted the triumph to a crowd in Wenceslas Square. Zorin returned to Moscow.

The Communists proceeded to seize complete power. Their most active enemies were arrested. The news was completely controlled. Western publications were banned. An election was staged with only one slate of candidates. One of the ousted cabinet officers attempted suicide. Jan Masaryk was found dead under his office window: The Communists called it suicide; the people assumed it was murder.

Twenty years later, during the "Prague Spring," the Czechoslovak Communist government reopened the Masaryk case. Testimony was presented that on the night of his death Masaryk's quarters had been found in utter disorder, as though there had been a struggle, and that his body showed signs of violence in addition to his fall. Before the investigation could be completed during that brief glimpse of freedom in 1968, Soviet tanks rolled into Prague. But to the Czechoslovaks the evidence confirmed what they had believed since 1948.[3]

As for President Eduard Beneš, he retired to his country home and resigned in June 1948. Three months later—a few days before he died—he told his secretary: "My greatest mistake was that I refused to believe to the very last that even Stalin lied to me...."[4]

In Poland, which was the most important geographically, and where anti-Soviet feeling was strongest, the Soviets moved faster than in Czechoslovakia. By early 1946 the country was wrenched by political pressures as it approached the election scheduled for January 1947. The Polish Peasant Party, which actually represented a strong majority of the population, was given only 52 seats out of more than 400 in the provisional parliament. Then the police arm pressured the Peasant Party to purge its members. A number of branches were suspended, and some parliament members were expelled. In July the land reform and agricultural planning functions were taken from Mikolajczyk, thus sharply cutting his already limited role.

In August the British and U.S. governments began serving notice that they expected a free election. In September the parliament passed an election law that favored the Communist forces. The latter pressured the Socialist and other leftist elements to join in a so-called Government Bloc for election purposes. Arrests and intimidation of those daring to oppose Communist policies were intensified.

Through this period outraged protests came from Mikolajczyk, from the British and U.S. ambassadors in Moscow, and from Arthur Bliss Lane, the U.S. ambassador in Warsaw. The voting was on January 19, 1947, with the Government Bloc winning 394 out of 444 seats in the parliament.

The election had been so blatantly rigged that Lane resigned as ambassador. Though the spectacle was precisely what the London Poles had feared and the Western powers had tried to prevent, the United States and Britain continued to recognize the Polish government. Despite Churchill's determination not to be cheated over Poland, the British and the Americans, and the Poles themselves, were now thoroughly cheated.

The Communists proceeded to consolidate their power. On February 5 Bierut was chosen president of Poland, and three days later a new cabinet—

completely dominated by Communists—was formed. In May, Gomulka decreed that the Socialist Party must merge with the Polish Workers (Communist) Party. During the summer of 1947 Moscow prohibited Poland from participating in the Marshall Plan, as it had also prohibited Czechoslovakia. The Cominform—a revival of the Comintern that Stalin had suspended during the war—was created at a congress held in Poland.

Finally, the purge of independent thinkers was expanded. On October 20, 1947, the parliament lifted the immunity from arrest that had protected four of its members, including Mikolajczyk. The latter promptly fled the country, escaping to the British occupation zone in Germany.

No voice for freedom remained in Poland or, within a few months, anywhere in Eastern Europe. Churchill had described the situation as early as March 1946 in a speech at Fulton, Missouri, with President Truman on the platform:

From Stettin in the Baltic to Trieste in the Adriatic, an iron curtain has descended across the Continent. . . . this is certainly not the Liberated Europe we fought to build up. Nor is it one which contains the essentials of permanent peace.

Since Stalin had exclusive power east of that curtain by the beginning of 1945, why did he take three more years to secure his grip? The answer seems to be two-fold.

First, from the start of World War II it was clear that the Soviets wished to cloak their actions with legitimacy. They denied the existence of the secret protocol in the Ribbentrop-Molotov agreement that handed them eastern Poland; instead they claimed their Polish invasion was done on behalf of the Poles. They held phony elections to sanction their seizure of eastern Poland and the Baltic states. Similar window dressing was used in their seizure of Bessarabia from Romania and Ruthenia from Czechoslovakia in 1945, as well as their step-by-step actions in transforming democracies into puppet states in Eastern Europe.

Why? In the late 1940s Stalin was looking beyond Eastern Europe to the rest of the continent. He knew that modern wars were followed by popular movements to the left. After World War I it was the Socialists, with their respectability, who had dampened Communist chances. Now France and Italy were especially vulnerable. In both countries the Communist Party made a strong bid for popular support. These prizes in the industrial West were worth courting; a too-heavy hand in Eastern Europe could alarm and alienate their voters.

Second, at the end of World War II, Stalin had not yet taken the measure of U.S. resolve. His agents had undoubtedly told him of U.S. atomic power, even before he learned of it from Truman at Potsdam, and before it was demonstrated at Hiroshima. The extent to which the United States would exert this unique power in world politics was unknown. Stalin could hardly imagine that any nation would fail to flex this kind of muscle.

Thus his earliest actions in Eastern Europe may be seen, in one sense, as probes to test his adversary; as the response proved weak, the actions became bolder. Just as Soviet military offensives had been cautiously planned, so were Soviet postwar political ventures—not risking a confrontation that would require a face-losing retreat. Unlike Hitler, the Soviets did not have a swift timetable based on personal ego; since they considered their eventual triumph as inevitable, they could afford to make haste slowly.

The larger issue is that if the sovietization of Eastern Europe was inevitable once it came under Stalin's power, the really crucial time to have saved the independence of that region was during the war itself. From 1941 to 1945, what could Britain and the United States have done to limit the impact of Soviet occupation?

The answers fall into two main categories: first, binding agreements enforced by quid pro quos, where the Western powers could withhold their part of the deal in case of nonfulfillment by the Soviet Union, and, second, prior military occupation.

In the first category, Churchill and Eden were experienced in European politics and recognized as early as 1941 the need for quid pro quos in dealing with Moscow. On the other hand, Roosevelt and Hull rejected power politics in international affairs and favored agreements based on mutual trust. This was certainly a legitimate approach, but should have been discounted from the start in view of Soviet behavior in attacking Poland and Finland and occupying the Baltic states and part of Romania during the period of alliance with Hitler from 1939 to 1941.

Thus in 1941 and 1942, when the British and Soviets were negotiating a treaty, Moscow wanted to legitimize its seizures in those countries through British diplomatic recognition. Eden was ready to do this, except for Poland, in return for a guarantee of the integrity of the rest of Europe, including the use of confederations.

But Roosevelt and Hull intervened to block British recognition of Soviet annexations, leaving Eden no lever to get his quid pro quo. Admittedly, if the deal had materialized, the Balts would have felt betrayed by Britain. Yet it was clear that whether the Germans or the Russians won on the eastern front, the Baltic states would not regain their independence.

In the end, not only the Balts but all Eastern European peoples lost their freedom. It is by no means certain that this could have been prevented by a quid pro quo with Stalin but, as the British realized, his bargaining power was at its weakest in 1941 and 1942; if the Soviet Union survived, it could only get stronger later.

Would Stalin have kept such an agreement after his Red Army occupied the ground? Probably not if the quid pro quo treaty was the only lever. But opportunities to reinforce it with other safeguards would soon arise.

Roosevelt evidently realized that when he blocked the recognition of Soviet territorial gains, the Soviets felt they were being denied part of their war aims. To help assure that Moscow would not make a separate peace, he pledged the second front in 1942. This empty promise created a new danger, which he then tried to mitigate by the unconditional surrender declaration at Casablanca. That, in turn, assured that the Germans would resist to the end, and that the war would last until the Red Army had swept all the way across Eastern Europe into Germany.

Starting in the spring of 1944, Churchill and Eden tried again to strike a quid pro quo with Stalin—this time limited largely to the Balkans. Again Roosevelt and Hull rejected it on the grounds that "spheres of influence" were intrinsically wrong. As a result Churchill had to bargain with Stalin alone, and all he saved was Greece.

It seems likely that if the United States had thrown its weight onto the Balkan scales throughout the war, instead of refusing any responsibility, more than Greece could have been won. This is not to say that the Balkans could have been kept in the Western camp. But the Soviets showed they were willing to settle for a neutral Finland and a neutral Austria. A strong U.S. policy in the Balkans might at least have extended such neutralization and left millions breathing the air of freedom.

Still less understandable is the attitude of both Britain and the United States toward Czechoslovakia. The United States had midwifed the birth of that nation in 1918; Britain should have felt compelled to embrace it out of shame for the Munich betrayal. But neither power made any offer of a treaty to President Beneš to assure him that he need not seek security in the arms of the Russian bear.

As for Poland, Churchill and Eden saw clearly enough that a settlement should be made early, before the Red Army moved in. But the cause of Poland's independence became hostage to the strife over the eastern frontier. Here the Poles themselves allowed strategy to be ruled by emotion. If they had any logic in their position, it was that in World War I, Germany and Russia had both been defeated, allowing a new Poland to rise between them, and that the same would happen in World War II.

Churchill knew that Poland could save itself only by agreeing early to the Curzon Line; but it would not. Meanwhile, both Roosevelt and Churchill made the mistake of acquiescing in the Curzon Line at Tehran while getting no concession from Stalin in return. Tehran was their last chance to use this bargaining lever to get a strong formula for Polish independence, including internationally supervised elections, before the Red Army engulfed the country.

After that, the negotiations on Poland were clearly lopsided; by the time of Yalta the Allied objective had been reduced to seeking little more than the appearance of Polish independence to mollify public opinion at home. Eden at least was right in opposing an agreement at any price. No agreement at all would have been better than one that misled the Poles and the world.

From the beginning of lend-lease to the Soviet Union in 1941, this assistance constituted an opportunity for leverage. Though some Soviets tried to minimize its importance, Stalin himself acknowledged that without it they could not have won the war.

The U.S. chargé d'affaires in Moscow, George Kennan, argued that the United States should have dealt with the Soviet Union not as an ally but as a co-belligerent who was on its best behavior while receiving lend-lease aid. More than once Averell Harriman suggested that the United States threaten to withhold lend-lease if the Soviets persisted in breaking their agreements. Churchill proposed the same, especially in the frustration of the Warsaw Rising. The argument against this by Cordell Hull is persuasive:

If we made the threat and Russia still refused to accede to our demands, we would then have faced a dilemma. Would we cut off military aid and thereby hurt ourselves militarily? Or would we continue it, thereby proving that our threat had been an empty one? And if we did cut it off, and let Moscow go its own way, could we then have the slightest hope of reaching a general postwar agreement with the Soviet Government?[5]

Still, such a lever need not have been applied on an "either-or" basis with the usual all-out American approach. Wielding this power at the bargaining table could simply have been a reasonable counter to Stalin's Red Army. As it was, the Western Allies understood well the power Stalin possessed in Eastern Europe, and they acted accordingly—that is, they acceded to his demands. But they failed to exercise the power that they possessed. Just as Stalin did not have to remind them of his power, so they did not have to threaten, in so many words, to use theirs. It would have been the task of diplomacy to make Stalin, who respected only power, understand this.

Most advantageous of all would have been to incorporate lend-lease at the outset in a general agreement on treatment of liberated peoples. But this never occurred to either the U.S. or the British leadership.

The second category of possible Allied moves to save Eastern Europe's independence was prior military occupation. The opportunities for this alternative came up in three areas—Southeast Europe, Germany, and Czechoslovakia. For all three, Churchill was the exponent and the U.S. leaders the opponents.

At one time just before Tehran, it appeared that Roosevelt might favor a Balkan invasion if it were desired by Stalin, but when the latter sternly opposed it at Tehran, Churchill was left as the sole proponent. From the beginning General Marshall opposed the venture as a dilution of the main second front planned for France.

But the real key to Churchill's plans for invasion at the head of the Adriatic was the progress of fighting in Italy. As long as the Germans kept the Allies out of the Po Valley, an Adriatic landing could not have a secure rear. Up to the summer of 1944 a thrust into the mountains of northern Yugoslavia toward Budapest and Vienna would have been highly risky without a second pincers coming from Red Army troops in the east. But at the very moment when the Red Army's drive through the Balkans made the Adriatic invasion militarily feasible, U.S. troops were taken from Italy for the invasion of southern France, leaving the Allies as weak as the Germans on the peninsula. A strictly military decision concentrating on the western front ruled the day, and the last chance to influence the future of Southeast Europe had gone.

Whether the political gain in the Balkans would have been worth more than the military gain in the west, and whether Churchill's military plan in southeast Europe would have succeeded, are both subject to question. But the Americans never considered the choice.

In Germany, it appears that U.S. troops could have reached Berlin as early as the Soviets and shared with them the capture of the capital. Reaching so far into the future Soviet zone of occupation would have given the West some leverage in countering Soviet violations of agreements, which at that time were rampant and outrageous. Partly on the argument that the Americans would have to pull back to their own zone sooner or later, General Eisenhower refused to drive for Berlin, despite the urgings of Churchill.

The case was even more clear-cut in Czechoslovakia. Here Eisenhower, instead of staking out Prague as an objective when he contacted the Soviets for theirs, let them speak first for the Czechoslovak capital. Then, although General Patton could have reached Prague two days before Marshal Konev and rescued the rebelling Czechs from German counterattacks, Eisenhower confined him to a toehold in Czechoslovakia. Again, Churchill was rebuffed in his pleadings.

In all three of these cases the decisions had been made by military men, on military grounds. Except for Churchill, Allied political leaders abdicated their responsibility. The political objectives for which wars are fought become doubly important toward the end of coalition wars, when the several victorious allies may each have different objectives. But neither Roosevelt nor Truman understood this, nor did they understand Churchill's fears of Soviet conquest that would negate for half of Europe the original Allied war objectives. Truman later understood, and led the way in saving Western Europe through the Truman Doctrine, the Marshall Plan, the Berlin Airlift, and the NATO alliance.

At a more general level one can fault Roosevelt for failing to heed the warnings of ambassadors such as Harriman and numerous foreign service officers who saw Soviet strategy at first hand; for failing to heed Churchill and Eden, whose experience in dealing with the Soviet Union and Eastern Europe should have been valued as an Allied asset; for being too anxious for Soviet entry into the Japanese war when Soviet interest pointed to its entry in any case; for pinning all hopes of future peace in the world on an international United Nations organization; for believing that the Soviets would honor agreements with no penalties for violation; and for believing that diplomatic success could be won by personal charm.

But to state these "should have beens" is to call for a different cast of characters in the U.S. leadership of World War II. Roosevelt's capability in all other wartime demands was superb, but in European geopolitics he was no match for Stalin. The qualities that made him peerless in the U.S. domestic arena did not work in Eastern Europe, where the foundations of power were not votes but divisions. He adopted the foolish posture of a neutral between Churchill and Stalin, trusting the British less and the Soviets more than history should have told him. By his aloofness from the East European issues he played into Stalin's hands and left Churchill to bargain alone—a position that Churchill finally had to abandon with bitter misgivings on the last day at Yalta.

As for Churchill, he had feared as early as 1943 that the principles of national independence for which Britain had gone to war would be swamped by the Soviet tide—that Europe would be saved from one dictator only to be seized by another. Unlike the Americans, he did not regard the enemy to be communism as such, but Russian imperialism—Stalin was using Communist regimes as instruments of Soviet expansion. The partition of Europe confirmed Churchill's foreboding and fed his increasing fits of depression. The presence of Soviet power only 75 miles from the North Sea filled him with apprehension. Not only Britain's security but the world balance of power could be overturned if the Soviet Union controlled all Europe.

On one of his last birthdays, while the world was eulogizing him in the press and over the airwaves, Churchill told his daughters, "I have achieved a great deal to achieve nothing in the end."[6]

In the large picture, one more of history's "what ifs" should be cited, and here Churchill may stand at fault. Starting with the North African invasion in 1942, the Mediterranean strategy that Churchill championed could be stamped a monumental strategic error. As Marshall pointed out, the "soft underbelly" of Hitler's Europe was not soft. The mountainous terrain made it more defensible than France. Allied commitment to slogging up the rugged spine of Italy took 20 months to reach—what? Europe's most formidable barrier, the Alps. By the time this barrier was reached, the main victory in Germany was won.

As Marshall also warned, the diversion to the Mediterranean meant that the true second front across the English Channel would be delayed not just to 1943, but to 1944. This in turn meant that the Red Army would have a longer reach into Europe, and the Western Allies a shorter one, before the two would meet and end the war. Besides prolonging the war, this had an obvious political impact on Central Europe.

To pursue this speculation on a country-by-country basis is to carry speculation too far. We need not speculate—we know from experience the tragic result of the war that was actually fought and the division of Europe that was actually made. It was, first of all, a European tragedy. Through a catastrophic war the continent had been saved from one oppression. But in the process half of it was turned over to another oppression and the other half was saved from this fate mainly by a terrifying nuclear deterrent.

Napoleon and Hitler had each in his turn tried to rule the whole continent, but their successes soon turned to disaster. Yet Stalin, unchallenged by rival powers, won half of Europe for Soviet dominance through more than four decades. It was a feat unsurpassed since Charlemagne.

In the end it is not action by the West, but an economic collapse in the East, that has caused a Soviet retreat. The withdrawal of Soviet military support from the six puppet regimes of Eastern Europe has brought a swift and astonishing upheaval in all six nations. Though glorious, the fresh wind of independence could not bring back the years of suffocation for two generations of 100 million people.

But the tragedy of Eastern Europe went far beyond the continent. Had those six nations held their independence, even as neutral buffers between East and West, Soviet power would not have hung so ominously over Western Europe. Through the late twentieth century the industrial strength of Western Europe has been the crucial makeweight in the world balance of power. That precarious balance has been defined by the cleft across the face of Europe from the Baltic to the Adriatic. And the threat of unhinging that balance of power has been the basis of the Cold War and the arms race. To maintain the balance, the people of the world have been held hostage by the terror of nuclear holocaust, by an arms race measured only in degrees of madness.

Here, too, a stunning change in Soviet policy has been precipitated by domestic crisis and courageous leadership. Between the superpowers, arms control is supplanting the arms race, true peace is supplanting the Cold War. After nearly half a century of dangerous confrontation, leaders and people on both sides may look to an era in which war, though not eliminated, will not mean global annihilation. And, with the superpowers cooperating more than contending, even the United Nations may become the peacekeeper that Roosevelt intended.

Notes

CHAPTER 1   DESPERATE ALLIANCE

1. Sir John Wheeler-Bennett, ed., *Action This Day: Working with Churchill* (New York and London, 1969), p. 89.

2. W. Averell Harriman and Elie Abel, *Special Envoy to Churchill and Stalin, 1941–1946* (New York, 1975), p. 536.

3. Arthur Bryant. *Triumph in the West* (Garden City, N.Y., 1959), p. 62.

4. Anthony Eden, *The Memoirs of Anthony Eden*, vol. 2, *The Reckoning* (Boston, 1965), p. 595.

5. Samuel I. Rosenman, *The Public Papers and Addresses of Franklin D. Roosevelt* (New York, 1950), 1943 vol., p. 550.

6. Violet Bonham Carter, *Winston Churchill: An Intimate Portrait* (New York, 1965), p. 4.

7. A. J. P. Taylor, et al., *Churchill Revised: A Critical Assessment* (New York, 1969), p. 251.

8. Sir John Colville, *The Fringes of Power: 10 Downing Street Diaries, 1939–1955* (New York and London, 1985), p. 554.

9. Arthur Bryant, *The Turn of the Tide* (Garden City, N.Y., 1957), p. 13.

10. Robert J. Gannon, *The Cardinal Spellman Story* (New York, 1962), p. 246.

11. Robert E. Sherwood, *Roosevelt and Hopkins: An Intimate History* (New York, 1948), p. 138.

12. Gannon, *Cardinal Spellman*, pp. 243–244.

13. William C. Bullitt, "How We Won the War and Lost the Peace," *Life*, August 30, 1948, p. 94.

14. Elliott Roosevelt and Joseph P. Lash, eds., *F. D. R., His Personal Letters, 1928–1945*, vol. 2 (New York, 1950), p. 1177.

15. *U.S. News and World Report*, April 26, 1971, p. 70.

16. Frances Perkins, *The Roosevelt I Knew* (New York, 1946), pp. 382–383.

17. Gustav Hilger and Alfred G. Meyer, *The Incompatible Allies* (New York, 1953), p. 300.

18. U.S. Department of State, *Nazi-Soviet Relations, 1939–1941: Documents from the Archives of the German Foreign Office*, Raymond James Sontag and James Stuart Beddie, eds. (Washington, D.C., 1948), p. 75.

19. General Sikorski Historical Institute, *Documents on Polish-Soviet Relations, 1939–1945*, vol. 1 (London, 1961), p. 48.

20. Ibid., p. 65.

21. *Correspondence Between the Chairman of the Council of Ministers of the U.S.S.R. and the Presidents of the U.S.A. and the Prime Ministers of Great Britain During the Great Patriotic War of 1941–1945* (Moscow, 1957), vol. 1, pp. 11–13.

22. Ibid., p. 21.

23. Winston S. Churchill, *The Grand Alliance* (Boston, 1950), pp. 455–460; Ivan Maisky, *Memoirs of a Soviet Ambassador* (New York, 1967), pp. 188–192; Eden, *The Reckoning*, pp. 318–319.

24. Churchill, *Grand Alliance*, pp. 527–530; Maisky, *Memoirs*, pp. 198–202.

25. *Correspondence Between the Chairman*, vol. 1, pp. 33, 35; Churchill, *Grand Alliance*, pp. 529, 531–532.

CHAPTER 2   BATTLE OF THE BOUNDARIES

1. Hastings Lionel Ismay, *The Memoirs of General Lord Ismay* (New York, 1960), p. 327.

2. Kenneth Young, ed., *The Diaries of Sir Robert Bruce Lockhart, 1939–1965*, vol. 2 (London, 1980), p. 338.

3. John Gilbert Winant, *Letter from Grosvenor Square* (Boston, 1947), pp. 92, 96.

4. Young, *Diaries . . . Lockhart*, vol. 2, pp. 328, 550.

5. Winston S. Churchill, *Their Finest Hour* (Boston, 1949), p. 571.

6. U.S. Department of State, *Foreign Relations of the United States (FRUS). Diplomatic Papers 1941*, vol. 1 (Washington, D.C., 1958), pp. 192–194.

7. Ibid., pp. 194–195; Cordell Hull, *The Memoirs of Cordell Hull*, vol. 2 (New York, 1948), pp. 1165–1167; W. Averell Harriman and Elie Abel, *Special Envoy to Churchill and Stalin* (New York, 1975), p. 110; Anthony Eden, *The Memoirs of Anthony Eden, Earl of Avon*, vol. 2, *The Reckoning* (Boston, 1965), pp. 330–331.

8. Eden, *The Reckoning*, p. 334.

9. Charles E. Bohlen, *Witness to History, 1929–1969* (New York, 1973), p. 131.

10. Quentin James Reynolds, *Only the Stars are Neutral* (New York, 1942), p. 94.

11. Orville H. Bullitt, ed., *For the President: Personal and Secret* (Boston, 1972), p. 66.

12. David Dilks, ed., *The Diaries of Sir Alexander Cadogan, 1938–1945* (London, 1971), p. 422.

13. This and other quotes from the December 16 session are from British Foreign Office, Russia Correspondence, FO 371, 1941, vol. 29655, Eden to Foreign Office and Prime Minister, 17 December 1941; Eden, *The Reckoning*, pp. 334–342; Ivan Maisky, *Memoirs of a Soviet Ambassador* (New York, 1967), p. 231; Graham Ross, ed.,

The Foreign Office and the Kremlin: British Documents on Anglo-Soviet Relations, 1941–1945 (Cambridge, 1984), pp. 82–85.

14. The second and third sessions are derived from Eden, *Reckoning*, pp. 342–345; Ross, *Foreign Office and Kremlin*, pp. 85–87; Dilks, *Diaries... Cadogan*, pp. 421–422; Maisky, *Memoirs*, p. 232; and especially British Foreign Office, Russia Correspondence, FO 371, 1941, vol. 29655, Eden to Foreign Office (two messages), 18 December 1941; FO 371, 1942, vol. 32879, "Memorandum by Secretary of State on Conversations with M. Stalin, December 16–20, 1941," dated 25 December 1941; and Pierson Dixon memorandum on Anglo-Soviet treaty, 15 April 1942.

15. Eden, *Reckoning*, p. 347.

16. Elisabeth Barker, *Churchill and Eden at War* (London, 1978), p. 138.

17. British Foreign Office, Russia Correspondence, FO 371, 1942, vol. 32876, no. 931, Eden to Halifax, 10 February 1942.

18. Ibid., no. 932, Eden to Halifax, 10 February 1942.

19. Ibid., nos. 971 and 1013, Halifax to Eden, 19 and 20 February, 1942.

20. Eden, *Reckoning*, p. 375.

21. British Foreign Office, Russia Correspondence, FO 371, 1942, vol. 32876, Dominion Office to Dominion prime ministers, 9 April 1942.

22. Francis L. Loewenheim, Harold A. Langley, and Manfred Jonas, *Roosevelt and Churchill: Their Secret Wartime Correspondence* (New York, 1975), p. 186.

23. British Foreign Office, Russia Correspondence, FO 371, 1942, vol. 32877, Churchill to Stalin, 9 March 1942.

24. Ibid., Halifax to Eden, 9 March 1942.

25. Ibid., Eden to Halifax, 10 March 1942.

26. Ibid., Halifax to Eden, 11 March 1942.

27. Ibid., vol. 32876, Eden to Dominion prime ministers, 18 March 1942; vol. 32877, Armine Dew to Halifax, 13 March 1942; minute by Eden, 15 March 1942.

28. Loewenheim et al., *Roosevelt and Churchill*, p. 196.

29. British Foreign Office, Russia Correspondence, FO 371, 1942, vol. 32876, Dominion Office to Dominion prime ministers, 31 March 1942; U.S. Dept. of State, *FRUS, Diplomatic Papers*, 1942, vol. 3 (Washington, D.C., 1961), p. 536n.

30. British Foreign Office, Russia Correspondence, FO 371, 1942, vol. 32878, Eden to Halifax, 27 March 1942.

31. *FRUS, Diplomatic Papers*, 1942, vol. 3, p. 538.

32. Robert E. Sherwood, *Roosevelt and Hopkins* (New York, 1948), p. 526.

33. Dilks, *Diaries... Cadogan*, p. 449.

34. Ibid., p. 450.

35. Eden, *Reckoning*, p. 379.

36. The discussions over the Anglo-Soviet treaty between Eden's return from Moscow and Molotov's visit to London are in British Foreign Office, Russia Correspondence, FO 371, 1942, vols. 32876–32878; the Prime Minister's Operational Correspondence (PREM), 1942, 3/395/12; and *FRUS, Diplomatic Papers*, 1942, vol. 3, pp. 491–556.

37. Harriman and Abel, *Special Envoy*, p. 94.

38. Quentin Reynolds, *Only the Stars Are Neutral* (New York, 1942), p. 91.

39. Eden, *Reckoning*, p. 481.

40. Dilks, *Diaries... Cadogan*, p. 454n.

41. Bohlen, *Witness*, p. 380.

42. Winston S. Churchill, *The Gathering Storm* (Boston, 1948), p. 368.

43. The subsequent negotiations between Molotov and Eden in London are described in PREM, 1942, 3/399/4–5, 21–25 May and 9 June 1942; Ross, *Foreign Office and Kremlin*, pp. 103–106; Eden, *Reckoning*, pp. 380–382; Dilks, *Diaries . . . Cadogan*, pp. 453–455; Maisky, *Memoirs*, pp. 265–267; Winston S. Churchill, *The Hinge of Fate* (Boston, 1950), pp. 332–339; *FRUS, Diplomatic Papers*, 1942, vol. 3, pp. 557–562, 564–566; Hull, *Memoirs*, pp. 1171–1173; Harriman and Abel, *Special Envoy*, p. 136.

44. Hull, *Memoirs*, pp. 1172–1173.

45. Warren F. Kimball, ed., *Churchill & Roosevelt: The Complete Correspondence*, vol. 1 (Princeton, 1984), p. 505; Elliott Roosevelt and Joseph P. Lash, eds., *F.D.R. His Personal Letters* (New York, 1950), vol. 2, p. 1329.

46. Harriman and Abel, *Special Envoy*, p. 136.

47. Eden, *Reckoning*, p. 382.

48. Ibid., p. 370.

49. Robert J. Gannon, *The Cardinal Spellman Story* (New York, 1962), p. 223.

50. Dilks, *Diaries . . . Cadogan*, p. 488.

51. Milovan Djilas, *Conversations with Stalin* (New York, 1962), p. 114.

CHAPTER 3   "SECOND FRONT NOW!"

1. Molotov's Washington visit is described in *FRUS. Diplomatic Papers*, 1942, vol. 3 (Washington, D.C., 1961), pp. 566–587; Robert E. Sherwood, *Roosevelt and Hopkins* (New York, 1948), pp. 557–577; Cordell Hull, *The Memoirs of Cordell Hull*, vol. 2 (New York, 1948), p. 1174; W. Averell Harriman and Elie Abel, *Special Envoy to Churchill and Stalin* (New York, 1975), pp. 136–139; Warren F. Kimball, ed., *Churchill & Roosevelt: The Complete Correspondence* (Princeton, N.J., 1984), vol. 1, p. 503.

2. Elliott Roosevelt and Joseph P. Lash, eds. *F.D.R. His Personal Letters, 1928–1945*, vol. 2 (New York, 1950), p. 1329.

3. Winston S. Churchill, *The Hinge of Fate* (Boston, 1950), p. 341.

4. Ibid., p. 342.

5. Soviet reaction to the second front promise is from *FRUS, Diplomatic Papers*, 1942, vol. 3, pp. 593–599; *Correspondence Between the Chairman of the Council of Ministers of the U.S.S.R. and the Presidents of the U.S.A. and the Prime Ministers of Great Britain During the Great Patriotic War of 1941–1945* (Moscow, 1957), vol. 1, pp. 53, 56; British Foreign Office, Russia Correspondence, FO 371, 1942, vol. 33017, Soviet Monitor, 11–13 June 1942.

6. *FRUS, Diplomatic Papers*, 1942, vol. 3, p. 598.

7. *Correspondence Between the Chairman*, vol. 1, p. 56.

8. Churchill, *Hinge of Fate*, pp. 473, 475.

9. Sources for Churchill's visit to Moscow are PREM, 1942, 3/76A/9, 11, and 12; Churchill, *Hinge of Fate*, pp. 476–502; *FRUS, Diplomatic Papers*, 1942, vol. 3, pp. 618–626; Warren F. Kimball, ed., *Churchill & Roosevelt: The Complete Correspondence* (Princeton, N.J., 1984), vol. 1, pp. 560–572; Francis L. Loewenheim, Harold D. Langley, and Manfred Jonas, *Roosevelt and Churchill: Their Secret Wartime Correspondence* (New York, 1975), pp. 234–240; W. Averell Harriman and Elie Abel, *Special Envoy to Churchill and Stalin* (New York, 1975), pp. 152–164; David Dilks, ed., *The Diaries of Sir Alexander Cadogan* (London, 1971), pp. 471–474; Arthur Bryant, *The Turn of the Tide* (Garden City, N.Y., 1957), pp. 372–383; A. H. Birse, *Memoirs of an*

Interpreter (London, 1967), pp. 97–104; Sir Charles Wilson (Lord Moran), *Churchill: Taken from the Diaries of Lord Moran. The Struggle for Survival, 1940–1965* (Boston, 1966), pp. 60–72.

10. *Roosevelt and Churchill*, p. 240; *Correspondence Between the Chairman* vol. 2, p. 33.

11. U.S. Department of State, *FRUS, The Conferences at Washington, 1941 and 1942, and Casablanca, 1943* (Washington, D.C., 1968), p. 506.

12. Elliott Roosevelt, *As He Saw It* (New York, 1946), p. 117. Elliott puts the date of the luncheon at January 23, but Churchill himself brought up the unconditional surrender subject in a formal meeting on the afternoon of January 18. The luncheon on that day is the more likely setting.

13. Churchill, *Hinge of Fate*, p. 684.

14. The decision on unconditional surrender is described in *FRUS, Conferences . . . Casablanca*, pp. 635, 704, 727, 833, 835, 837; Churchill, *Hinge of Fate*, pp. 684–691; Robert E. Sherwood, *Roosevelt and Hopkins* (New York, 1948), pp. 693–697; W. Averell Harriman and Elie Abel, *Special Envoy to Churchill and Stalin* (New York, 1975), pp. 87–90; Elliott Roosevelt, *As He Saw It* (New York, 1946), p. 117; Martin Gilbert, *Road to Victory: Winston S. Churchill, 1941–1945* (London, 1986), pp. 300–301, 309–310; and Albert C. Wedemeyer, *Wedemeyer Reports!* (New York, 1958), pp. 186–187.

15. For a thorough and convincing study on this subject, see Anne Armstrong, *Unconditional Surrender: The Impact of the Casablanca Policy upon World War II* (New Brunswick, N.J., 1961), esp. pp. 253–255.

16. See the extensive survey in H. W. Koch, "The Spectre of a Separate Peace in the East: Russo-German 'Peace Feelers', 1942–44," *Journal of Contemporary History* 10 (1975), 531.

17. *Correspondence Between the Chairman*, vol. 2, p. 71.

CHAPTER 4   THE MISSING 10,000

1. Count Edward Raczynski, *In Allied London* (London, 1962), pp. 163–164.

2. General Sikorski Historical Institute, *Documents on Polish-Soviet Relations*, vol. 1 (London, 1961), pp. 128–132; Ivan Maisky, *Memoirs of a Soviet Ambassador* (New York, 1967), pp. 172–173.

3. General Sikorski Institute, *Documents*, vol. 1, pp. 173–174; Stanislaw Kot, *Conversations with the Kremlin and Dispatches from Russia* (London, 1963), p. 51.

4. General Sikorski Institute, *Documents*, vol. 1, p. 233; Kot, *Conversations*, p. 142.

5. General Sikorski Institute, *Documents*, vol. 1, p. 519.

6. Anthony Eden, *Memoirs of Anthony Eden*, vol. 2, *The Reckoning* (Boston, 1965), p. 430.

7. Ibid., p. 432; British Foreign Office, Russia Correspondence, FO 371, 1943, vol. 37045, Eden to Halifax, 3 August 1942; PREM, 1943, 3/354/8, Eden to Clark Kerr, 1 May 1943; *FRUS, Diplomatic Papers*, 1943, vol. 3 (Washington, D.C., 1963), p. 15, memorandum by Harry L. Hopkins, March 15, 1943.

8. The Katyn announcement and reaction to it are cited in General Sikorski Institute, *Documents*, vol. 1, pp. 530–532, 539–540; Raczynski, *Allied London* pp. 140–141; Winston Churchill, *The Hinge of Fate* (Boston, 1950), pp. 757–61; David Dilks, ed., *The Diaries of Sir Alexander Cadogan* (London, 1971), pp. 520–521.

9. General Sikorski Institute, *Documents*, vol. 1, p. 527; see also *FRUS, Diplomatic Papers*, 1943, vol. 3, pp. 376–382.

10. *FRUS, Diplomatic Papers*, 1943, vol. 3, pp. 379, 386–400, 405; Raczynski, *Allied London*, p. 141.

11. *FRUS, Diplomatic Papers*, 1943, vol. 3, p. 530. These and related events are also chronicled in Louis Fitzgibbon, *Unpitied and Unknown* (London, 1975), pp. 13–23; and Polish Cultural Foundation, *The Crime of Katyn: Facts and Documents* (London, 1965), pp. 101–105.

12. *Correspondence Between the Chairman of the Council of Ministers of the U.S.S.R. and the Presidents of the U.S.A. and the Prime Ministers of Great Britain During the Great Patriotic War of 1941–1945* (Moscow, 1957), vol. 2, p. 60.

13. *FRUS, Diplomatic Papers*, 1943, vol. 3, p. 397.

14. W. Averell Harriman and Elie Abel, *Special Envoy to Churchill and Stalin* (New York, 1975), p. 200.

15. Among numerous books providing these and other data are Louis Fitzgibbon, *Unpitied and Unknown* (London, 1975); Polish Cultural Foundation, *Crime of Katyn*; and J. K. Zawodny, *Death in the Forest: The Story of the Katyn Forest Massacre* (Notre Dame, Ind., 1962). Other details are in Winston Churchill, *The Hinge of Fate* (Boston, 1950), pp. 759–761; Cordell Hull, *The Memoirs of Cordell Hull*, vol. 2 (New York, 1948), pp. 1267–1268; Warren F. Kimball, ed., *Churchill & Roosevelt: The Complete Correspondence* (Princeton, N.J., 1984), vol. 2, pp. 389–402; Stanislaw Mikolajczyk, *The Rape of Poland* (New York, 1948), pp. 28–38.

16. *New York Times*, April 14, 1990, p. 1; *Los Angeles Times*, April 14, 1990, p. A1.

17. Wladyslaw Anders, *An Army in Exile* (London, 1949), p. 124.

18. British Foreign Office, Russia Correspondence, FO 371, 1943, vol. 37045, Eden to Halifax, 24 July and 3 August 1943.

19. U.S. Department of State, *FRUS, The Conferences at Washington and Quebec, 1943* (Washington, D.C., 1970), pp. 1113–1116, Eden to Hull, August 23, 1943.

20. Jan Ciechanowski, *Defeat in Victory* (Garden City, N.Y., 1947), pp. 212–221.

21. Raczynski, *Allied London*, p. 167.

CHAPTER 5   DR. BENEŠ FACES EAST

1. Edward Taborsky, "The Triumph and Disaster of Eduard Beneš," *Foreign Affairs*, July 1958, p. 669.

2. Ibid., p. 670.

3. Winston S. Churchill, *Closing the Ring* (Boston, 1951), p. 452.

4. British Foreign Office, Russia Correspondence, FO 371, 1943, vol. 37009. Translation dated 19 June 1943.

5. Kenneth Young, ed., *The Diaries of Sir Robert Bruce Lockhart*, vol. 2 (London, 1980), p. 242.

6. British Foreign Office, Russia Correspondence, FO 371, 1943, vol. 37037, Eden to Philip B. Nichols, 16 June 1943; Eduard Beneš, *Memoirs of Dr. Eduard Beneš: From Munich to New War and New Victory*, trans. Godfrey Lias (Cambridge, 1954), pp. 185–186, 195–196.

7. British Foreign Office, Russia Correspondence, FO 371, 1943, vol. 37037, Eden to Nichols, 16 June 1943.

8. Ibid., Halifax to Eden, 7 July 1943.

9. Ibid., Eden to Nichols, 16 June 1943, and Eden to Halifax, 26 June 1943; Beneš, *Memoirs*, p. 244.

10. W. Averell Harriman and Elie Abel, *Special Envoy to Churchill and Stalin, 1941–1946* (New York, 1975), p. 246.

11. The discussion of the Czechoslovak-Soviet treaty at the Moscow conference is from U.S. Department of State, *FRUS*, 1943, vol. 1 (Washington, D.C., 1963), p. 626; British Foreign Office, Russia Correspondence, FO 371, N6921, "Record of the Proceedings of the Foreign Ministers' Conference Held in Moscow from 19th October to 30th October, 1943," 6th meeting, 24 October, 3 P.M.; Harriman and Abel, *Special Envoy*, pp. 245–246. Neither Eden's nor Hull's memoirs mention the Czechoslovak-Soviet treaty discussion in Moscow.

12. Beneš, *Memoirs*, p. 262.

13. The conversations among Beneš, Molotov, and Stalin in Moscow were recorded in notes by Jaromír Smutný, who was the head of Beneš's Chancellery and attended all the meetings. Deposited at Columbia University, they were translated into English by Vojtech Mastny and published in *Jahrbücher für Geschichte Osteuropas, new ser.* 20 (September 1972), 376–402.

14. Ibid., pp. 399, 402; Beneš, *Memoirs*, pp. 255–265; Edward Taborsky, "Benes and Stalin—Moscow, 1943 and 1945," *Journal of Central European Affairs*, July 1953, p. 165; *FRUS, Diplomatic Papers*, 1943, vol. 1, pp. 726–734 (Harriman correspondence to Washington); General Sikorski Institute, *Documents on Polish-Soviet Relations*, vol. 2 (London, 1967), p. 129 (transcript of Beneš's meeting with Mikolajczyk on his return from Moscow).

15. Beneš, *Memoirs*, p. 263; Taborsky, "Benes and Stalin," pp. 167, 178.

16. Beneš, *Memoirs*, p. 262.

17. Taborsky, "Beneš and Stalin," p. 168.

18. Beneš, *Memoirs*, p. 262.

19. *FRUS, Diplomatic Papers*, 1943, vol. 3, p. 732.

20. Mikolajczyk Papers, box 35, Committee of National Liberation, 1943–1944, letter from Klement Gottwald to Czechoslovak State Council, London, 21 December 1943.

21. Smutný, "Conversations," p. 398.

22. Charles de Gaulle, *The War Memoirs of Charles de Gaulle*, vol. 2, *Unity: 1942–1944*, trans. Richard Howard (New York, 1959), pp. 230–231.

23. Churchill, *Closing the Ring*, p. 452.

CHAPTER 6   THE EAGLES GATHER

1. Anthony Eden, *Memoirs of Anthony Eden*, vol. 2, *The Reckoning* (Boston, 1965), p. 482.

2. Ibid., pp. 469–470. Maisky's memoirs do not mention this talk.

3. John Harvey, ed., *The War Diaries of Oliver Harvey* (London, 1978), p. 304.

4. Winston Churchill, *Closing the Ring* (Boston, 1951), p. 283.

5. Charles E. Bohlen, *Witness to History, 1929–1969* (New York, 1973), p. 129.

6. David Dilks, ed., *The Diaries of Sir Alexander Cadogan* (London, 1971), pp. 553–554.

7. Hastings Lionel Ismay, *The Memoirs of General Lord Ismay* (New York, 1960), p. 324.

8. John Harvey, ed., *The War Diaries of Oliver Harvey* (London, 1978), p. 311.

9. W. Averell Harriman and Elie Abel, *Special Envoy to Churchill and Stalin* (New York, 1975), p. 236.

10. U.S. Dept. of State, *FRUS, Diplomatic Papers*, 1943, vol. 1 (Washington, D.C., 1963), pp. 522–523, 531–533, 596–602, 755–756; British Foreign Office, Russia Correspondence, FO 371, vol. 37031, Christopher Warner report to prime minister, received 15 November 1943.

11. British Foreign Office, Russia Correspondence, FO 371, vol. 37031, annex 7 to the secret protocol of the conference, signed 1 November 1943; *FRUS, Diplomatic Papers*, 1943, vol. 1, p. 762.

12. Harvey, *Diaries . . . Harvey*, p. 311.

13. British Foreign Office, Russia Correspondence, FO 371, vol. 37031, minute by Nevile Butler, 15 November 1943.

14. *FRUS, Diplomatic Papers*, 1943, vol. 1, p. 638; Cordell Hull, *Memoirs of Cordell Hull*, vol. 2 (New York, 1948), p. 1298.

15. The quotes in this exchange are from the British record of the meeting: British Foreign Office, Russia Correspondence, FO 371, vol. 37031, received 7 November 1943. The American record in *FRUS, Diplomatic Papers*, 1943, vol. 1, pp. 667–668, is shorter but similar.

16. U.S. Department of State, *FRUS, The Conferences at Cairo and Tehran, 1943* (Washington, D.C., 1961), p. 154, Harriman to Roosevelt, November 4, 1943.

17. Harriman and Abel, *Special Envoy*, p. 242.

18. British Foreign Office, Russia Correspondence, FO 371, vol. 37031, Clark Kerr to Foreign Office, 5 November 1943.

19. Ibid. Extract from London *Times*, 16 November 1943, and Foreign Office staff comments.

20. Ibid., minute by Frank Roberts, 16 November 1943.

21. General Sikorski Historical Institute, *Documents on Polish-Soviet Relations*, vol. 2 (London, 1967), pp. 83–86.

22. *FRUS, Diplomatic Papers*, 1943, vol. 3 (Washington, D.C., 1963), pp. 478–481.

23. Ibid., pp. 484–487.

24. Ibid., pp. 485–486, 488.

25. *FRUS, Cairo and Tehran*, p. 154.

26. Harriman and Abel, *Special Envoy*, p. 262.

27. British Foreign Office, Russia Correspondence, FO 371, vol. 39456, "Uncorrected Records of Tehran Conversations. Passages Concerning Poland," 28 November 1943.

28. Churchill, *Closing the Ring*, pp. 361–362; *FRUS, Cairo and Tehran*, pp. 510, 512.

29. *FRUS, Cairo and Tehran*, pp. 594, 884; Harriman and Abel, *Special Envoy*, p. 278; Bohlen, *Witness*, p. 151; *FRUS. The Conferences at Malta and Yalta, 1945* (Washington, D.C., 1955), pp. 667, 677.

30. Eden, *The Reckoning*, p. 496.

31. *FRUS, Cairo and Tehran*, p. 594.

32. Independent evidence substantiating these charges by Stalin has not come forth.

33. The discussion on the Polish issue at this Tehran session is from *FRUS, Cairo and Tehran*, pp. 596–601; Churchill, *Closing the Ring*, pp. 394, 397, 403; Eden, *The Reckoning*, p. 496; Bohlen, *Witness*, p. 152; "Tehran Conference of the Leaders of the

Three Great Powers, 1943," *International Affairs* (Moscow) 8 (August 1961), 121–122, "Round-table Sitting, December 1, 1943." Generally, Stalin's quotes are taken from this Soviet version.

34. Elliott Roosevelt and Joseph P. Lash, eds., *F.D.R. His Personal Letters*, vol. 2 (New York, 1950), p. 1498.

CHAPTER 7   THE INVASION THAT NEVER WAS

1. Elisabeth Barker, *British Policy in South-East Europe in the Second World War* (London, 1976), p. 227.

2. Arthur Bryant, *The Turn of the Tide* (Garden City, N.Y., 1957), p. 242.

3. Ibid., p. 290.

4. Arthur Bryant, *Triumph in the West* (Garden City, N.Y., 1959), p. 73.

5. W. Averell Harriman and Elie Abel, *Special Envoy to Churchill and Stalin* (New York, 1975), p. 445.

6. Henry L. Stimson, and McGeorge Bundy, *On Active Service in Peace and War* (New York, 1947), p. 664.

7. Michael Howard, *Grand Strategy* (London, 1972), pp. 498–499.

8. Winston Churchill, *The Hinge of Fate* (Boston, 1950), p. 826; Howard, *Grand Strategy*, p. 499.

9. Stimson and Bundy, *Active Service*, pp. 330–333.

10. U.S. Department of State, *FRUS, The Conferences at Washington and Quebec, 1943* (Washington, D.C., 1970), p. 499.

11. Harriman and Abel, *Special Envoy*, p. 226.

12. Robert Rhodes James, *Anthony Eden* (London, 1986), p. 275.

13. *FRUS, Washington and Quebec, 1943*, pp. 1213, 1289.

14. Bryant, *Triumph in the West*, p. 35.

15. John Harvey, ed., *The War Diaries of Oliver Harvey* (London, 1978), p. 314.

16. Bryant, *Triumph in the West*, p. 47.

17. U.S. Department of State, *FRUS, The Conferences at Cairo and Tehran, 1943* (Washington, D.C., 1961), p. 259.

18. Bryant, *Triumph in the West*, p. 47.

19. *FRUS, Cairo and Tehran*, p. 259.

20. Ibid., p. 332.

21. Ibid., pp. 480.

22. Ibid., pp. 492–493; Robert E. Sherwood, *Roosevelt and Hopkins* (New York, 1948), p. 780.

23. This discussion is in *FRUS, Cairo and Tehran*, pp. 493–495, 503–507.

24. Bryant, *Triumph in the West*, p. 63.

25. Sir Charles Wilson (Lord Moran), *Churchill: Taken from the Diaries of Lord Moran* (Boston, 1966), p. 143.

26. Ibid., p. 145.

27. Elliott Roosevelt, *As He Saw It* (New York, 1946), p. 184.

28. *FRUS, Cairo and Tehran*, pp. 535, 539, 541, 547, 551–552.

29. Wilson, *Churchill*, p. 153.

30. Ibid., p. 151.

31. Ibid., p. 155.

32. John North, ed., *The Alexander Memoirs, 1940–1945. Field-Marshal Earl Alexander of Tunis* (London, 1962), p. 138.

33. Alfred D. Chandler, Jr., and Stephen E. Ambrose, eds., *The Papers of Dwight David Eisenhower: The War Years*, vol. 3 (Baltimore, 1970), p. 1939.

34. Arthur Bryant, *Triumph in the West* (Garden City, N.Y., 1959), p. 166.

35. John Ehrman, *History of the Second World War: Grand Strategy*, vol. 5 (London, 1956), pp. 351–355; Winston S. Churchill, *Triumph and Tragedy* (Boston, 1953), pp. 63–64, 721; Warren F. Kimball, ed., *Churchill & Roosevelt* Vol. 3, (Princeton, N.J., 1984), pp. 213, 219.

36. Bryant, *Triumph in the West*, p. 167.

37. Churchill, *Triumph and Tragedy*, p. 723.

38. Harold Macmillan, *The Blast of War, 1939–1945* (New York, 1967), p. 416.

39. Harry C. Butcher, *My Three Years with Eisenhower* (New York, 1946), p. 644.

40. Frances Loewenheim et al., *Roosevelt and Churchill* (New York, 1975), pp. 546–548.

41. Kimball, *Churchill & Roosevelt*, vol. 3, p. 232.

42. Churchill, *Triumph and Tragedy*, pp. 691–692.

43. Wilson, *Churchill*, pp. 173–174.

44. Sources for this meeting are Forrest C. Pogue, *George C. Marshall: Organizer of Victory, 1943–1945* (New York, 1973), p. 414; Forrest C. Pogue, *The Supreme Command* (Washington, D.C., 1954), p. 225; Chandler and Ambrose, *Papers... Eisenhower*, vol. 4, pp. 2066–2067; Dwight D. Eisenhower, *Crusade in Europe* (Garden City, N.Y., 1952), pp. 281–284; James Nelson, ed., *General Eisenhower on the Military Churchill* (interview of Eisenhower by Alistair Cooke) (New York, 1970), pp. 42–43. In the latter reference, Eisenhower recalled that this meeting took place at his own headquarters, but he was undoubtedly thinking of an earlier one on July 9. Butcher's diary shows the August 9 meeting took place at 10 Downing Street.

45. Churchill, *Triumph and Tragedy*, p. 100.

46. This exchange between Churchill and Roosevelt is documented in Ehrman, *Grand Strategy*, vol. 5, p. 509; Churchill, *Triumph and Tragedy*, p. 100; U.S. Dept. of State, *FRUS, The Second Conference at Quebec, 1944* (Washington, D.C., 1972), p. 313.

47. *FRUS, Quebec 1944*, pp. 222–224, 229.

48. Chandler and Ambrose, *Papers... Eisenhower*, vol. 4, p. 2119.

49. *FRUS, Quebec 1944*, pp. 303, 314; Bryant, *Triumph in the West*, p. 204.

50. Churchill, *Triumph and Tragedy*, p. 155.

51. Wilson, *Churchill*, p. 207.

52. Ehrman, *Grand Strategy*, vol. 6, pp. 86–87.

53. Churchill, *Triumph and Tragedy*, p. 224.

54. This Churchill-Stalin exchange in Moscow in October 1944 is cited in U.S. Dept. of State, *FRUS, Diplomatic Papers*, 1944, vol. 4 (Washington, D.C., 1965), p. 1014; Ehrman, *Grand Strategy*, vol. 6, pp. 86–87.

55. Ehrman, *Grand Strategy*, vol. 6, pp. 51, 381.

56. *FRUS, Quebec 1944*, pp. 221–222.

57. Henry Maitland Wilson, *Eight Years Overseas* (London, 1948), pp. 239–240.

58. Churchill, *Triumph and Tragedy*, p. 101; Martin Gilbert, *Road to Victory* (London, 1986), p. 931.

59. U.S. Dept. of State, *FRUS, The Conferences at Malta and Yalta* (Washington, D.C., 1955), p. 543.

60. Sir John Colville, *The Fringes of Power* (New York and London, 1985), p. 555.

61. Bryant, *Triumph in the West*, p. 306.

62. Mark C. Clark, *Calculated Risk* (New York, 1950), p. 370.

63. Bryant, *Triumph in the West*, p. 38.

64. Pogue, *Marshall*, p. 419.

65. Ibid.

66. Ibid., pp. 415, 417.

CHAPTER 8   SAVE US FROM OUR ALLIES

1. Jozef Lettrich, *History of Modern Slovakia* (New York, 1955), p. 213.

2. U.S. Dept. of State, *FRUS, Diplomatic Papers*, 1944, vol. 3 (Washington, D.C., 1965), p. 523.

3. Lettrich, p. 211.

4. *FRUS, Diplomatic Papers*, 1944, vol. 3, p. 520.

5. Ibid., p. 518.

6. *Department of State Bulletin*, October 29, 1944, p. 497.

7. Lettrich, pp. 216–218.

8. *FRUS, Diplomatic Papers*, 1944, vol. 3, p. 523.

9. General Sikorski Historical Institute, *Documents on Polish-Soviet Relations*, vol. 2 (London, 1967), pp. 291, 297, 323, 357–362; *FRUS, Diplomatic Papers*, 1944, vol. 3, pp. 1369–1371; Stefan Korbonski, *The Polish Underground State. A Guide to the Underground, 1939–1945*, trans. Marta Erdman (New York, 1978), pp. 155–167; Jan M. Ciechanowski, *The Warsaw Rising of 1944* (London and New York, 1974), pp. 190–211.

10. K. K. Rokossovsky, *A Soldier's Duty* (Moscow, 1970), p. 254.

11. *Correspondence Between the Chairman of the Council of Ministers of the U.S.S.R. and the Presidents of the U.S.A. and the Prime Ministers of Great Britain During the Great Patriotic War of 1941–1945* (Moscow, 1957), vol. 1, p. 242.

12. Ibid.

13. Tadeusz Bór-Komorowski, *The Secret Army* (London, 1950), p. 212.

14. Rokossovsky, *Soldier's Duty*, p. 256.

15. Stanislaw Mikolajczyk, *The Rape of Poland: Pattern of Soviet Aggression* (New York, 1948), p. 74; *FRUS, Diplomatic Papers*, 1944, vol. 3, p. 1308.

16. Alexander Werth, *Russia at War, 1941–1945* (London, 1964), pp. 877–878.

17. General Sikorski Institute, *Documents*, vol. 2, p. 324.

18. Ibid., pp. 323–324.

19. Ibid., p. 311.

20. Winston Churchill, *Triumph and Tragedy* (Boston, 1953), p. 133.

21. Ibid.

22. This discussion is from *FRUS, Diplomatic Papers*, 1944, vol. 3, pp. 1374–1376.

23. W. Averell Harriman and Elie Abel, *Special Envoy to Churchill and Stalin* (New York, 1975), p. 339.

24. This conversation is from *FRUS, Diplomatic Papers*, 1944, vol. 3, pp. 1386–1389; Harriman and Abel, *Special Envoy*, pp. 339–341.

25. *FRUS, Diplomatic Papers*, 1944, vol. 3, pp. 1378–1379.

26. Ibid., pp. 1381–1382.
27. General Sikorski Institute, *Documents*, vol. 2, pp. 351–353.
28. *Correspondence Between the Chairman*, vol. 2, p. 356.
29. General Sikorski Institute, *Documents*, vol. 2, p. 356.
30. Warren F. Kimball, ed., *Churchill & Roosevelt* (Princeton, N.J., 1984), vol. 3, p. 294.
31. General Sikorski Institute, *Documents*, vol. 2, p. 381.
32. Ibid., p. 363.
33. Martin Gilbert, *Road to Victory* (London, 1986), p. 927.
34. Churchill, *Triumph and Tragedy*, p. 140.
35. Sir John Colville, *The Fringes of Power* (New York and London, 1985), p. 508.
36. Kimball, *Churchill & Roosevelt*, vol. 3, p. 313.
37. Churchill, *Triumph and Tragedy*, p. 140.
38. *FRUS, Diplomatic Papers*, 1944, vol. 3, p. 1396.
39. Rokossovsky, *Soldier's Duty*, p. 261.
40. Korbonski, *Polish Underground State*, p. 388.
41. Rokossovsky, *Soldier's Duty*, p. 261.
42. Korbonski, *Polish Underground State*, p. 395.
43. General Sikorski Institute, *Documents*, vol. 2, p. 398.
44. Heinz Guderian, *Panzer Leader* (London, 1952), p. 359.
45. General Sikorski Institute, *Documents*, vol. 2, p. 383.
46. George F. Kennan, *Memoirs, 1925–1950* (Boston, 1967), p. 211.
47. Churchill, *Triumph and Tragedy*, p. 141.

CHAPTER 9   CARVING THE BALKANS

1. The following exchange between Churchill and Eden is from British Foreign Office, Southern Europe Correspondence, FO 371, file 68, Southern R7380, Churchill to Eden, 4 May 1944; Eden to Churchill, 9 May 1944; Churchill to Eden, 21 May 1944; and Churchill, *Triumph and Tragedy* (Boston, 1953), p. 72–73.
2. British Foreign Office, Southern Europe Correspondence, FO 371, file 68, Southern R7903, Eden to Clark Kerr, 18 May 1944.
3. Ibid.
4. Ibid.
5. Churchill, *Triumph and Tragedy*, p. 73.
6. British Foreign Office, Southern Europe Correspondence, FO 371, file 68, Southern R7903, Eden to Halifax, 25 May 1944.
7. Churchill, *Triumph and Tragedy*, p. 74.
8. Ibid.
9. Cordell Hull, *Memoirs of Cordell Hull*, vol. 2 (New York, 1948), p. 1454.
10. Warren F. Kimball, ed., *Churchill & Roosevelt* (Princeton, N.J., 1984), vol. 3, p. 177; Churchill, *Triumph and Tragedy*, p. 75.
11. Churchill, *Triumph and Tragedy*, pp. 75–77; Kimball, *Churchill & Roosevelt*, vol. 3, pp. 178–180.
12. This and the following exchange between Roosevelt and Churchill are from Kimball, *Churchill & Roosevelt*, vol. 3, pp. 201–202, 207–208.
13. Hull, *Memoirs*, vol. 2, p. 1455.

14. British Foreign Office, Southern Europe Correspondence, FO 371, file 68, Southern R10483, Churchill to Eden, 10 July 1944.

15. This exchange between Churchill and Stalin is in *Correspondence Between the Chairman of the Council of Ministers of the U.S.S.R. and the Presidents of the U.S.A. and the Prime Ministers of Great Britain During the Great Patriotic War of 1941–1945* (Moscow, 1957), vol. 1, pp. 235–236, 238; Churchill, *Triumph and Tragedy*. pp. 79–80.

16. British Foreign Office, Southern Europe Correspondence, FO 371, file 68, Southern R11Y61, Churchill to Eden, 1 August 1944.

17. Sir Charles Wilson (Lord Moran), *Churchill: Taken from the Diaries of Lord Moran* (Boston, 1966), p. 173.

18. Ibid., p. 185.

19. Ibid., pp. 204–205.

20. Francis L. Loewenheim, Harold D. Langley, and Manfred Jonas, *Roosevelt and Churchill: Their Secret Wartime Correspondence* (New York, 1975), pp. 580–582.

21. Robert E. Sherwood, *Roosevelt and Hopkins: An Intimate History* (New York, 1948), pp. 833–834; Charles E. Bohlen, *Witness to History, 1929–1969* (New York, 1973), pp. 162–163.

22. *Correspondence Between the Chairman*, vol. 2, pp. 162–163; W. Averell Harriman and Elie Abel, *Special Envoy to Churchill and Stalin* (New York, 1975), pp. 353–356; U.S. Dept. of State, *FRUS, Diplomatic Papers 1944*, vol. 4 (Washington, D.C., 1965), pp. 1002–1005; Kimball, *Churchill & Roosevelt*, vol. 3, p. 344.

23. *Correspondence Between the Chairman*, vol. 2, pp. 162–163.

24. Kimball, *Churchill & Roosevelt*, vol. 3, p. 345.

25. *FRUS, Diplomatic Papers*, 1944, vol. 4, pp. 1004–1005; Harriman and Abel, *Special Envoy*, pp. 355–356.

26. Churchill, *Triumph and Tragedy*, pp. 217, 219.

27. Harriman and Abel, *Special Envoy*, p. 355.

28. The following discussions in Moscow over the "percent agreement" are recorded in PREM 1944, 3/434/2–5, "Records of Meetings at the Kremlin, Moscow, October 9–October 12, 1944"; Winston Churchill, *Triumph and Tragedy* (Boston, 1953), pp. 227–234; Martin Gilbert, *Road to Victory* (London, 1986), pp. 989–1001; Anthony Eden, *The Memoirs of Anthony Eden, Earl of Avon*, vol. 2, *The Reckoning* (Boston, 1965), p. 559; W. Averell Harriman and Elie Abel, *Special Envoy to Churchill and Stalin* (New York, 1975), pp. 356–358; *FRUS, Diplomatic Papers*, 1944, vol. 4, pp. 1009–1010; Sir Llewellyn Woodward, *British Foreign Policy in the Second World War* (London, 1962), p. 308.

29. *FRUS, Diplomatic Papers*, 1944, vol. 4, p. 1015.

30. Gilbert, *Road to Victory*, p. 1056.

31. Valentin Berezhkov, *History in the Making: Memoirs of World War II Diplomacy* (Moscow, 1983), pp. 371–372.

32. Vladimir Dedijer, *Tito* (New York, 1953), p. 233.

CHAPTER 10   THE AGONY OF POLAND

1. Stanislaw Mikolajczyk, *The Rape of Poland* (New York, 1948), pp. 49–50; U.S. Dept. of State, *FRUS, Diplomatic Papers*, 1944, vol. 3 (Washington, D.C., 1965), pp. 1216–1217.

2. Anthony Eden, *Memoirs of Anthony Eden*, vol. 2, *The Reckoning* (Boston, 1965), pp. 504–505.

3. *Correspondence Between the Chairman of the Council of Ministers of the U.S.S.R. and the Presidents of the U.S.A. and the Prime Ministers of Great Britain During the Great Patriotic War of 1941–1945* (Moscow, 1957), vol. 1, p. 182.

4. *FRUS, Diplomatic Papers*, 1944, vol. 3, pp. 1217–1220.

5. Ibid., p. 1228.

6. Ibid., p. 1231.

7. This meeting is from General Sikorski Historical Institute, *Documents on Polish-Soviet Relations*, vol. 2 (London, 1967), pp. 144–149.

8. Ibid., pp. 165–166.

9. This meeting at Chequers is from *FRUS, Diplomatic Papers*, 1944, vol. 3, pp. 1249–1257; PREM, 1944, 3/355/8; General Sikorski Institute, *Documents*, vol. 2, pp. 165–171.

10. *FRUS, Diplomatic Papers*, 1944, vol. 3, p. 1266.

11. General Sikorski Institute, *Documents*, vol. 2, pp. 196–197, 200.

12. Sir John Colville, *The Fringes of Power* (New York and London, 1985), p. 476.

13. *Correspondence Between the Chairman*, vol. 1, p. 392.

14. The following exchange between Churchill and Stalin is from *Correspondence Between the Chairman*, vol. 1, pp. 212–213; *FRUS, Diplomatic Papers*, 1944, vol. 3, pp. 1269–1270; General Sikorski Institute, *Documents*, vol. 2, pp. 212–214.

15. General Sikorski Institute, *Documents*, vol. 2, p. 223.

16. Ibid., p. 227.

17. Mikolajczyk, *Rape of Poland*, p. 57.

18. Ibid., p. 59. Other accounts of the Mikolajczyk-Roosevelt meetings are in *FRUS, Diplomatic Papers*, 1944, vol. 3, pp. 1280–1289; General Sikorski Institute, *Documents*, vol. 2, pp. 249–270; Jan Ciechanowski, *Defeat in Victory* (Garden City, N.Y., 1947), pp. 291–314.

19. Eden, *The Reckoning*, vol. 2, p. 541.

20. Mikolajczyk, *Rape of Poland*, p. 77. This quote does not appear in records of the meetings in General Sikorski Institute, *Documents*, vol. 2, pp. 325–333, 765–772, but these are specified as incomplete.

21. Mikolajczyk, *Rape of Poland*, p. 93.

22. This meeting on October 13 is from General Sikorsky Institute, *Documents*, vol. 2, pp. 405–414; Mikolajczyk, *Rape of Poland*, pp. 93–97; *FRUS, Diplomatic Papers*, 1944, vol. 3, pp. 1322–1323.

23. Mikolajczyk Papers, box 31, "Prime Minister's Papers Relating to Second Trip to Moscow," letter from Mikolajczyk to Harriman, October 16, 1944; W. Averell Harriman and Elie Abel, *Special Envoy to Churchill and Stalin* (New York, 1975), pp. 359–360.

24. Winston Churchill, *Triumph and Tragedy* (Boston, 1953), p. 235; Eden, *The Reckoning*, p. 563.

25. The principal sources for this Moscow meeting on Poland are General Sikorski Institute, *Documents*, vol. 2, pp. 416–421; and Mikolajczyk, *Rape of Poland*, pp. 97–99.

26. General Sikorski Institute, *Documents*, vol. 2, pp. 423–424; Mikolajczyk, *Rape of Poland*, p. 99. This exchange took place at the second meeting, with Churchill alone, but Mikolajczyk treats the two as a single meeting.

27. Sir Charles Wilson (Lord Moran), *Churchill: Taken from the Diaries of Lord Moran* (Boston, 1966), p. 217.

28. Eden, *The Reckoning*, p. 563.

29. General Sikorski Institute, *Documents*, vol. 2, p. 449.

30. Ibid., p. 462.

31. This meeting is detailed in ibid., pp. 450–456.

32. Ibid., pp. 468–471; *FRUS, Diplomatic Papers*, 1944, vol. 3, pp. 134–135.

33. General Sikorski Institute, *Documents*, vol. 2, 471–474; *FRUS, Diplomatic Papers*, 1944, vol. 3, pp. 1335–1336; Mikolajczyk, *Rape of Poland*, pp. 103–105.

34. Mikolajczyk, *Rape of Poland*, p. 105.

CHAPTER 11   LAST BATTLE OF THE CRIMEA

1. British Foreign Office, Poland Correspondence, FO 371, file 47575. Churchill to Stalin, 5 January 1945.

2. Winston Churchill, *Triumph and Tragedy* (Boston, 1953), p. 366.

3. U.S. Dept. of State, *FRUS, The Conferences at Malta and Yalta 1945* (Washington, D.C., 1955), pp. 227–229.

4. U.S. Dept. of State, *FRUS, Diplomatic Papers*, 1945, vol. 5 (Washington, D.C., 1967), p. 119.

5. *FRUS*, Malta and Yalta, pp. 230–234.

6. Thomas M. Campbell and George C. Herring, eds., *The Diaries of Edward R. Stettinius, 1943–1946* (New York, 1975), p. 214.

7. Sir John Colville, *The Fringes of Power* (New York and London, 1985), pp. 513–514.

8. Ibid., p. 560; David Dilks, ed., *Diaries of Sir Alexander Cadogan* (London, 1971), p. 702.

9. W. Averell Harriman and Elie Abel, *Special Envoy to Churchill and Stalin* (New York, 1945), p. 390.

10. Anthony Eden, *The Memoirs of Anthony Eden, Earl of Avon*, vol. 2, *The Reckoning* (Boston, 1965), p. 592.

11. Campbell and Herring, *Diaries . . . Stettinius*, pp. 227–228; Eden, *The Reckoning*, p. 591; Edward R. Stettinius, *Roosevelt and the Russians: The Yalta Conference*, ed. Walter Johnson (Garden City, N.Y., 1949), p. 64.

12. Robert Rhodes James, *Anthony Eden* (London, 1986), p. 289.

13. This and subsequent quotations from the third plenary session, February 6, are from *FRUS, Malta and Yalta*, pp. 667–681. Throughout the Yalta conference, the principal U.S. minutes were taken by Charles Bohlen, but those taken by H. Freeman Mathews are also useful and are often used here because they give direct quotes. Discussions on Poland were held at the plenary sessions and at four foreign ministers' meetings in the period February 6–11 (pp. 660–929). A Soviet transcript in English of the plenary sessions only is in *International Affairs* (Moscow), June–September 1965. A principal difference between the U.S. and Soviet versions is that the latter sometimes omits certain passages. For example, in this particular citation it does not mention Churchill's plea for Lwów (June 1965, p. 107).

14. This opposition to the Lublin government is referred to in the Mathews minutes (p. 677–678) but not in Bohlen's.

15. That this touched a Soviet nerve is shown in the Soviet version (*International*

Affairs, June 1965, p. 107). Where Churchill declared that Britain had "entered the war to defend Poland from German aggression," the only footnote in the entire Soviet text states: "Here Churchill obviously erred against the truth. When Hitler Germany attacked Poland on September 1, 1939, Britain, formally declaring war on Germany, did nothing to implement her guarantees given Poland earlier."

16. Eden, *The Reckoning*, p. 598; Churchill, *Triumph and Tragedy*, p. 372; *FRUS, Malta and Yalta*, pp. 726–728.

17. The discussions on Poland in this fourth plenary session, February 7, are in *FRUS*, Malta and Yalta, pp. 711, 716–720, 725–726.

18. Stettinius, *Roosevelt and the Russians*, p. 184.

19. *FRUS, Malta and Yalta*, p. 720.

20. Ibid., p. 792.

21. Ibid., pp. 869–870.

22. The Polish discussion in the fifth plenary session, February 8, is in *FRUS, Malta and Yalta*, pp. 776–781, 786–790.

23. Discussion on the Polish issue at the February 9 meeting of the foreign ministers is in *FRUS, Malta and Yalta*, pp. 803–807, 811–813.

24. Discussion on Poland in the sixth plenary session, February 9, is in *FRUS, Malta and Yalta*, pp. 842–843, 846–848, 850–854.

25. Eden, *The Reckoning*, p. 599.

26. The Polish issue in the foreign ministers' meeting, February 9, is in *FRUS, Malta and Yalta*, pp. 867–868, 870–871. See also Stettinius, *Roosevelt and the Russians*, pp. 246–248.

27. Eden, *The Reckoning*, p. 599.

28. Discussion of the Declaration on Liberated Europe in the sixty plenary session on February 9 is in *FRUS, Malta and Yalta*, pp. 848–849, 853–954. The text of the U.S. draft is on pp. 862–863.

29. Ibid., p. 868.

30. Ibid., p. 873.

31. Ibid., pp. 847–848, 854. The Soviet transcript (*International Affairs*, August 1965, p. 111) puts the latter quote: "Roosevelt would like the Polish elections to be, like Caesar's wife, above suspicion. Stalin remarked that Caesar's wife only had that kind of reputation. Actually, she wasn't all that lily-white."

32. *FRUS, Malta and Yalta*, p. 872.

33. Churchill, *Triumph and Tragedy*, p. 385.

34. Stettinius, *Roosevelt and the Russians*, p. 258.

35. William D. Leahy, *I Was There* (New York, 1950), pp. 315–316.

36. Stettinius, *Roosevelt and the Russians*, p. 303.

37. Quoted in James, *Anthony Eden*, p. 291.

38. Harriman and Abel, *Special Envoy*, pp. 412–413.

39. Charles E. Bohlen, *Witness to History* (New York, 1973), p. 192.

40. Although no U.S. minutes were taken of the last plenary session, this exchange is in the notes taken by Alger Hiss (*FRUS, Malta and Yalta*, p. 928). Abbreviations in Hiss's notes have been rendered here in complete words. The Soviet version reads: "He anticipated great criticism of the British Government, especially by the London Poles, and accusations that it had surrendered its positions to the U.S.S.R."

41. *International Affairs*, September 1965, p. 135.

42. PREM, 1945, 3/352/9 and 3/356/3.

43. Nigel Nicholson, ed., *The Diaries and Letters of Harold Nicholson*, vol. 2, *The War Years, 1939–1945* (New York, 1967), p. 437.

CHAPTER 12   "WHO WILL TAKE BERLIN?"

1. The September exchange between Eisenhower and Montgomery is documented in Bernard Law Montgomery, *The Memoirs of Field-Marshal the Viscount Montgomery of Alamein* (Cleveland and New York, 1958), pp. 241–252; Alfred D. Chandler, Jr., and Stephen E. Ambrose, eds., *The Papers of Dwight David Eisenhower*, vol. 4 (Baltimore and London, 1970), pp. 2120–2122, 2148–2149, 2164–2166.

2. *U.S. News & World Report*, April 26, 1971, "Why Ike Didn't Capture Berlin: An Untold Story," p. 70.

3. Winston Churchill, *Triumph and Tragedy* (Boston, 1953), p. 547.

4. Montgomery, *Memoirs*, p. 484.

5. Arthur Bryant, *The Turn of the Tide* (Garden City, N.Y., 1957), p. 431.

6. Montgomery, *Memoirs*, p. 484.

7. Churchill, *Triumph and Tragedy*, pp. 278–279; *Correspondence Between the Chairman of the Council of Ministers of the U.S.S.R. and the Presidents of the U.S.A. and the Prime Ministers of Great Britain During the Great Patriotic War of 1941–1945* (Moscow, 1957), vol. 1, pp. 294–295.

8. In his *The Road to Berlin* (Boulder, Colo., 1983), John Erickson thoroughly documents the German threat and the need to destroy it before proceeding to Berlin. Chapter 7, "The Assault on the Reich: January–March 1945" (pp. 431–529), is convincing, not to say exhaustive, on this point.

9. Sir John Colville, *The Fringes of Power* (New York and London, 1985), p. 563.

10. U.S. Dept. of State, *FRUS, The Conferences at Malta and Yalta, 1945* (Washington, D.C., 1955), p. 570. Manila fell the next day.

11. Arthur Bryant, *Triumph in the West* (Garden City, N.Y., 1959), p. 337.

12. Omar Nelson Bradley and Clay Blair, *A General's Life* (New York, 1983), p. 406.

13. Stephen E. Ambrose, *Eisenhower* (New York, 1983), p. 393.

14. Harry C. Butcher, *My Three Years with Eisenhower* (New York, 1946), p. 788.

15. Chandler and Ambrose, *Papers . . . Eisenhower*, vol. 4, p. 2551.

16. Ibid., p. 2562.

17. Churchill, *Triumph and Tragedy*, pp. 463–464.

18. Warren F. Kimball, ed., *Churchill & Roosevelt* (Princeton, N.J., 1984), vol. 3, pp. 603–605; Churchill, *Triumph and Tragedy*, pp. 464–466.

19. Chandler and Ambrose, *Papers . . . Eisenhower*, vol. 4, pp. 2567–2574.

20. Churchill, *Triumph and Tragedy*, p. 467.

21. Georgi K. Zhukov, *The Memoirs of Marshal Zhukov* (New York, 1971), pp. 587–589. This meeting shows that Stalin was already planning to step up his Berlin assault before receiving Eisenhower's message.

22. W. Averell Harriman and Elie Abel, *Special Envoy to Churchill and Stalin* (New York, 1975), p. 435.

23. Chandler and Ambrose, *Papers . . . Eisenhower*, vol. 4, pp. 2583–2584.

24. Stalin's meeting with Zhukov and Konev on April 1 is documented in Zhukov, *Memoirs*, pp. 589–591; Seweryn Bialer, ed., *Stalin and His Generals* (New York, 1969), see I. S. Konev, "The Strike from the South," pp. 516–520; and Sergei M. Shtemenko, *The Soviet General Staff at War, 1941–1945*, trans. Robert Daglish (Moscow,

1970), pp. 319–320. General Shtemenko was chief of operations of the Soviet General Staff.

25. Chandler and Ambrose, *Papers... Eisenhower*, vol. 4, pp. 2576–2577.

26. These exchanges are from ibid., pp. 2592–2595.

27. Martin Blumenson, ed., *The Patton Papers*, vol. 2, *1940–1945* (Boston, 1974), p. 685.

28. Omar N. Bradley, *A Soldier's Story* (New York, 1951), pp. 535, 537.

29. Chandler and Ambrose, *Papers... Eisenhower*, vol. 4, p. 2615.

30. S. L. A. Marshall, writing in the *New York Times Book Review*, February 13, 1966, p. 1; March 27, 1966, pp. 30, 32.

31. William H. Simpson, in *New York Times Book Review*, June 12, 1966, p. 34.

32. James M. Gavin, *On to Berlin* (New York, 1978), p. 317.

33. Chandler and Ambrose, *Papers... Eisenhower*, vol. 4, p. 2611.

34. Cornelius Ryan, *The Last Battle* (New York, 1966), p. 332.

35. Bialer, *Stalin and His Generals*, pp. 519, 527.

36. Chandler and Ambrose, *Papers... Eisenhower*, vol. 4, pp. 2632–2633.

37. James Nelson, ed., *General Eisenhower on the Military Churchill* (New York, 1970), pp. 55–56.

38. Forrest C. Pogue, *George C. Marshall: Organizer of Victory, 1943–1945* (New York, 1973), p. 571.

39. Chandler and Ambrose, *Papers... Eisenhower*, vol. 4, p. 2592.

40. Stephen E. Ambrose, *Eisenhower and Berlin, 1945* (New York, 1967), pp. 86–87, quoting a private communication to the author from Eisenhower.

41. Simpson, letter in *New York Times Book Review*, p. 34.

42. Bradley, *A Soldier's Story*, p. 536.

43. Edward Crankshaw, ed., *Krushchev Remembers* (Boston, 1970), p. 221.

CHAPTER 13   "ON TO CZECHOSLOVAKIA!"

1. Edward Taborsky, "Beneš and Stalin," *Journal of Central European Affairs*, July 1953, p. 165.

2. Ibid., p. 167.

3. Ibid.

4. F. Nemec and V. Moudry, *The Soviet Seizure of Subcarpathian Ruthenia* (Toronto, 1955), pp. 89–124, 210–287. Nemec headed the delegation sent by Beneš to administer Ruthenia.

5. Taborsky, "Beneš and Stalin," p. 174.

6. Ibid.

7. Eduard Beneš, "Postwar Czechoslovakia," *Foreign Affairs*, April 1946, p. 397.

8. C. L. Sulzberger, *A Long Row of Candles* (New York, 1969), p. 204.

9. Jozef Lettrich, *History of Modern Slovakia* (New York, 1955), p. 230.

10. Taborsky, "Beneš and Stalin," p. 177.

11. This and the preceding description are taken from Chapter 2 of Jan Stransky, *East Wind over Prague* (New York, 1951). Soviet excesses are corroborated in other sources, though less graphically.

12. Taborsky, "Beneš and Stalin," p. 176.

13. Ibid., p. 179.

14. This memorable speech is cited in ibid., pp. 179–180, and in a letter by

Harriman on March 31, 1945, in U.S. Dept. of State, *FRUS, Diplomatic Papers*, 1945, vol. 4 (Washington, D.C., 1968), p. 431.

15. *FRUS, Diplomatic Papers*, 1945, vol. 4, p. 429.

16. Victor S. Mamatey and Radomir Luza, eds., *A History of the Czechoslovak Republic, 1918–1948* (Princeton, N.J., 1973), pp. 388–389.

17. Paul E. Zinner, *Communist Strategy and Tactics in Czechoslovakia, 1918–1948* (New York, 1963), p. 94.

18. Josef Korbel, *The Communist Subversion of Czechoslovakia, 1938–1948* (Princeton, N.J., 1959), p. 115.

19. Paul E. Zinner, "Marxism in Action: The Seizure of Power in Czechoslovakia," *Foreign Affairs*, July 1950, p. 648.

20. Kenneth Young, ed., *Diaries of Sir Robert Bruce Lockhart*, vol. 2 (London, 1980), p. 411; Taborsky, "Beneš and Stalin," p. 180.

21. Taborsky, "Beneš and Stalin," p. 181.

22. Korbel, *Communist Subversion*, p. 120.

23. Ibid., p. 123.

24. Ibid., p. 126.

25. *FRUS, Diplomatic Papers*, 1945, vol. 4, p. 426.

26. Ibid., pp. 429–430.

27. Ibid., p. 435.

28. Ibid., pp. 443–444.

29. Ibid., p. 455.

30. Zinner, *Communist Strategy*, p. 100.

31. Ivo D. Duchacek, *The Strategy of Communist Infiltration: The Case of Czechoslovakia* (New Haven, 1949), pp. 8–9.

32. Chandler and Ambrose, *Papers . . . Eisenhower*, vol. 4, pp. 2632–2633.

33. Ibid., p. 2633.

34. John Ehrman, *Grand Strategy*, vol. 6 (London, 1956), p. 157.

35. Dwight Eisenhower, *Crusade in Europe* (Garden City, N.Y., 1952), p. 347.

36. Anthony Eden, *Memoirs of Anthony Eden*, vol. 2 *The Reckoning* (Boston, 1965), p. 615.

37. Ibid., p. 613.

38. Ibid., p. 615; *FRUS, Diplomatic Papers*, 1945, vol. 4, p. 445.

39. Eden, *The Reckoning*, p. 615.

40. Walter Ullman, *The United States in Prague, 1945–1948* (New York, 1978), p. 12.

41. Chandler and Ambrose, *Papers . . . Eisenhower*, vol. 4, p. 2662.

42. Ibid.

43. *FRUS, Diplomatic Papers*, 1945, vol. 4, p. 451.

44. Harry C. Butcher, *My Three Years with Eisenhower* (New York, 1946), p. 827.

45. *FRUS, Diplomatic Papers*, 1945, vol. 4, p. 451.

46. Omar Bradley, *A Soldier's Story* (New York, 1951), pp. 547–548.

47. Chandler and Ambrose, *Papers . . . Eisenhower*, vol. 4, p. 2662.

48. Churchill, *Triumph and Tragedy*, p. 506.

49. Harry S. Truman, *Year of Decisions* (Garden City, N.Y., 1955), p. 79.

50. Ibid., pp. 216–217.

51. Ibid.

52. Chandler and Ambrose, *Papers . . . Eisenhower*, vol. 4, pp. 2663–2664.

53. Martin Blumenson, ed., *The Patton Papers*, vol. 2 (Boston, 1974), p. 696.
54. Chandler and Ambrose, *Papers...Eisenhower*, vol. 4, pp. 2679–2680.
55. John R. Deane, *The Strange Alliance* (New York, 1947), p. 159.
56. Ehrman, *Grand Strategy*, vol. 6, pp. 159–160; Chandler and Ambrose, *Papers ...Eisenhower*, vol. 4, p. 2680.
57. Deane, *Strange Alliance*, p. 159.
58. Ehrman, *Grand Strategy*, vol. 6, p. 160.
59. Bradley, *A Soldier's Story*, p. 551; I. Konev, "Nineteen Forty-Five," *International Affairs* (Moscow), February 1966, pp. 87–88.
60. Bradley, *A Soldier's Story*, p. 549.
61. Blumenson, *Patton Papers*, vol. 2, p. 696.
62. George S. Patton, Jr., *War as I Knew It* (London, n.d.), p. 327.
63. *FRUS, Diplomatic Papers*, 1945, vol. 4, pp. 448–449.
64. Churchill, *Triumph and Tragedy*, p. 507.
65. Dana Adams Schmidt, *Anatomy of a Satellite* (Boston, 1952), pp. 90–91; Alan Levy, *Good Men Still Live!* (Chicago, 1974), pp. 39–53.
66. British Foreign Office, Czechoslovakia file, FO 371, 1945, file N5657/5217/12, "Report on Fighting in Prague, May 18, 1945."
67. Jan Kren and Jiří Dolezal, *Czechoslovakia's Fight, 1938 to 1945* (Prague: Committee on the History of the Czechoslovak Resistance Movement, 1964), p. 110.
68. Schmidt, *Anatomy*, p. 87.
69. Blumenson, *Patton Papers*, vol. 2, p. 696.
70. Ibid., p. 699.
71. Kren and Dolezal, *Fight*, p. 112.
72. Hubert Ripka, *Czechoslovakia Enslaved: The Story of the Communist Coup d'Etat* (London, 1950), p. 37. Ripka was minister of foreign trade in the Beneš cabinet.
73. Edward Taborsky, "The Triumph and Disaster of Eduard Beneš," *Foreign Affairs*, July 1958, p. 680; the Prague public's disappointment at the U.S. failure to appear is described in British Foreign Office, Czechoslovakia file, FO 371, 1945, file N5804/27/12, Nichols to Eden, 18 May 1945.
74. Schmidt, *Anatomy*, pp. 87, 88, 91.
75. Georgi Zhukov, *Memoirs of Marshal Zhukov* (New York, 1971), p. 640.
76. Igor Vitukhin, ed., *Soviet Generals Recall World War II* (New York, 1981), p. 392.
77. Konev, "Nineteen Forty-Five," pp. 92–93.
78. Forrest C. Pogue, *The Supreme Command*, vol. 3, pt. 4 (Washington, D.C., 1954), pp. 565–566.
79. Forrest C. Pogue, *George C. Marshall: Organizer of Victory, 1943–1945* (New York, 1973), p. 573.

CHAPTER 14   "LET THE SPARROWS TWITTER!"

1. Walter Bedell Smith, *My Three Years in Moscow* (Philadelphia and New York, 1950), p. 17.
2. U.S. Dept. of State, *FRUS, Diplomatic Papers*, 1945, vol. 5 (Washington, D.C., 1967), pp. 486–487.
3. Ibid., pp. 487–488, 502.
4. Ibid., p. 503.

5. Evidence on British reluctance to act in the Balkans due to the percent agreement is abundant; Anthony Eden, *The Memoirs of Anthony Eden, Earl of Avon*, vol. 2, *The Reckoning* (Boston, 1965), p. 605; Winston Churchill, *Triumph and Tragedy* (Boston, 1953), p. 420; Sir John Colville, *The Fringes of Power* (New York and London, 1985), p. 565; British Foreign Office, Russian Correspondence, FO 371, 1945, vol. 47881, undated Foreign Office memo (approx. 6 January 1945), "Russian Behavior in Eastern Europe and on Control Commission"; ibid., Southern Europe Correspondence, 1945, file 45–17–47941, Clark Kerr to Eden, 2 March 1945.

6. *FRUS, Diplomatic Papers*, 1945, vol. 5, p. 504.

7. Ibid., p. 505–506; Churchill, *Triumph and Tragedy*, pp. 419–421; Warren F. Kimball, ed., *Churchill & Roosevelt* (Princeton, N.J., 1984), vol. 3, pp. 547–548.

8. Kimball, *Churchill & Roosevelt*, vol. 3, p. 562.

9. *FRUS, Diplomatic Papers*, 1945, vol. 5, pp. 507–508.

10. Ibid., pp. 194, 528.

11. Ibid., p. 511.

12. British Foreign Office, Russia Correspondence, FO 371, 1945, vol. 47881, "Notes on Conversation at Dinner at Livadia on 4 February 1945."

13. U.S. Congress, 83rd Congress, 2nd Session, House of Representatives, "Communist Takeover and Occupation of Hungary," Fifth Interim Report of Hearings Before the Subcommittee on Hungary of the Select Committee on Communist Aggression (Washington, D.C., 1954), testimony of Bishop Alexander St. Ivanyi, p. 250.

14. National Archives, U.S. Army, Allied Control Commission, Hungary, 1945, letter from Brigadier General William S. Key to Major General J. E. Hull, assistant chief of staff, May 19, 1945.

15. Ibid., Secretary of State James F. Byrnes to H. F. Arthur Schoenfeld, October 26, 1945.

16. Nigel Nicholson, ed., *The Diaries... of Harold Nicholson*, vol. 2 (New York, 1967), p. 439.

17. This so-called Bern incident is documented in *FRUS, Diplomatic Papers*, 1945, vol. 3, pp. 722–757; Churchill, *Triumph and Tragedy*, pp. 441–453. The preliminary talks in Switzerland concerning a German surrender in Italy are in Allen Dulles, *The Secret Surrender* (New York, 1966).

18. Colville, *Fringes of Power*, p. 566.

19. Kimball, *Churchill & Roosevelt*, vol. 3, p. 552.

20. Ibid., p. 562.

21. Ibid., p. 565.

22. Ibid., p. 588–589.

23. *Correspondence Between the Chairman of the Council of Ministers of the U.S.S.R. and the Presidents of the U.S.A. and the Prime Ministers of Great Britain During the Great Patriotic War of 1941–1945* (Moscow, 1957), vol. 2, p. 202.

24. C. L. Sulzberger, *A Long Row of Candles* (New York, 1969), p. 253.

25. *FRUS, Diplomatic Papers*, 1945, vol. 5, pp. 202, 204.

26. W. Averell Harriman and Elie Abel, *Special Envoy to Churchill and Stalin* (New York, 1975), p. 444.

27. *FRUS, Diplomatic Papers*, 1945, vol. 3, pp. 756–757.

28. The Polish issue in the Tripartite Commission meetings up to Roosevelt's death on April 12, 1945, is documented in *FRUS, Diplomatic Papers*, 1945, vol. 5,

pp. 153–210; Churchill, *Triumph and Tragedy*, pp. 421–439; Harriman and Abel, *Special Envoy*, pp. 426–440.

29. Eden, *The Reckoning*, p. 595.

30. Churchill, *Triumph and Tragedy*, pp. 497, 501.

31. Ibid., p. 503.

32. The staff meeting in the Oval Office on April 23 is covered in: *FRUS, Diplomatic Papers*, 1945, vol. 5, pp. 252–255; Harry S. Truman, *Year of Decisions* (Garden City, N.Y., 1955), pp. 77–79; Henry L. Stimson and McGeorge Bundy, *On Active Service in Peace and War* (New York, 1947), p. 609; Walter Millis, ed., *The Forrestal Diaries* (New York, 1951), pp. 49–51; Harriman and Abel, *Special Envoy*, pp. 451–453; William D. Leahy, *I Was There: The Personal Story of the Chief of Staff to Presidents Roosevelt and Truman Based on His Notes and Diaries Made at the Time (New York, 1950), p. 351; Charles E. Bohlen, Witness to History, 1929–1969* (New York, 1973), pp. 212–213.

33. The meeting between Truman and Molotov on April 23 is described in *FRUS, Diplomatic Papers*, 1945, vol. 5, pp. 256–258; Truman, *Year of Decisions*, pp. 79–82; Harriman and Abel, *Special Envoy*, p. 453; Leahy, *I Was There*, pp. 351–352; and Bohlen, *Witness*, p. 213.

34. Bohlen, *Witness*, p. 214.

35. Ibid., p. 215.

36. Information on the arrest of the 16 Polish leaders is in *FRUS, Diplomatic Papers*, 1945, vol. 5, pp. 281–284, 286–288; Stanislaw Mikolajczyk, *The Rape of Poland: Pattern of Soviet Aggression* (New York, 1948), pp. 111–112; Stefan Korbonski, *The Polish Underground State. A Guide to the Underground, 1939–1945*, trans. Marta Erdman (Boulder, Colo., 1978), pp. 216–219; General Sikorski Historical Institute, *Documents on Polish-Soviet Relations, 1939–1945*, vol. 2 (London, 1967), pp. 556–558, 573–574; Mikolajczyk Papers, box 36, Correspondence and Memoranda, January–June 1945, account of the Polish government-in-exile, April 6, 1945, and statement by Stanislaw Mikolajczyk, May 7, 1945.

37. Hopkins's negotiations with Stalin in Moscow are documented in *FRUS, Diplomatic Papers*, 1945, vol. 5, pp. 299–324, 326–328; Robert E. Sherwood, *Roosevelt and Hopkins: An Intimate History* (New York, 1948), pp. 887–912; Harriman and Abel, *Special Envoy*, pp. 459–471; Bohlen, *Witness*, pp. 215, 218–221.

38. Churchill, *Triumph and Tragedy*, pp. 560–561.

39. Robert Rhodes James, *Anthony Eden* (London, 1986), pp. 295, 305.

40. Churchill, *Triumph and Tragedy*, p. 555.

41. Ibid., pp. 573–574.

42. Ibid., p. 609.

43. Rohan Butler and M. E. Pelly, eds., *Documents on British Policy Overseas*, series 1, vol. 1, *The Conference at Potsdam, July–August, 1945* (London, 1984), p. 3.

44. U.S. Dept. of State, *FRUS, The Conference of Berlin (The Potsdam Conference), 1945*, vol. 2 (Washington, D.C., 1960), p. 166.

45. Ibid., pp. 230–231.

46. Ibid., p. 394.

47. Ibid., p. 360.

48. Ibid., p. 362.

49. Ibid., p. 555.

50. *FRUS, Diplomatic Papers*, 1945, vol. 4 (Washington, D.C., 1968), p. 856.

51. David Dilks, ed., *Diaries of Sir Alexander Cadogan* (London, 1971), p. 778.

52. Bohlen, *Witness*, p. 219.

CHAPTER 15   THE CURTAIN DESCENDS

1. Josef Korbel, *The Communist Subversion of Czechoslovakia, 1938–1948* (Princeton, N.J., 1959), p. 183.

2. Dana Adams Schmidt, *Anatomy of a Satellite* (Boston, 1952), p. 121.

3. *New York Times*, April 4, 1968, p. 7; April 7, 1968, p. 18; April 17, 1968, pp. 1, 46. See also Claire Sterling, *The Masaryk Case* (New York, 1968).

4. Edward Taborsky, "Beneš and Stalin—Moscow, 1943 and 1945," *Journal of Central European Affairs*, July 1953, p. 162n.

5. Cordell Hull, *The Memoirs of Cordell Hull*, vol. 2 (New York, 1948), p. 1272.

6. Sarah Churchill, *A Thread in the Tapestry* (New York, 1967), p. 17.

Bibliography

The story of how Europe was divided by the Allied Powers during World War II is derived from a wealth of both manuscript and published primary sources, including letters, reports, diaries, memoirs, testimony, and transcripts of conversations of the principal figures involved. Particularly fruitful are the correspondence of the British Foreign Office, the prime minister's operational correspondence, and the voluminous diplomatic papers on the foreign relations of the United States—all for the years 1941 to 1945. These provide firsthand exchanges among the top U.S., British, and Soviet leaders—not only at the three summit conferences at Tehran, Yalta, and Potsdam but more especially at numerous other meetings and in ongoing correspondence over the period. A great many other volumes of private diaries, letters, and reminiscences of key figures are also invaluable.

The Soviet transcripts of the principal conferences, published in English, are useful; we have a number of memoirs of Soviet generals and diplomats. However, Soviet archives on foreign affairs during this period and afterward are not open to foreign researchers. Access even for Soviet historians still appears to be limited. In September 1989, V. K. Volkov, director of the Institute of Slavonic and Balkan studies in Moscow, told a Paris conference on the "Fiftieth Anniversary of the Opening of the Second World War" that there were many gaps in the Soviet foreign affairs archives. Many documents, he said, disappeared during the Stalin era. It therefore seems doubtful that we will ever have much insight into the internal Soviet discussions on the division of Europe.

PRIMARY SOURCES

Manuscripts and Microfilms

British Foreign Office. Czechoslovakia, Hungary, and Poland files, including Southern Europe Correspondence. FO 371, 1943 to 1945. British Government Ar-

chives, Public Records Office, Kew Gardens, London.
———. Russia Correspondence. FO 371, 1941 to 1945, vols. 29655 to 47987. Microform Office, Research Library, University of California at Los Angeles.
British Prime Minister's Operational Correspondence, 1941 to 1945 (PREM 3/352 to 3/399). Microtext Office, Cecil H. Green Library, Stanford University.
Papers of Stanislaw Mikolajczyk, 1938 to 1966. Holding no. 1793. Hoover Institution, Stanford University.
War Department General Staff. European Theater Section, Allied Control Commission, Hungary, 1945. Series RG 338. U.S. National Archives, Federal Records Center, Suitland, Md.

Government Publications

Great Britain

Butler, J. R. M., ed. United Kingdom Military Series. *History of the Second World War*.
    Ehrman, John. *Grand Strategy*. Vols. 5 and 6. London, 1956
    Howard, Michael. *Grand Strategy*. Vol. 4. London, 1972
Butler, Rohan, and M. E. Pelly, eds. *Documents on British Policy Overseas*. Series 1, vols. 1 and 2 (1945). London, 1984.

Soviet Union

Correspondence Between the Chairman of the Council of Ministers of the U.S.S.R. and the Presidents of the U.S.A. and the Prime Ministers of Great Britain During the Great Patriotic War of 1941–1945. 2 vols. Moscow, 1957.
"Documents: The Crimea and Potsdam Conferences of the Leaders of the Three Great Powers, 1945." *International Affairs* (Moscow), June–December 1965, January–May 1966.
"Documents: The Tehran Conference of the Leaders of the Three Great Powers, 1943." *International Affairs* (Moscow), July and August 1961.
Berezhkov, Valentin. *History in the Making: Memoirs of World War II Diplomacy*. Moscow, 1983.
Konev, I. "Nineteen Forty-Five." *International Affairs* (Moscow), February 1966.
Ponomaryov, B., A. Gromyko, and V. Khvostov, eds. *History of Soviet Foreign Policy, 1917–1945*. Moscow, 1969.
Rokossovsky, K. K. *A Soldier's Duty*. Moscow, 1970.
Shtemenko, Sergei M. *The Soviet General Staff at War, 1941–1945*. Trans. Robert Daglish. Moscow, 1976.

United States

United States Congress, 80th Congress. House of Representatives, Committee on Foreign Affairs. *The Coup d'Etat in Prague*. Supplement 3, *Country Studies. The Strategy and Tactics of World Communism*. Washington, D.C., 1949.

——. 80th Congress. House of Representatives, Committee on Foreign Affairs. *The Coup d'Etat in Prague.* Supp. 3, *Country Studies. The Strategy and Tactics of World Communism.* Washington, D.C., 1949.

——. 80th Congress. House of Representatives, Committee on Foreign Affairs. *National and International Movements. The Strategy and Tactics of World Communism.* Washington, D.C., 1949.

——. 81st Congress, 1st Session. House of Representatives, Committee on Foreign Affairs. *The Strategy and Tactics of World Communism.* Supp. 2, *Official Protests of the United States Government Against Communist Policies or Actions, and Related Correspondence (July 1945–December 1947).* Washington, D.C., 1948.

——. 83rd Congress, 2nd Session. House of Representatives. *Communist Takeover and Occupation of Hungary.* Fifth Interim Report of Hearings Before the Subcommittee on Hungary of the Select Committee on Communist Aggression. Washington, D.C., 1954.

——. 83rd Congress, 2nd Session. House of Representatives. *Report of Committee to Investigate Communist Aggression and Forced Incorporation of the Baltic States into the USSR.* Washington, D.C., 1954.

U.S. Department of the Army. *The United States Army in World War II—the European Theater of Operations.*
MacDonald, Charles B. *The Last Offensive.* Vol. 3, pt. 9. Washington, D.C., 1954.
Pogue, Forrest C. *The Supreme Command.* Vol. 3, pt. 4. Washington, D.C., 1954.

U.S. Department of State. *Department of State Bulletin*, October 29, 1944. (Message from President Roosevelt to President Beneš on the anniversary of Czechoslovak independence.)

——. *Nazi-Soviet Relations, 1939–1941: Documents from the Archives of the German Foreign Office.* Ed. Raymond James Sontag and James Stuart Beddie. Washington, D.C., 1948.

——. *Foreign Relations of the United States* (FRUS). *The Conferences at Malta and Yalta, 1945.* Washington, D.C., 1955.

——. *FRUS. Diplomatic Papers.* Washington, D.C.
1941. Vol. 1. 1958.
1942. Vol. 3. 1961.
1943. Vol. 1. 1963.
1943. Vol. 3. 1963.
1944. Vol. 3. 1965.
1944. Vol. 4. 1965.
1945. Vol. 2. 1967.
1945. Vol. 3. 1968.
1945. Vol. 4. 1968.
1945. Vol. 5. 1967.
1946. Vol. 2. 1970.
1946. Vol. 6. 1969.
1947. Vol. 3. 1972.
1947. Vol. 4. 1972.
1948. Vol. 4. 1974.

——. *FRUS. The Conference of Berlin (The Potsdam Conference), 1945.* Vols. 1 and 2.

Washington, D.C., 1960.

———. *FRUS. The Conferences at Cairo and Tehran, 1943.* Washington, D.C., 1961.

———. *FRUS. The Conferences at Washington, 1941 and 1942, and Casablanca, 1943.* Washington, D.C., 1968.

———. *FRUS. The Conferences at Washington and Quebec, 1943.* Washington, D.C., 1970.

———. *FRUS. The Conference at Quebec, 1944.* Washington, D.C., 1972.

Other Primary Books

Acheson, Dean. *Present at the Creation: My Years in the State Department.* New York, 1969.

Alliluyeva, Svetlana. *Twenty Letters to a Friend.* New York, 1967.

Anders, Wladyslaw. *An Army in Exile.* London, 1949.

Auty, Phyllis, and Richard Clogg, eds. *British Policy Towards Wartime Resistance in Yugoslavia and Greece.* London, 1975.

Beneš, Eduard. *Memoirs of Dr. Eduard Beneš: From Munich to New War and New Victory.* Trans. Godfrey Lias. Cambridge, 1954.

Berezhkov, Valentin. *History in the Making: Memoirs of World War II Diplomacy.* Moscow, 1983.

Bialer, Seweryn, ed. *Stalin and His Generals.* New York, 1969.

Birse, A. H. *Memoirs of an Interpreter.* London, 1967.

Blumenson, Martin, ed. *The Patton Papers,* Vol. 2, *1940–1945.* Boston, 1974.

Bohlen, Charles E. *Witness to History, 1929–1969.* New York, 1973.

Bonham Carter, Violet. *Winston Churchill: An Intimate Portrait.* New York, 1965.

Bór-Komorowski, Tadeusz. *The Secret Army.* London, 1950.

Bradley, Omar N. *A Soldier's Story.* New York, 1951.

Bradley, Omar N., and Clay Blair. *A General's Life.* New York, 1983.

Bryant, Arthur. *The Turn of the Tide: A History of the War Years Based on the Diaries of Field-Marshal Lord Alan Brooke, Chief of the Imperial General Staff.* Garden City, N.Y., 1957.

———. *Triumph in the West: A History of the War Years Based on the Diaries of Field-Marshal Lord Alan Brooke, Chief of the Imperial General Staff.* Garden City, N.Y., 1959.

Bullitt, Orville H., ed. *For the President: Personal and Secret: Correspondence Between Franklin D. Roosevelt and William C. Bullitt.* Boston, 1972.

Butcher, Harry C. *My Three Years with Eisenhower.* New York, 1946.

Byrnes, James F. *Speaking Frankly.* New York, 1947.

———. *All in One Lifetime.* New York, 1958.

Campbell, Thomas M., and George C. Herring, eds. *The Diaries of Edward R. Stettinius Jr., 1943–1946.* New York, 1975.

Chandler, Alfred D., Jr., and Stephen E. Ambrose, eds. *The Papers of Dwight David Eisenhower.* Vols. 3 and 4. Baltimore and London, 1970.

Chuikov, Vasili I. *The End of the Third Reich.* Trans. Ruth Kisch. London, 1967.

Churchill, Sarah. *A Thread in the Tapestry.* New York, 1967.

Churchill, Winston S. *The Second World War.* 6 vols.

    The Gathering Storm. Boston, 1948.

    Their Finest Hour. Boston, 1949.

The Grand Alliance. Boston, 1950.

The Hinge of Fate. Boston, 1950.

Closing the Ring. Boston, 1951.

Triumph and Tragedy. Boston, 1953.

Ciechanowski, Jan. *Defeat in Victory*. Garden City, N.Y., 1947.

Clark, Mark C. *Calculated Risk*. New York, 1950.

Colville, Sir John. *Winston Churchill and His Inner Circle*. New York, 1981.

———. *The Fringes of Power: 10 Downing Street Diaries 1939–1955*. New York and London, 1985.

Crankshaw, Edward, ed. *Khrushchev Remembers*. Boston, 1970.

Deane, John R. *The Strange Alliance*. New York, 1947.

Dedijer, Vladimir. *Tito*. New York, 1953.

de Gaulle, Charles. *The War Memoirs of Charles de Gaulle*. Vol. 2, *Unity: 1942–1944*. Trans. Richard Howard. New York, 1959.

Dennett, Raymond, and Robert K. Turner, eds. *Documents on American Foreign Relations*. Vols. 6–9 (1944–1947). Princeton, N.J., 1949.

Dilks, David, ed. *The Diaries of Sir Alexander Cadogan, 1938–1945*. London, 1971.

Djilas, Milovan. *Conversations with Stalin*. New York, 1962.

Dönitz, Karl. *Memoirs: Ten Years and Twenty Days*. Trans. R. H. Stevens. London, 1959.

Dulles, Allen. *The Secret Surrender*. New York, 1966.

Eden, Anthony. *The Memoirs of Anthony Eden, Earl of Avon*. Vol. 2, *The Reckoning*. Boston, 1965.

Eisenhower, Dwight D. *Crusade in Europe*. Garden City, N.Y., 1952.

Gavin, James M. *On to Berlin: Battles of an Airborne Commander, 1943–1946*. New York, 1978.

General Sikorski Historical Institute. *Documents on Polish-Soviet Relations, 1939–1945*. Vol. 1, 1939–1943. London, 1961. Vol. 2, 1943–1945. London, 1967.

Gorlitz, Walter, ed. *The Memoirs of Field-Marshal Keitel*. Trans. David Irving. New York, 1966.

Grew, Joseph C. *Turbulent Era: A Diplomatic Record of Forty Years, 1904–1945*. Ed. Walter Johnson. Vol. 2. Boston, 1952.

Griffis, Stanton. *Lying in State*. New York, 1952.

Guderian, Heinz. *Panzer Leader*. London, 1952.

Harriman, W. Averell, and Elie Abel. *Special Envoy to Churchill and Stalin, 1941–1946*. New York, 1975.

Harvey, John, ed. *The War Diaries of Oliver Harvey*. London, 1978.

Hilger, Gustav, and Alfred G. Meyer. *The Incompatible Allies. A Memoir-History of German-Soviet Relations, 1918–1941*. New York, 1953.

Hull, Cordell. *The Memoirs of Cordell Hull*. Vol. 2. New York, 1948.

Ismay, Hastings Lionel. *The Memoirs of General Lord Ismay*. New York, 1960.

Karski, Jan. *Story of a Secret State*. Boston, 1944.

Kennan, George F. *Memoirs, 1925–1950*. Boston, 1967.

Kimball, Warren F., ed. *Churchill & Roosevelt: The Complete Correspondence*. 3 vols. Princeton, N.J., 1984.

Korbonski, Stefan. *Fighting Warsaw: The Story of the Polish Underground State, 1939–1945*. London, 1956.

———. *The Polish Underground State. A Guide to the Underground, 1939–1945*. Trans.

Marta Erdman. Boulder, Colo., 1978.

Kot, Stanslaw. *Conversations with the Kremlin and Dispatches from Russia*. Trans. H. C. Stevens. London, 1965.

Lane, Arthur Bliss. *I Saw Poland Betrayed: An American Ambassador Reports to the American People*. New York, 1948.

Leahy, William D. *I Was There: The Personal Story of the Chief of Staff to Presidents Roosevelt and Truman Based on His Notes and Diaries Made at the Time*. New York, 1950.

Levy, Alan. *Good Men Still Live!* Chicago, 1974.

Lochner, Louis P., ed. and trans. *The Goebbels Diaries, 1942–1943*. Garden City, N.Y., 1948.

Lockhart, R. H. Bruce. *Comes the Reckoning*. London, 1947.

Loewenheim, Francis L., Harold D. Langley, and Manfred Jonas. *Roosevelt and Churchill: Their Secret Wartime Correspondence*. New York, 1975.

Maclean, Fitzroy. *Eastern Approaches*. London, 1949.

Macmillan, Harold. *The Blast of War, 1939–1945*. New York, 1967.

——. *War Diaries. Politics and War in the Mediterranean, January 1943–May 1945*. New York, 1984.

Maisky, Ivan. *Memoirs of a Soviet Ambassador*. New York, 1967.

Mikolajczyk, Stanislaw. *The Rape of Poland: Pattern of Soviet Aggression*. New York, 1948.

Millis, Walter, ed. *The Forrestal Diaries*. New York, 1951.

Montgomery, Bernard Law. *The Memoirs of Field-Marshal the Viscount Montgomery of Alamein*. Cleveland and New York, 1958.

Murphy, Robert. *Diplomat Among Warriors*. Garden City, N.Y., 1964.

Nagy, Ferenc. *The Struggle Behind the Iron Curtain*. New York, 1948.

Nelson, James, ed. *General Eisenhower on the Military Churchill*. New York, 1970. (Interview of Eisenhower by Alistair Cooke.)

Nemec, F., and V. Moudry. *The Soviet Seizure of Subcarpathian Ruthenia*. Toronto, 1955.

Nicholson, Nigel, ed. *The Diaries and Letters of Harold Nicholson*. Vol. 2, *The War Years, 1939–1945*. New York, 1967.

North, John, ed. *The Alexander Memoirs, 1940–1945. Field-Marshal Earl Alexander of Tunis*. London, 1962.

Patton, George S., Jr. *War as I Knew It*. London, n.d.

Perkins, Frances. *The Roosevelt I Knew*. New York, 1946.

Polish Cultural Foundation. *The Crime of Katyn: Facts and Documents*. London, 1965.

Raczynski, Count Edward. *In Allied London*. London, 1962.

Reynolds, Quentin James. *Only the Stars Are Neutral*. New York, 1942.

Richardson, Stewart, ed. *The Secret History of World War II*. New York, 1986.

Roosevelt, Elliott. *As He Saw It*. New York, 1946.

Roosevelt, Elliott, and Joseph P. Lash, eds. *F. D. R. His Personal Letters, 1928–1945*. Vol. 2. New York, 1950.

Rosenman, Samuel I. *The Public Papers and Addresses of Franklin D. Roosevelt*. Vols. 1941, 1942, 1943, and 1944–1945. New York, 1950.

Ross, Graham, ed. *The Foreign Office and the Kremlin: British Documents on Anglo-Soviet Relations, 1941–1945*. Cambridge, 1984.

Salisbury, Harrison E. *A Journey for Our Times: A Memoir*. New York, 1983.

Smith, Walter Bedell. *My Three Years in Moscow*. Philadelphia and New York, 1950.

Standley, William. *Admiral Ambassador to Russia*. Chicago, 1955.

Stettinius, Edward R., Jr. *Roosevelt and the Russians: The Yalta Conference*. Ed. Walter Johnson. Garden City, N.Y., 1949.

Stimson, Henry L., and McGeorge Bundy. *On Active Service in Peace and War*. New York, 1947.

Stransky, Jan. *East Wind over Prague*. New York, 1951.

Sulzberger, C. L. *A Long Row of Candles. Memoirs and Diaries 1934–1954*. New York, 1969.

Truman, Harry S. *Memoirs*. 2 vols.: *Year of Decisions* and *Years of Trial and Hope*. Garden City, N.Y., 1955.

Vitukhin, Igor, ed. *Soviet Generals Recall World War II*. New York, 1981.

Wedemeyer, Albert C. *Wedeyer Reports!* New York, 1958.

Wheeler-Bennett, Sir John, ed. *Action This Day: Working with Churchill*. New York and London, 1969.

Wilson, Sir Charles (Lord Moran). *Churchill: Taken from the Diaries of Lord Moran. The Struggle for Survival, 1940–1965*. Boston, 1966.

Wilson, Sir Henry Maitland. *Eight Years Overseas: 1939–1947*. London, 1948.

Winant, John Gilbert. *Letter from Grosvenor Square*. Boston, 1947.

Young, Kenneth, ed. *The Diaries of Sir Robert Bruce Lockhart, 1939–1965*. Vol. 2. London, 1980.

Zhukov, Georgi K. *The Memoirs of Marshal Zhukov*. New York, 1971.

Primary Sources in Periodicals

Beneš, Eduard. "Postwar Czechoslovakia," *Foreign Affairs*, April 1946, pp. 397–410.

Bess, Demaree. "Our Agents Behind the Iron Curtain," *Saturday Evening Post*, August 24, 1946, pp. 18–19, 117–118.

Bullitt, William C. "How We Won the War and Lost the Peace," *Life*, August 30, 1948, pp. 82–97.

Marshall, S. L. A. *New York Times Book Review*, February 13, 1966, p. 1; March 27, 1966, pp. 30, 32.

Nagy, Ferenc. "How the Russians Grabbed My Government," *Saturday Evening Post*, August 23, 1947, pp. 18–19, 76–78; August 30, 1947, pp. 24–25, 83–86, 105; September 6, 1947, pp. 28, 137–140, 161.

Schoenfeld, H. F. Arthur. "What Russia Has Done in Hungary," *Vital Speeches*, October 15, 1947, pp. 28–32.

———, "Soviet Imperialism in Hungary," *Foreign Affairs*, April 1948, pp. 554–566.

Simpson, William H. *New York Times Book Review*, June 12, 1966, p. 34.

Smutný, Jaromír, transcriber, and Mastny, Vojtech, translator. "The Beneš-Stalin-Molotov Conversations in December 1943: New Documents," *Jahrbücher für Geschichte Osteuropas, n.f.* 20, heft 3 (September 1972): 367–402.

Taborsky, Edward. "Beneš and the Soviets," *Foreign Affairs*, January 1949, pp. 302–314.

———. "Beneš and Stalin—Moscow, 1943 and 1945," *Journal of Central European Affairs*, July 1953, pp. 154–181.

———. "The Triumph and Disaster of Eduard Beneš," *Foreign Affairs*, July 1958, pp. 669–684.

SECONDARY SOURCES

Books

Ambrose, Stephen E. *Eisenhower and Berlin, 1945: The Decision to Halt at the Elbe.* New York, 1960.
———. *The Supreme Commander; the War Years of General Dwight D. Eisenhower.* Garden City, N.Y., 1976.
———. *Eisenhower.* New York, 1983.
Armstrong, Anne. *Unconditional Surrender: The Impact of the Casablanca Policy upon World War II.* New Brunswick, N.J., 1961.
Baldwin, Hanson W. *Great Mistakes of the War.* New York, 1949.
Barker, Elisabeth. *British Policy in South-East Europe in the Second World War.* London, 1976.
———. *Churchill and Eden at War.* London, 1978.
Betts, R. R., ed. *Central and South East Europe, 1945–1948.* London, 1950.
Bosordy, Stephen. *The Triumph of Tyranny: The Nazi and Soviet Conquest of Central Europe.* New York, 1960.
Bruce, George. *The Warsaw Uprising.* London, 1972.
Brzezinski, Zbigniew K. *The Soviet Bloc: Unity and Conflict.* Cambridge, Mass., 1960.
Bullitt, William C. *The Great Globe Itself: A Preface to World Affairs.* New York, 1946.
Burns, James McGregor. *Roosevelt: The Soldier of Freedom.* New York, 1970.
Ciechanowski, Jan M. *The Warsaw Rising of 1944.* London and New York, 1974.
Clark, Alan. *Barbarossa: The Russian-German Conflict, 1941–45.* New York, 1965.
Clemens, Diane Shaver. *Yalta.* New York, 1970.
Coutouvidis, John, and Jayme Reynolds. *Poland 1939–1947.* Leicester, 1986.
Davis, Lynn Etheridge. *The Cold War Begins: Soviet-American Conflict over Eastern Europe.* Princeton, N.J., 1974.
Deakin, William, Elisabeth Barker and Jonathan Chadwick, eds. *British Political and Military Strategy in Central, Eastern and Southern Europe in 1944.* London, 1988.
Divine, Robert A. *Roosevelt and World War II.* Baltimore, 1969.
Duchacek, Ivo D. *The Strategy of Communist Infiltration: The Case of Czechoslovakia.* New Haven, 1949.
Erickson, John. *The Road to Berlin: Continuing the History of Stalin's War with Germany.* Boulder, Colo., 1983.
Eubank, Keith. *The Summit Conferences, 1919–1960.* Norman, Okla., 1966.
———. *Summit at Teheran.* New York, 1985.
Feis, Herbert. *Churchill-Roosevelt-Stalin: The War They Waged and the Peace They Sought.* Princeton, N.J., 1957.
———. *Between War and Peace: The Potsdam Conference.* Princeton, N.J., 1960.
Fitzgibbon, Louis. *Unpitied and Unknown.* London, 1975.
Friedman, Otto. *The Breakup of Czech Democracy.* Westport, Conn., 1971.
Gannon, Robert J. *The Cardinal Spellman Story.* New York, 1962.
Garlinski, Josef. *Poland, SOE and the Allies.* Trans. Paul Stevenson. London, 1969.
Gilbert, Martin. *Road to Victory: Winston S. Churchill, 1941–1945.* London, 1986.
Glaser, Kurt. *Czechoslovakia: A Critical History.* Caldwell, Idaho, 1961.
Hamilton, Nigel. *Monty: The Field-Marshal, 1944–1976.* London, 1986.

Higgins, Trumbull. *Winston Churchill and the Second Front, 1940–1943*. New York, 1957.

———. *Soft Underbelly: The Anglo-American Controversy over the Italian Campaign, 1939–1945*. New York and London, 1968.

Howard, Michael. *The Mediterranean Strategy in the Second World War*. London, 1968.

Ingersoll, Ralph. *Top Secret*. New York, 1946.

Irving, David. *The War Between the Generals*. New York, 1981.

James, Robert Rhodes. *Anthony Eden*. London, 1986.

Kacewicz, George V. *Great Britain, the Soviet Union and the Polish Government in Exile 1939–1945*. The Hague, 1979.

Kennan, George F. *Russia and the West Under Lenin and Stalin*. Boston, 1960.

Kertesz, Stephen D. *Diplomacy in a Whirlpool: Hungary Between Nazi Germany and Soviet Russia*. Notre Dame, Ind., 1953.

———. *Between Russia and the West: Hungary and the Illusion of Peacemaking, 1945–1947*. Notre Dame, Ind., 1984.

———, ed. *The Fate of East Central Europe* Notre Dame, Ind., 1956.

Kitchen, Martin. *British Policy Towards the Soviet Union During the Second World War*. New York, 1986.

Kolko, Gabriel. *The Politics of War: The World and United States Foreign Policy, 1943–1945*. New York, 1968.

Korbel, Josef. *The Communist Subversion of Czechoslovakia, 1938–1948*. Princeton, N.J., 1959.

Kovrig, Bennett. *The Myth of Liberation: East-Central Europe in U.S. Diplomacy and Politics Since 1941*. Baltimore, 1973.

Kren, Jan, and Jiří Dolezal. *Czechoslovakia's Fight, 1938 to 1945*. Prague: Committee on the History of the Czechoslovak Resistance Movement, 1964.

Kuby, Erich. *The Russians and Berlin, 1945*. Trans. A. J. Pomerans. New York, 1968.

Kusnierz, D. Bronislaw. *Stalin and the Poles*. London, 1949.

LaFeber, Walter. *America, Russia and the Cold War 1945–1971*. New York, 1972.

Lettrich, Jozef. *History of Modern Slovakia*. New York, 1955.

Liddell Hart, Sir Basil H. *The Other Side of the Hill*. London, 1948.

———. *History of the Second World War*. New York, 1970.

Lukacs, John A. *The Great Powers and Eastern Europe*. New York, 1953.

———. *1945: Year Zero*. Garden City, N.Y., 1978.

Mamatey, Victor S., and Radomir Luza, eds. *A History of the Czechoslovak Republic, 1918–1948*. Princeton, N.J., 1973.

Mastny, Vojtech. *Russia's Road to the Cold War: Diplomacy, Warfare, and the Politics of Communism, 1941–1945*. New York, 1979.

Mayle, Paul D. *Eureka Summit: Agreement in Principle and the Big Three at Tehran, 1943*. Cranbury, N.J., 1987.

McNeill, William H. *America, Britain and Russia: Their Cooperation and Conflict, 1941–1946*. London, 1953.

Medvedev, Roy. *Let History Judge. The Origins and Consequences of Stalinism*. New York, 1989.

Mee, Charles L., Jr. *Meeting at Potsdam*. New York, 1975.

Neumann, William L. *After Victory: Churchill, Roosevelt, Stalin and the Making of the Peace*. New York, 1967.

O'Connor, Raymond G. *Diplomacy for Victory: FDR and Unconditional Surrender*. New York, 1971.

Pogue, Forrest C. *George C. Marshall: Organizer of Victory, 1943–1945*. New York, 1973.

Polonsky, Antony. *The Great Powers and the Polish Question*. London, 1976.

Ripka, Hubert. *Czechoslovakia Enslaved: The Story of the Communist Coup d'Etat*. London, 1950.

———. *Eastern Europe in the Post-War World*. New York, 1961.

Roberts, Walter R. *Tito, Mihailović and the Allies, 1941–1945*. New Brunswick, N.J., 1973.

Rose, Lisle A. *Dubious Victory: The United States and the End of World War II*. Kent, Ohio, 1973.

Rothwell, Victor. *Britain and the Cold War, 1941–1947*. London, 1982.

Roucek, Joseph S., ed. *Moscow's European Satellites*. Annals of the American Academy of Political and Social Science, 271. (September 1950).

Rozek, Edward J. *Allied Wartime Diplomacy: A Pattern in Poland*. New York, 1958.

Ryan, Cornelius. *The Last Battle*. New York, 1966.

Ryan, Henry Butterfield. *The Vision of Anglo-America. The US–UK Alliance and the Emerging Cold War, 1943–1946*. Cambridge, 1987.

Saimsbury, Keith. *The Turning Point: Roosevelt, Stalin, Churchill and Chiang Kai-Shek, 1943*. Oxford, 1985.

Schmidt, Dana Adams. *Anatomy of a Satellite*. Boston, 1952.

Seton-Watson, Hugh. *The East European Revolution*. London, 1956.

———. *Neither War nor Peace: The Struggle for Power in the Postwar World*. New York, 1960.

Sherwood, Robert E. *Roosevelt and Hopkins: An Intimate History*. New York, 1948.

Snell, John L. *Illusion and Necessity: The Diplomacy of Global War, 1939–1945*. Boston, 1963.

Snell, John L., ed.; Forrest C. Pogue, Charles F. Delzell, and George A. Lensen. *The Meaning of Yalta: Big Three Diplomacy and the New Balance of Power*. Baton Rouge, La., 1956.

Sterling, Claire. *The Masaryk Case*. New York, 1968.

Stern, Harold. *The Struggle for Poland*. Washington, 1953.

Stoler, Mark A. *The Politics of the Second Front, 1941–43*. Westport, Conn., 1977.

Taylor, A. J. P., Robert Rhodes James, J. H. Plumb, Sir Basil H. Liddell Hart, and Anthony Storr. *Churchill Revised: A Critical Assessment*. New York, 1969.

Toland, John. *The Last 100 Days*. New York, 1965.

Tolstoy, Nikolai. *Stalin's Secret War*. London, 1981.

Ulam, Adam B. *Stalin: The Man and His Era*. New York, 1973.

———. *Expansion and Co-Existence: Soviet Foreign Policy, 1917–73*. New York, 1974.

Ullman, Walter. *The United States in Prague, 1945–1948*. New York, 1978.

Umiatowski, Roman. *Poland, Russia and Great Britain, 1941–1945: A Study of Evidence*. London, 1946.

Welles, Sumner. *The Time for Decision*. New York, 1944.

———. *Seven Decisions that Shaped History*. New York, 1950.

Werth, Alexander. *Russia at War, 1941–1945*. London, 1964.

Wheeler-Bennett, Sir John, and Anthony Nicholls. *The Semblance of Peace: The Political Settlement After the Second World War*. London, 1972.

Wilmot, Chester. *The Struggle for Europe.* New York, 1952.

Woodward, Sir Llewellyn. *British Foreign Policy in the Second World War.* London, 1962.

Zawodny, Janusz Kazimierz. *Death in the Forest: The Story of the Katyn Forest Massacre.* Notre Dame, Ind., 1962.

Zinner, Paul E. *Communist Strategy and Tactics in Czechoslovakia, 1918–48.* New York, 1963.

Zochowski, Stanislaw. *British Policy in Relation to Poland in the Second World War.* New York, 1987.

Newspapers and Periodicals

Ambrose, Stephen. "Refighting the Last Battle—the Pitfalls of Popular History," *Wisconsin Magazine of History,* Summer 1966, pp. 294–301.

Hamilton, Nigel. "Did Eisenhower Let Stalin Grab Europe?" *U.S. News and World Report,* September 1, 1986, pp. 28–30.

Koch, H. W. "The Spectre of a Separate Peace in the East: Russo-German 'Peace Feelers', 1942–44," *Journal of Contemporary History* 10 (1975): 531–547.

Los Angeles Times. April 14, 1990, p. A1.

New York Times. April 4, 1968, p. 7; April 7, 1968, p. 18; April 17, 1968, pp. 1, 46; April 14, 1990, p. 1.

U.S. News and World Report. "Why Ike Didn't Capture Berlin: An Untold Story," April 26, 1971, pp. 70–73.

Zinner, Paul E. "Marxism in Action: The Seizure of Power in Czechoslovakia," *Foreign Affairs,* July 1950, pp. 644–658.

Index

ABOUT THE AUTHOR

REMI NADEAU earned his bachelor's degree in history at Stanford University in 1942 and his Ph.D. in modern European history at the University of California at Santa Barbara in 1987. During World War II he served three years in the Mediterranean and European theaters as an intelligence officer and gunnery officer with the U.S. Army Air Force. In a business career of more than 30 years he was a journalist with West Coast newspapers and served in top public affairs positions with major international corporations. Since 1948 he has written eight nonfiction books including *City-Makers*, *The Water Seekers*, *California: The New Society*, and *Fort Laramie and the Sioux*. He has written many historical articles for such magazines as *American Heritage* and has contributed to seven American history anthologies.